500
3-INGREDIENT
RECIPES

500
3-INGREDIENT
RECIPES

SIMPLE AND SENSATIONAL
RECIPES FOR EVERYDAY COOKING

ROBERT HILDEBRAND AND CAROL HILDEBRAND

FAIR WINDS
PRESS
GLOUCESTER, MASSACHUSETTS

Text © 2004 by Carol Hildebrand and Robert Hildebrand

First published in the USA in 2004 by
Fair Winds Press
33 Commercial Street
Gloucester, MA 01930

ISBN 1-59233-094-0

Library of Congress Cataloging-in-Publication Data available

Cover design: Mary Ann Smith
Book design: *tabula rasa* graphic design

Printed and bound in USA

Dedications

CJH:
To my husband Don Eburne, for his unfailing love, enthusiasm, and support, not to mention his heroic ingestion of all sorts of experimental recipes. I love you more than butter.

RFH:
To my wife Sarah, for her loving encouragement and support in pursuing my dreams.

Both:
To our mother, Margery Hildebrand, who perfected the art of cooking while hemmed in by kitchen chairs topped with small nosy children. We love food because you always cook with love. And to our father, George Hildebrand, who always shows appreciation for any food placed before him.

Contents

1

Introduction

When we told people we were doing a cookbook of recipes that have three ingredients, people invariably responded in one of two ways: "How the heck can you cook anything with only three ingredients?" or "Oh, man, that book is for me! I want to cook better, but I get intimidated by the recipes!"

Those reactions reflect what we think of as a classic dichotomy when it comes to cooking and eating today. People want to eat well. The fact that we dine out far more than our parents did means that we are exposed to new and sophisticated flavors, and our palates reflect that. And the flood of new and exciting produce and international foods in grocers nationwide has further sparked culinary enthusiasm. People want more than the traditional plate of meat, starch, and two vegetables, or they want it to be reinvented in a fresher fashion.

But . . .

There is a vast chasm between the thought of cooking well and the act. In many cases, the urge to come home and slice, sauté, and present a sprightly and original meal based on garden-fresh ingredients crumbles in the grip of the time crucible most of us call life. We've got work, and housekeeping chores, and the endless ongoing juggling of tasks that marks the typical family these days.

And many times, our hands haven't caught up with our palates. We don't want to settle for meatloaf, but we might not have the skills necessary to prepare and serve complicated food at our next dinner party.

Perhaps, too, that cornucopia of food overflowing in our supermarkets is intimidating as well as exhilarating. Should we grill the swordfish with mango or papaya? What about starfruit? So many choices can induce "analysis paralysis," and we end up with the safe choice—the meatloaf, the spaghetti with meat sauce, the baked chicken—dinners we've made a thousand times. Boring but acceptable.

In other words, we may want to serve food that's original and good, but we don't quite know how to go about doing it, and we don't have the time to devote to extensive training and research.

That's where this book comes in. Imposing a limit of three ingredients may sound draconian, but it forces cooks to pare down their recipes to the distilled core of taste, to the things that each dish must have. Then, too, it helps to break that bewildering impasse that too many choices can create. Three ingredients gives fearful cooks a comforting territory from which to explore new tastes and cooking techniques.

Three ingredients also simplifies shopping—with these recipes, it's a snap to pick up the necessary ingredients for dinner with a ten-minute jog through the market. We tried to stay with ingredients that we found at our local supermarkets and convenience stores. As one rural inhabitant and one suburban dweller, we hope that our stores are fairly typical. However, we do realize that our regional stores—we're both in New England—

might offer different foodstuffs from stores in the rest of the world. Wherever possible, we've offered substitutes.

The Recipes

You might think that recipes with three ingredients will sound like the following: "Immerse pasta in boiling water. Add salt. Cook."

In all actuality, however, they're a little more complicated than that.

First, we start out with a small set of "free" ingredients: water, salt, pepper, oil, and butter, ingredients that serve as the framework for much cooking. These items don't count in the ingredient count for each recipe.

Every recipe has another secret ingredient that heavily influences taste, too: the cooking method. In three-ingredient recipes, how you cook the food plays even more of a starring role. Why? With only three ingredients to play with, we found that we needed to focus sharply on the flavor basics in order to make our concepts translate to the plate. We needed to add complexity with technique rather than with ingredients. For example, we could take an ear of corn, which is basically sweet, and add bitterness by grilling it. We could add sweetness to a dish containing onions by slowly caramelizing them. We could use the mellowness of slow-cooked garlic and highlight it with the sharpness of garlic added right at the end of cooking. Same ingredient, two flavors.

In this cookbook, you'll see recipes that take advantage of cooking techniques to add depth to a dish. For example, there's lots of searing of meat, which adds flavor through caramelizing, and lots of braising, which slowly cooks food in a liquid to alchemize various flavors into an entirely new taste.

Three-ingredient recipes also use the ingredients in new ways to extract the most value from each item. For example, we'll boil corn cobs in water to extract every ounce of corn flavor for our Tarragon Corn Chowder, or we'll use grapes for their juice in a sauce as well as a sautéed element in Chicken with Green Grapes.

Pantry

Nobody can count on having fresh produce and meat available at all times—there's always going to be an evening when you survey the contents of the fridge and try to figure out how to build a meal based on half a jar of olives, a hard-boiled egg, and one desiccated orange. That's life. However, you can tilt the odds in your favor by having a basic stock of what we think of as building-block foods. If you have a jar of pesto and some grated Parmesan cheese on hand, you're just a pot of boiling water and some pasta away from a reasonable meal. (Well, a salad to go with it wouldn't be a bad idea, either, but you get the gist.)

We know that very few people have the time to make demi-glace and freeze it in individual portions, ready to use for an unctuous sauce for that Wednesday night rack of lamb. Most people have trouble keeping the ice cube tray full, for goodness sake. We know that planned-ahead cooking is hard to do, and certainly the world will not end if it doesn't get done. That said, however, if you can make a big pot of a simple marinara sauce, or chicken stock, and freeze the stuff, you'll be happier and healthier in the long run. Oh, and you'll save money.

Here are the things we like to keep on hand:

- hoisin sauce
- soy sauce
- good olive oil (virgin or extra virgin)
- garlic olive oil
- vegetable oil
- vinegar: red wine and balsamic
- a jar of pesto
- Parmesan cheese
- garlic
- onion
- flour
- simple marinara sauce (bottled or homemade)
- chicken stock or broth (homemade or canned)
- Vanilla Sugar (recipe, page 37)
- hot sauce

Ingredients

You might think that limiting the recipes to three ingredients would result in simple food with certain flavors dominating each dish, that the limit on the number of flavors we could add to a dish meant having to focus the flavors, to simplify the techniques, and to lose subtlety.

In practice, we have found that this is not necessarily so. We have discovered the joy of taking a single ingredient and using it in several ways. Limiting your ingredients makes you think how many ways you could use the same ingredient to gain different flavors and textures in the same dish.

Paring a recipe down to its vital core means that you have to count on your ingredients to provide the biggest bursts of flavor possible. For that, the ingredients needed to be as fresh and pure as possible. We fully support the use of seasonal fruits and vegetables whenever possible—corn straight from the field and bursting with sweetness is bound to pack more of a flavor punch than the prepackaged variety plucked from the freezer section of the grocery store, for example.

There's another element at play here, too. The proliferation of wonderfully diverse fresh ingredients over the past decade or so has really given horsepower to the concept of culinary minimalism. The onset of winter no longer means that we are stuck with tomatoes that look as though they were cultivated a stone's throw from Three Mile Island. Instead, we are presented with a dizzying variety. Even in deep winter we can choose from a staggering array of tomatoes: vine-ripened, low-acid yellow tomatoes, cherry tomatoes, tiny plum tomatoes, Romas, and heirloom tomatoes, to name just a few.

Fruits that once seemed exotic are now available on a daily basis. We can get mango at our local neighborhood convenience store, and our kids eat them as often as they do apples and bananas.

Ironically, the other major development in ingredients is the continuing sophistication of packaged goods. It used to be unusual to find pesto at the grocer. Now you'll have to choose between traditional pesto, sun-dried tomato pesto, bottled pesto, fresh pesto—the permutations are almost endless.

The quality has improved over the years, too. The bottled spaghetti sauces of 20 years ago, heavy on sugar and salt, have given way to products that have moved beyond the realm of "It'll do in a pinch" into the category of "good eats."

What that means for the three-ingredient cook is that we can make our ingredients work harder. We can choose a lemon-pepper marinade with a reasonable assurance of getting all the tastes advertised. Thus, our first order of business was to go to various supermarkets, clipboard in hand, and walk up and down the aisles looking for stuff we could use. We tried to think outside the box (or jar, if you will), using bottled pasta sauces as braising sauces, for example. Our recipes reflect the best of what we found.

In the end, what we've discovered is that three-ingredient cooking isn't boring cooking. It is, to some extent, simple cooking in that you don't have to wrestle with a laundry list of confusing ingredients. But it's not mundane cooking. It's a way to simplify the daily task of getting three square meals on the table without removing the joy and creativity that can make cookery so worthwhile.

2

Techniques
and Terms

*In this chapter, we've outlined some basic things
we think every cook should know.*

Searing Meats

Searing meat does not lock in moisture, as many folks suppose. It is, however, essential to many dishes for the flavor it adds. When you sear meat you develop caramelization, which is bittersweet. Searing is not burning—burnt meat is just bitter. The caramelized brown bits left in the pan after searing are sometimes called the "fond."

To sear meat, you want to use a heavy-bottomed pan. You want the pan to be hot—not so hot that you will burn the meat, but hot enough to give off a satisfying sizzle when the meat hits the pan. So let the pan heat up, pour in the oil, and just when it starts to smoke, add the meat. The oil will also look as though it is shimmering when it is hot enough. How do you know what level of heat to use? You know your stove. High heat on some stoves is too hot for searing; on others it is just right. We usually specify medium-high for searing, but adjust to your stove's idiosyncrasies.

Don't crowd the pan. This is especially a pitfall when searing stew meat. Give the meat room to get hot, or you will end up steaming it and the meat will spill all of its juices right then. You want those juices in the sauce later. We usually sear in batches, but again, be careful that the oil and especially any flour coating on the meat does not just form a burnt crust on the bottom of the pan. If it does, just rinse out the pan, wipe it dry, and heat it to continue your searing. If you do end up with burnt stuff in your pan, and the recipe calls for deglazing the pan (using wine or another liquid to scrape up the fond), don't deglaze these cinders. It will make the dish bitter. You are better off losing the fond than adding the bitterness that will ultimately ruin the dish. Just deglaze with water and dump the results down the drain.

Braising and Stewing

Braising and stewing are both moist-heat methods of cooking. This gentle heat, usually at a simmer, allows the collagen in tough cuts of meat to break down. This is why pot roast is so tender. If you tried grilling the same cut of meat, it would be awfully tough. "Braising" usually refers to larger cuts of meat, such as a pot roast, and means that one-third to one-half of the meat is covered by the liquid.

With stewing, the meat is usually cut into smaller pieces and the meat is fully covered with the cooking liquid.

Knowing When the Meat Is Done

We recommend that you have an instant-read meat thermometer (see equipment), especially for roasts. When cooking chops or steaks, or even a rack of lamb, however, we usually rely on the touch method to determine the doneness of the meat. Once you get the hang of it, this is a really simple method. As meat cooks, the protein coagulates and becomes stiffer. Prod the meat with your finger—give it a good poke. Then compare the feel of the meat to the feel you get when pressing on these parts of your face: your chin, the tip of your nose, and your forehead. Your chin is rare, the tip of your nose is medium, and your forehead is well done. Medium rare will feel somewhere in between your chin and nose (no, don't prod your lips). Also, it is a good idea to try poking raw meat, to get the idea of how soft it is in that state.

Different cuts of meat will feel different—filet mignon will feel different from sirloin. You just need to get a little experience and you will be on your way. The last thing you want to do to test meat's doneness is to remove it from the grill and cut it. All the nice juices will end up on your platter, not in the meat, where they belong. This is also why we are always yammering at you to rest the meat before cutting it. When the meat comes off the heat, all the juices are driven to the center. They need a bit of time to collect themselves and re-distribute throughout the meat. Larger cuts, such as a roast, require 10 to 15 minutes for this process. A steak will need just a couple of minutes.

Cutting Up a Bird

Any supermarket has chickens already cut up, or packages of breasts, leg quarters, or other chicken parts. For many of our recipes, those are fine. However, for some recipes, we use the whole bird, different parts in different ways. It is also the case that you will seldom find a duck already cut up. You may be able to get the meat department to do this task for you, but if the duck is frozen—as many supermarket ducks are—then this task will fall to you.

So here is how to cut up a bird. Once you do it a couple of times, you will find it is quick and easy. In fact, you may notice that you can save quite a bit of money, as whole chickens are usually much cheaper than the cut-up parts. Boning knives usually have a thin, flexible blade about 6 inches long. Any knife you have that is close to this description will work.

1. Off with the legs. First, wash the chicken with cold water, pat dry, and place, breast side up, on cutting board. Pull one leg and thigh away from the chicken body and slice through the skin between the body and thigh. Pull the leg away from the body and put your fingers under the thigh near the carcass. Apply pressure upward until you feel the ball pop out of the ball-and-socket joint of the thigh. Slice down through the separation in the joint, staying close to the backbone, until the leg quarter is cut off. Try to keep the "oyster" with the leg; it's the nugget of meat just beyond the leg joint. Repeat the process with the other leg. At this point, you can leave the thigh and leg as one piece, or you can cut them into two pieces by slicing through the joint that ties the drumstick to the thigh.

2. Cut off the wings. Pull each wing away from the body and cut through the ball joint that attaches it to the breast.

3. Cut the bird in half. Pull out the wishbone by hooking it in your finger and pulling it out. If it doesn't come out in one piece, worry not. Turn the bird upside down, with the exposed backbone from the leg area up and the back facing you. Slice right down the backbone on either side. Cut right through the ribs—they won't offer much resistance. Do this on either side and you will have removed the backbone. This should leave you with two chunks: the whole breast, and the back portion of the bird.

4. Halve the breast. Turn the breast portion so that the skin side is down on the cutting board. Using a heavier knife if you wish, cut through the breastbone and through the meat and skin to separate the breasts. Expect a few crunches, but it's pretty easy to slice through the bone if you are firm about it.

Now you have a chicken cut into 8 pieces (or 10, if you bisected the leg and thigh segments), with the back, the wingtips, and (if they gave you one) the neck to make a stock. As always when working with raw meat, be careful to avoid cross-contamination. Be sure to clean up well with a disinfectant or antimicrobial cleaner, and don't use the cutting board for other ingredients until it is washed.

Under the constraint of three ingredients, we are having you cut up a whole bird if we need a stock to make a dish. In reality, you may have stock in your freezer (see Chapter 4: "Pantry Basics") or use canned broth. In that case, you can buy the cut parts from the store.

Fryer Chicken versus Roasting Chicken

We often specify a fryer chicken or a roasting chicken. A fryer is simply a younger, smaller bird. They are also sometimes called broilers. Fryer chickens typically weigh 2½ to 3½ pounds per bird. Roasters are larger, 5 to 7 pounds on average. Unless the package says roaster parts, packages of chicken parts are from fryer chickens.

Trussing a Fowl

To truss a fowl, lay it breast side up on a cutting board with the legs facing you. Cut a piece of butcher twine about 2 feet (60 cm) long. Slide the middle of the length of string under the bird on the neck end until it is halfway along the wings. Pull the ends up to pin the wings and cross them at the tip of the leg-end cavity just under the breast bone, and pull the twine taut, but not tight, using the breast bone as your fulcrum. Now wrap the ends under the drumsticks and, using the string, pull them together and tight. Cross the ends of the twine around the ends on the legs and tie together. Cut off excess string.

Cooking Green Vegetables

With a few exceptions, such as a long-simmered pot of collard greens, we want to cook green vegetables in such a way that they remain bright green. We need to be nice to the chlorophyll to avoid the army-green look. There are a couple of cooking methods that work. When boiling green vegetables, make sure you have a large pot of salted water. You may want to cook them in batches if you are cooking a large amount. The trick is to get back to a boil as soon as possible. Also, you never want to cover the pot when cooking green vegetables. As they cook, the vegetables release acids. These need to disperse in the steam. If covered they go back into the cooking water and destroy your nice bright green chlorophyll. Another way of cooking green vegetables is to sauté them in hot oil—again, not crowding the pan, or you will be steaming them. The oil will cook the veggies quickly (oil transfers heat much more efficiently than water) and the they will be crisp and green. This is the principle behind Chinese wok cooking.

Yellow and white vegetables are much more forgiving, so go ahead and cover the pot.

Using a Pasta Maker

A crank-operated pasta maker is a great addition to any kitchen. Along with a mixer that has a dough hook, you can whip up a batch of fresh pasta in no time. As a bonus, kids love to get involved in making the pasta and cranking it through the machine.

Some helpful hints on pasta machines:

◆ Dust the machine with flour before using.

◆ Never wash your pasta machine with water. Just brush it off and put it away.

◆ Run the dough through several times on the lowest setting, to make the dough silky smooth, before moving to higher settings.

◆ If the dough is sticking to the rollers, dust lightly with more flour.

◆ Work with small pieces of dough. By the time you have run it through on the higher settings that little piece will have gotten long and unwieldy.

◆ A good trick when making pasta alone, since it seems to take more than two hands, is to press the two ends of the dough together to form a continuous loop, which will feed itself through the machine and be less likely to stick together. We even sometimes use a rolling pin as a tension on the side of the loop away from the pasta machine.

◆ Line a baking sheet with waxed paper and sprinkle flour over it. Let the pasta dry for a half hour or so, either spread out well on the baking sheet, or in the traditional way over a broom handle.

◆ Your water has to be at a strong rolling boil, or you risk making mushy pasta at best and flour soup at worst.

◆ Fresh pasta takes only a few minutes to cook. When it rises to the top of the water, it is done.

Working with Phyllo Dough

We can't imagine making our own phyllo dough from scratch. Fortunately, we don't have to, because it is to be found in the freezer section of almost any supermarket. Even with this head start, the stuff can be frustrating to work with. A few tips make it easier:

♦ Thaw the phyllo in the box for a day in the refrigerator before using it.

♦ Have a damp (not wet) towel large enough to cover the unused dough as you work. Phyllo sheets dry out very quickly, but this will prevent that.

♦ Don't worry if a sheet tears while you are working with it. Just reassemble it as best as you can. Rolling it into several layers with the butter will take care of those tears.

♦ Wrap unused phyllo in plastic and store it in the refrigerator. It will last a week or so.

Mounting a Sauce

We finish many of our sauces with a little butter. This addition provides flavor, richness, and a smooth mouthfeel to the sauce. This technique is called mounting a sauce with butter (in French, a beurre monté). The goal is to get a smooth sauce into which the butter has emulsified. Some care is required, as you can break a sauce and this will result in the butter separating and the sauce becoming greasy. To mount a sauce, first cut the butter into pieces of roughly 1 tablespoon (15 g). The butter should not be soft, but it does not need to be rock solid either. We usually say to whisk in the sauce, but in his kitchen at the Three Stallion Inn, Bob usually uses a tablespoon for this task. Certainly a whisk is the right tool when tackling a larger batch of sauce. Next, drop 1 to 2 tablespoons in at a time and whisk until they are almost melted, then add more. You want to watch the heat, moving the pot on and off the heat as you whisk. Continue until all the butter is incorporated and then remove the sauce from the heat and keep it in a warm place until use.

Deglazing a Pan

When we say to deglaze the pan, we are saying to pour a liquid into a hot pan that has been used to sear or sauté something. The idea here is to begin building a sauce with the fond (caramelization from the earlier cooking in the pan) and a reduction of the added liquid, usually stock, wine, or both.

3

Equipment

We thought of some great recipe ideas that use obscure equipment, but in the interest of making this book as useful as possible, we focused on using equipment that most of us are likely to have, or that can be purchased without great expense.

- Good knives. By that we mean knives that are forged steel instead of stamped, and that sharpen well. We like a set that includes a chef's knife, a paring knife, a bread knife (also great for fruit and tomatoes), a boning knife, and a slicing/carving knife. A cleaver is a great tool for pounding, but you can also use a meat tenderizer and use the flat side. The knives should be kept sharp.
- A set of pans, including heavy sauté pans in 6-, 10-, and 12-inch sizes (small, medium, and wide), a 12-inch (about 30 cm) cast-iron skillet, heavy-bottomed 1-, 2-, and 4-quart (or liter) saucepans with covers, and a stockpot of 2- to 4-gallon (7½- to 15-liter) capacity, with cover. And at least one 6-inch (15-cm) nonstick sauté pan kept in great shape—hide it; this is for eggs and omelets and needs to retain its nonstick surface. Try to get pots and pans with handles that can be put into the oven.
- A steamer with lid.
- A Dutch oven with cover. We love a heavy cast-iron version. This is an indispensable tool for searing on the stovetop, then braising in the oven.
- Baking sheets of heavy-gauge aluminum.
- Cookie sheets.
- A variety of casserole dishes, 1-, 2-, and 4-quart (or liter). These need to be oven safe. Pyrex dishes will work, but the table presentation will suffer. We like the oval French style with straight, fluted sides, 1 to 2 inches (2½ to 5 cm) tall.
- A food processor.
- A blender.
- A stand mixer with paddle, whip, and dough-hook attachments.
- In addition to a stove and oven, we will often ask that you have a grill.
- Roasting pan and rack.
- Tongs.
- Slotted metal cooking spoons.
- Wooden spoons.
- Ladles.
- A spider (wire mesh skimmer).
- A rolling pin.
- A couple of whisks.

- ◆ Potato masher or a potato ricer.
- ◆ Heat-resistant rubber spatulas.
- ◆ A lettuce spinner.
- ◆ A good colander.
- ◆ A set of metal mixing bowls in a variety of sizes.
- ◆ Large cutting boards—plastic for meats and veggies.
- ◆ A big wooden bread board for baking.

Also nice to have:
- ◆ Piping bags and a variety of piping tips.
- ◆ An immersion blender.

That's about all the equipment you will need to pull off these recipes. We are sure that you will find plenty of other stuff—as we have—at local kitchen-supply stores that you feel you must have. We say go for it, then find a recipe that justifies the purchase.

4

Pantry Basics

Certain recipes we come back to time and again, either as the building blocks for more complicated efforts, or as workhorses that see heavy use day after day. These are the sauces and condiments that you want to have on hand, in the fridge or freezer. Some, like the Quick and Basic Marinara Sauce, offer a cheaper (and tastier, of course) alternative to the myriad bottled pasta sauces on the market. Others, like demi-glace, provide a stepping-stone to kick up recipes to a more sophisticated level.

It may seem like more work than it's worth to follow recipes that aren't going to end in something concrete, like dinner. And certainly, there are many prepared alternatives to these basic items. But by investing a little time and effort up front—and for many of these recipes, the effort is very slight indeed—you can save yourselves both time and money in the long run. Your food will be the better for it, too.

PARSLEY-INFUSED OLIVE OIL

You can use other herbs, such as basil, tarragon, dill, and rosemary to make similar oils.

1 bunch parsley, flat or curly
1 cup (235 ml) extra-virgin olive oil

Rinse the parsley well. Heat a pot of water to a boil, and holding the stems of the parsley, dunk the leaves in the boiling water for 5 to 10 seconds. Rinse under cold water immediately. Chop the parsley, stems and all, and put it into a blender. Now heat the olive oil in a small pot over low heat until it is warm but not smoking. Add the oil to the blender and blend until the parsley is thoroughly chopped. Strain the oil through a fine sieve and discard the parsley. Refrigerate the oil but bring it to room temperature for use. It will keep for several weeks in the refrigerator.

YIELD: 1 cup (235 ml)

GARLIC-INFUSED OLIVE OIL

1 large bulb of garlic (about 8 cloves)
1 cup (235 ml) extra-virgin olive oil

Separate the garlic into cloves, peel, and chop into 2 or 3 pieces per clove. In a small pot, combine the garlic and oil and cook over low heat until warm. Let cool. If you want a really intense garlic flavor, let the oil steep longer—up to 2 days. Strain through a fine sieve or a cheesecloth and discard the garlic.

Refrigerate the oil but bring it to room temperature for use. It will keep for several weeks in the refrigerator.

YIELD: 1 cup (235 ml)

BASIC VINAIGRETTE

Many times we call for vinaigrette. There are good bottled versions available, which we often use, but this is even better and takes only seconds to make. This is a separating dressing, but you can just shake it up in a bottle, or rewhisk it anytime.

¼ **cup (60 ml) red wine vinegar**
1 cup (235 ml) extra-virgin olive oil
  (or for a lighter dressing, a blend of olive and other vegetable oils)
1 teaspoon minced garlic
1 teaspoon Dijon mustard
2 tablespoons (30 ml) water

In a small mixing bowl combine all the ingredients and season with salt and pepper to taste. Whisk together and toss with salad.

YIELD: About 1½ cups (350 ml)

EMULSIFIED BALSAMIC VINAIGRETTE

We make this dressing as our house dressing at the Three Stallion Inn. Emulsifying the oil makes for a smoother, less sharp vinegar flavor. Usually, egg yolks are used as an emulsifier, but since this version works without the egg, you don't have to worry about this dressing going bad on you. It will stay emulsified for several days in the refrigerator. If it starts to separate a bit, shake the bottle and it will come back together.

½ cup (120 ml) balsamic vinegar
2 cloves garlic, minced
2 tablespoons (30 g) Dijon mustard
½ cup (120 ml) hot water
3 cups (700 ml) olive oil

Put the vinegar, garlic, and mustard into a fairly narrow and tall container, such as a cleaned quart (liter) yogurt container. Add the oil. Using an immersion blender and starting from the bottom, blend the dressing while slowly adding the hot water, carefully moving the blender up as the bottom is emulsified and being very careful to not break the surface of the oil until you get the rest emulsified. Don't try this in a shallow container. You need to get the emulsion working from the bottom up.

If the dressing breaks while you are emulsifying, don't fret. Let it sit and try again. If it still won't emulsify, then just use it as a regular dressing—no need to waste.

YIELD: 4 cups (950 ml)

MAYONNAISE

Although most kitchens these days have a food processor, we still reach for the bottled mayo. And that's too bad, because mayonnaise is easy, fast, and cheap to make, and the taste is out of this world. Homemade mayo won't keep for long, however, so make small batches and use it up. If you are worried about salmonella, there are pasteurized egg yolks in most supermarkets these days. They come in 1 pint (½ liter) cartons, or smaller.

2 egg yolks
½ teaspoon lemon juice
½ teaspoon red wine vinegar (or other vinegar)
1½ cups (350 ml) vegetable oil (you can use olive oil if you want)

Put the yolks, lemon juice, and vinegar in a food processor fitted with the metal blade. Add about ½ teaspoon salt and ½ teaspoon pepper. With the processor running, add the oil in a slow and steady stream through the hole in the cover. If the mayo gets too thick, add just a bit of water. It will keep for 3 to 4 days in the refrigerator.

YIELD: About 2 cups (475 ml)

ADD IT!
You can add all sorts of things to this basic recipe, such as garlic, tarragon, basil, tomato paste, pickle—the list goes on—to make aioli, flavored mayonnaise, or even a quick tartar sauce.

HOLLANDAISE

This is one of the "mother sauces" of classic French cuisine. It is rich but also undeniably good. There are as many variations on the hollandaise theme as there are French chefs. Béarnaise uses tarragon and a little vinegar instead of lemon, Choron adds a touch of tomato, and the list goes on. Once you get the basic concept of this emulsified butter sauce down, then you can think up your own variation and name it whatever you want.

A note on the butter: some prefer clarifying the butter; some do not. The sauce will be thicker with clarified butter, as you are not adding the water in the milky part. You can use either, depending on the result you want. You can use either unsalted or salted butter, but you will need to add little, if any, salt if you are using salted butter.

> 8 tablespoons (115 g) butter
> **2 egg yolks**
> **Juice from 1 lemon**
> **Dash of hot pepper sauce, if desired**

Melt the butter in a small pan over low heat. Clarify the butter if you wish by spooning off the milk solids that rise to the top. Set aside. In another small saucepan, heat 2 inches (5 cm) or so of water to a simmer. Put the egg yolks, the lemon juice, and the hot pepper sauce into a stainless steel bowl. Place the bowl over the simmering water and whisk until the mixture is pale yellow and slightly foamy, and you can see streaks of the bowl through the egg as you whisk. This should take 5 to 6 minutes. Remove from the heat and, while whisking, slowly dribble in the melted butter. You need to start this almost a drop at a time. Once you get the emulsion started, you can speed up the butter a little, but it should still be a thin stream. Add the butter too fast and you will break the sauce. Once all the butter is incorporated, season to taste with salt and pepper.

YIELD: About 1 cup (235 ml)

Salsa Verde (Green Sauce)

A northern Italian staple, salsa verde is usually served with such dishes as bollito misto (mixed boiled meats) or fish. But this is a versatile sauce that can find its way into many dishes. It is also useful as a quick dip for raw veggies and bread, or as a bruschetta topping.

2 bunches flat-leaf parsley
2 tablespoons (20 g) minced garlic
1 tablespoon (15 ml) red wine vinegar
2 cups (475 ml) extra-virgin olive oil

Bring a small pot of water to a boil. Wash the parsley well. Then, holding it by the stems, dip the leaves into the water for 5 to 10 seconds. Rinse under cold water immediately. Chop the parsley leaves and put them into a blender, along with the garlic, the vinegar, and salt and pepper to taste. Add the olive oil and puree for several minutes.

YIELD: About 2 cups (475 ml)

Basic and Quick Marinara Sauce

This is useful as a basis for many dishes.

1 medium-size onion
2 tablespoons (30 ml) olive oil
4 cloves garlic, minced
1 can (28 ounces, or 825 g) crushed tomatoes

Peel the onion and cut it into small dice. Put the oil, onion, and garlic into a heavy-bottomed 2-quart (2-L) pot and place over medium-low heat. Cover and allow the vegetables to cook slowly (known as sweating the onions) for 8 to 10 minutes, until they are soft and translucent. Add the tomatoes, and season to taste with salt and pepper. Turn up the heat to medium-high and bring to a fast simmer or low boil. Cook, uncovered, for 15 to 20 minutes, stirring periodically. Puree with an immersion blender or in a food processor, or leave the sauce chunky if you prefer.

YIELD: About 3 to 4 cups (¾ to 1 L)

GORGONZOLA CREAM SAUCE

Here's an alternative to bottled marinara sauce when you need to pour something over a bowl of pasta at the end of a long, tiring day.

½ cup (60 g) Gorgonzola or other blue cheese, crumbled
½ cup (120 g) mascarpone cheese
½ cup (120 ml) light cream

Mix all the ingredients, along with salt and pepper to taste, in a 1-quart (1-L) saucepan. Cook over low heat until the cheeses are melted together into the cream.

YIELD: 1¼ cups (294 ml)

ALL-PURPOSE PORK BRINE

Brining pork for a day or so makes for a wonderfully flavorful roast or chop. The salt in the brine removes water from the meat, while the sugar moves water—along with flavor—into the meat.

½ cup (150 g) kosher salt
½ cup (100 g) sugar
¼ cup (25 g) pickling spice mix
½ gallon (2 L) boiling water

Mix all ingredients until sugar and salt are dissolved. Let cool and then add the meat. The brine should completely cover the meat. Let the meat sit in the brine for at least a few hours and up to two days, according to your recipe's specification. (Different cuts of meats should be brined for different periods of time, according to their size and thickness.)

YIELD: 2 quarts (2 L) brine, enough for 3 to 4 pounds (1¼ kg to 1¾ kg) of pork loin. The brine will also work for the same amount of beef or chicken.

CHICKEN STOCK

You can buy chicken broth at any store, and it is fine for many applications. It is not, however, stock. Stock adds a richness and mouthfeel that the canned broths will never match. Although you can usually get away with substituting broth, try making chicken stock to have on hand. You'll find that it is easy, economical, and, if you store it frozen in resealable plastic bags, convenient. If you don't have bones or want to cut up chicken, buy cheap leg quarters instead. One more thing: Don't ever salt stock. You might want to reduce it later for a sauce and will find the salt too concentrated. Save the salt for when you use the stock in the final dish.

This is a three-ingredient cookbook. Here we are cheating just a bit by combining three vegetables into an ingredient called mirepoix, which is 50 percent diced onion and 25 percent each diced carrot and celery.

> 2 pounds (900 g) chicken bones (necks, backs, wing tips, etc.)
> 1 pound (450 g) mirepoix
> 2 bay leaves
> 4 whole black peppercorns

Put the chicken bones in a large pot and add 4 quarts (4 L) water. Bring to a boil, and when the water just boils, skim off the foam that rises to the top. Skim two or three times, until the foam stops gathering. Add the mirepoix, the bay leaves, and the peppercorns.

Reduce the heat to a strong simmer and cook, uncovered, for 4 to 6 hours, adding water if needed to keep the level of the water above the bones. Drain the stock through a medium-mesh strainer, pressing down on the vegetables and bones. Discard the contents of the strainer. Refrigerate the stock, and when it is cold, remove and discard the solidified fat from the top—you can spoon it right off. Stock will keep for 3 to 4 days in the refrigerator, or several months in the freezer. We like to store it in resealable plastic bags.

YIELD: 3 to 4 quarts (3 to 4 L)

DEMI-GLACE

Why are we bothering with this one? Because it will open wide, new vistas of sauce making and will improve even your everyday pot roast or stew immeasurably. We don't call for demi-glace in this book much, because many folks find it intimidating, and it's not readily available at the supermarket. However, if you ever get semi-serious about cooking, try it at least once. You can keep it frozen in little resealable plastic bags for future use. (We have a slight addiction to resealable plastic bags.)

This is a modern demi-glace. The classic version involves steps you really don't want to bother yourself with. In fact, we have done side-by-side testing of the two versions and like this simpler recipe better. This is the way most commercial kitchens that still bother to make their own stocks (not as many as you would think) generally make it, with one minor exception: Most cooks like to roast their veal bones first. We don't, as we think it lessens the amount of gelatin extracted from the bones. Besides, with all the reducing involved with this demi-glace, we still end up with a nice caramel-colored and rich-flavored product. However, if you want to roast, go ahead. Just be sure to not burn those bones—that will add bitterness. When making demi-glace we make stock from the same bones twice. The first is the veal stock, which has most of the flavor. The second is called remoulage (or second wash). It is cooked for a shorter time and has less flavor, but it contains lots of the gelatin that we want.

As we did with the chicken stock, we are combining three vegetables into an ingredient called mirepoix, which is 50 percent diced onion and 25 percent each diced carrot and celery.

5 pounds (2½ kg) veal bones
2 pounds (900 g) mirepoix
2 bay leaves
8 whole black peppercorns

Put the veal bones in a 4-gallon (15-L) pot and add 6 to 8 quarts (6 to 8 L) water—enough to cover the bones, plus a couple of inches (5 cm). Bring to a boil, and when the water just boils, skim off the foam that rises to the top. Skim two to three times, until the foam stops gathering. Add the mirepoix, the bay leaves, and the peppercorns. Reduce heat to a simmer and cook, uncovered, for 12 to 14 hours, adding water as needed to keep the level of the water above the bones. Drain the stock through a medium-mesh strainer, pressing down on the vegetables and bones. Put the contents of the strainer (the bones and veggies) back in the stockpot, add 4 quarts (4 L) of water to the stockpot with the bones in it, and put it back on the stove. Cook at a low boil for 3 to 4 hours.

After you get the remoulage back on the stove, strain the stock you have made through a fine-mesh strainer lined with cheesecloth. Refrigerate until cold—if you want, you can shock the stock (cool it quickly) by immersing the container it is in in ice water. (Just be sure to have the level of water in your ice bath no higher than the stock inside the container—floating is not good, as the container will try to tip over.) When the remoulage is done, strain as before, but this time discard the contents (the bones and veggies) of the strainer. Refrigerate this batch too. When the stocks are cold, remove and discard the solidified fat from the top—you can spoon it right off. The stock should be jelled. Combine the two stocks into one stockpot, noting how far up the side of the pot it comes. Bring to a boil and boil fairly rapidly until reduced by half. This is demi-glace. It can be stored in the freezer in resealable plastic bags, or you can pour it into paper coffee cups or an ice cube tray before freezing.

YIELD: About 2 quarts (2 L)

FLAVORED CREAM CHEESE

We often call for a flavored cream cheese in the recipes in this book. You can certainly buy these premade at any supermarket or bagel store, but they are also easy and much cheaper to make at home. Here are two varieties.

SCALLION CREAM CHEESE

    8 ounces (225 g) cream cheese
    2 scallions, green and white parts

Put the cream cheese in a food processor fitted with the metal blade. Chop the scallion fine. Add the scallion to the food processor and process until the ingredients are well mixed.

YIELD: About 1 cup (225 g)

ORANGE-GINGER CREAM CHEESE

    8 ounces (225 g) cream cheese
    1 teaspoon minced fresh ginger
    ¼ cup (75 g) orange marmalade

Combine all ingredients in a food processor fitted with the metal blade. Process until well blended.

YIELD: About 1¼ cups (300 g)

FRENCH TOAST STUFFING

Spoon or pipe this into thick slices of French or Italian bread with a pocket cut into them, then fry like regular French toast—loved by kids of all ages.

- 8 ounces (225 g) cream cheese
- ½ cup (150 g) strawberry preserves
- ½ cup (50 g) confectioner's sugar

Combine all the ingredients in a food processor fitted with the metal blade. Process until well blended.

YIELD: About 1¼ cups (425 g)

VANILLA SUGAR

The enticing flavor and aroma of the vanilla bean permeates the sugar. Vanilla beans are expensive, but a little goes a long way.

- 1 vanilla bean
- 8 cups (1600 g) sugar

Split the vanilla bean in half. Bury it in the sugar in a resealable jar. Leave it alone for 2 to 3 weeks. Use in desserts, baking, or even in your coffee.

YIELD: 8 cups (1600 g)

CINNAMON SUGAR

You can buy this at the store, but why would you when it is so ridiculously easy to make?

- 1 cup (100 g) white sugar
- 1 tablespoon (7 g) ground cinnamon

Combine the two ingredients well. Store in an airtight container—it keeps indefinitely.

YIELD: 1 cup (100 g)

Starters

5

Appetizers

Any wedding reception will prove our point—appetizers are often the most interesting food at an event. Be it a platter of passed canapés or a more composed starter at a multicourse dinner, appetizers can provide the fun and spark to either get the ball rolling at a cocktail party or set the stage for an entire evening of dining.

Appetizers have come a long way from the '60s classic of mushy white bread rolled around canned asparagus spears. Produce is fresher and more varied, and our culinary influences have expanded to include many cuisines from around the world. Use these recipes to jump-start your next party.

ARTICHOKE PHYLLO PURSES

Artichokes are one of the few select vegetables beloved of all four Hildebrand kids—perhaps because each leaf serves as a convenient utensil with which one can shovel in the accompanying melted butter and vinegar. Anything that involves the ingestion of massive amounts of butter is good by us.

Even for adults, there's something endearing about a vegetable that makes us work so hard to attain the nuggets of subtle, green goodness at its heart, and we continue to love artichokes served every way imaginable.

A note on the phyllo: Please see Chapter 2: "Techniques and Terms" for more tips on using phyllo dough.

> 1 jar (6 ounces, or 175 g) marinated artichoke hearts, drained
> 4 ounces (115 g) cream cheese
> 4 sheets phyllo dough, thawed, each 14 x 18 inches (about 35 x 46 cm)
> 8 tablespoons (115 g) butter, melted

Preheat oven to 400°F (200°C, gas mark 6). Line a baking pan with parchment paper.

Put the artichoke hearts and the cream cheese in a food processor fitted with the metal blade and process until smooth. Store the phyllo under a damp towel to keep it moist. Take 1 phyllo sheet, lay it out on the counter, and brush it with melted butter. Put a second sheet on top and brush it with butter. Cut the phyllo into 2-inch (5-cm) squares. Put 1 teaspoon or so of the artichoke mixture in the center of each square. Bring the corners together and twist; place each purse on the baking sheet. Repeat with the 2 remaining phyllo sheets.

Bake for 10 to 12 minutes, until golden brown.

YIELD: 8 to 10 servings

🧂 ADD IT!
Fold a tablespoon of chopped fresh oregano into the food processor along with the artichoke hearts and the cream cheese.

ASPARAGUS ROLL-UPS

Here's an update of the popular appetizer of the '60s that involved flattened Wonder Bread rolled around canned asparagus spears. Here, the asparagus stays bright green and crisp, and the crackling phyllo adds a delicious mouthfeel to the package.

A note on the phyllo: Please see Chapter 2: "Techniques and Terms" for more tips on using phyllo dough.

> **16 asparagus spears**
> **2 sheets phyllo dough, thawed, each 14 x 18 inches (about 35 x 46 cm)**
> 4 tablespoons (55 g) butter, melted
> **½ cup (40 g) crumbled feta cheese**

Preheat oven to 400°F (200°C, gas mark 6).

Cut off the top 3 inches of the asparagus spears and blanch them for 2 minutes in boiling salted water. Drain and immediately plunge the asparagus under cold water. Drain and set aside.

Store the phyllo under a damp towel to keep it moist. Lay a phyllo sheet on a flat surface. Brush with the melted butter and lay the other sheet on top. Brush with butter and cut the phyllo into 2-inch (5-cm) squares. Lay 2 asparagus spears on each square and top with some of the feta. Roll the square so that the tops and bottoms of the asparagus stick out. Place, seam side down, on a baking sheet.

Bake for 10 to 12 minutes, until the phyllo is golden brown.

YIELD: 4 servings

BACON-WRAPPED SCALLOPS WITH DILL

We spice up this classic with the distinctive taste of dill.

- 16 large sea scallops
- 8 pieces bacon
- 16 dill fronds,1 to 2 inches (2½ to 5 cm) long

Preheat the oven to 400°F (200°C, gas mark 6).

Scrape the side muscle off the sea scallops, if there is one. Cut each bacon piece in half, crosswise.

Lay a dill frond down the vertical center of each piece of bacon and then wrap both around a scallop. Secure with a toothpick. Put the scallops on a baking sheet and bake for 10 to 12 minutes, until the bacon is crisp and the scallops just cooked through.

YIELD: 4 servings

BAGNA CAUDA

This infused olive oil derives its name from bagno caldo, Italian for "hot bath." It's a terrific hot bath indeed when used as a dip for veggies. It's wonderfully versatile: Dip bread into it, drizzle it over mashed potatoes, brush it on grilled meats and fish, or serve with a platter of sliced fresh vegetables—baby carrots, sliced yellow peppers, plum tomatoes, blanched asparagus spears, and endive, to suggest just a few. You'll want to have some around all of the time.

- 2 cups (475 ml) extra-virgin olive oil
- 16 cloves garlic, peeled
- 2 anchovy fillets
- 1 dried red hot pepper

Put the oil in a small saucepan. With the side of a knife, slightly crush the garlic cloves. Add them to the oil. With the side of a knife, mash the anchovy fillets into a paste. Add to the oil. Add the pepper and cook over very low heat for 45 minutes, until the garlic is beginning to soften. Do not let this get anywhere near a simmer—the heat needs to stay gentle, or the olive oil will lose its fruitiness and become bitter. Serve warm or at room temperature, but store it refrigerated.

ELD: 15 to 20 servings

BARBARA'S BACON-WRAPPED BREADSTICKS

This recipe comes to us courtesy of Barbara Rogers and her husband, Chris, two very accomplished and ingenious cooks. Barbara loves to serve this at cocktail parties, where it's always sure to disappear quickly. She says, "This appetizer (affectionately called bacon on a stick) is a very popular appetizer for those guests with a hungry appetite. It is very hearty and delicious. The brown sugar caramelizes on the bacon as it cooks to create a tasty coating."

10 slices bacon
20 Italian breadsticks
1 cup (145 g) brown sugar, unpacked

Preheat the oven to 450°F (230°C, gas mark 8). Line a cookie sheet with foil.

Cut each slice of bacon in half, crosswise. Wrap the bacon around the breadstick in a spiral from the top of the breadstick to one-fourth to one-half of the way down it. Roll the bacon-wrapped breadstick in the brown sugar to liberally coat it. Place the breadsticks on the cookie sheet, leaving space between each breadstick. Bake for 10 minutes, turning over the breadsticks after 5 minutes. Serve immediately.

YIELD: 6 to 8 servings

ADD IT!
Mix a tablespoon of Mexican chile powder into the brown sugar.

BASIC BAKED POTATO SKINS

Perfect for using leftover baked potatoes, but we know folks who will bake spuds just for this purpose.

> 4 baked potatoes, preferably russet, cooled
> 4 strips bacon, cooked
> 2 cups (225 g) cheddar cheese, shredded

Preheat the oven to 400°F (200°C, gas mark 6).

Cut the potatoes in half, lengthwise, and scoop out most of the inside, but leave a pretty thick wall of potato under the skin. Set aside the potato innards for potato pancakes or some such. Put the 8 potato halves on a baking sheet. Chop the bacon and divide among the potatoes. Divide the cheese among the potatoes.

Bake for 15 to 20 minutes, until the cheese is melted and bubbling and a bit browned on top.

YIELD: 4 servings

ADD IT!
Other accoutrements for these spuds can be sour cream, salsa, chopped scallions, chopped chives, or whatever else you like.

BASIC QUESADILLAS

4 flour tortillas, 12 inches (about 30 cm) in diameter
1 cup (125 g) shredded cheese, such as Monterey Jack
1 cup (225 g) salsa, fresh if possible
½ cup (120 ml) cooking oil

Lay out a tortilla and cover half with ¼ cup (30 g) cheese and ¼ cup (55 g) salsa. Fold the other half over, pressing down. Repeat with remaining tortillas. Heat a wide sauté pan over medium-high heat. Heat 2 tablespoons (30 ml) of the oil in the pan and put in 1 tortilla. After 3 to 4 minutes, carefully flip it over—the bottom side should be golden brown. Continue cooking for 3 to 4 more minutes, then remove the quesadilla and keep it warm. Repeat with the remaining tortillas, adding oil as needed.

Cut the quesadillas into 4 wedges each.

YIELD: 4 servings

ADD IT!
You can add many things inside or outside the quesadillas. Inside you can add cooked shredded chicken, beef, black beans, or shrimp. Outside, you can serve them with sour cream, guacamole, and more salsa. However, they make a great quick lunch or snack just as they are.

BLACK BEAN AND CORN SALSA

If you double this recipe, it also makes a perfectly acceptable black bean salad for dinner.

1 can (14 ounces, or 400 g) black beans
½ pound (225 g) frozen corn kernels, thawed
1½ cups (335 g) fresh salsa

Drain the beans and put them in a mixing bowl. Add the corn and salsa and mix well. Serve with tortilla chips to dip. This also makes a good salsa over grilled meats and is good tossed with pasta.

YIELD: 6 to 8 servings

ADD IT!
Squeeze fresh lime over the salad and add chopped green chiles or fresh cilantro.

BOURSIN-STUFFED MUSHROOMS

Looking like tiny little bowls, mushrooms just beg to be filled with a variety of tasty combinations. They're finger food that requires a minimum of hand cleansing, making them even more irresistible to the party planners of the world.

> 16 large mushrooms
> 8 ounces (225 g) Boursin cheese
> 1 cup panko (see note)

Preheat the oven to 400°F (200°C, gas mark 6).

Wash each mushroom, pat dry, and snap off its stem at the base. Use a spoon to clean out the mushroom innards to create a shallow little bowl.

Spoon a teaspoon or so of the Boursin into each of the mushroom caps, then dip each, cheese side down, into the panko, so that they stick to the cheese. Put the mushroom caps, cheese side up, on a shallow baking pan, and pour ¼ cup water into the pan. Bake the mushrooms for 10 to 12 minutes, until they have softened and the crumbs have browned a bit.

YIELD: 4 servings

NOTE: *Panko, or Japanese bread crumbs, are very coarse white-bread crumbs used in Japanese cooking to coat foods before frying. They absorb less grease than regular bread crumbs, and produce a delectably crunchy, golden brown crust. We find ours at the supermarket, but if you can't dig any up, use fresh bread crumbs.*

Cajun Cheddar Pinwheels

In confessing our continuing love affair with things dairy, we'll go on record as also adoring melted cheese—it's an important member of our Dairy Hall of Fame, where it joins fellow inductees Real Butter and Whipped Cream.

1 sheet puff pastry, thawed, 9 x 10 inches (23 x 25½ cm)
2 cups (225 g) shredded cheddar cheese
2 tablespoons (15 g) Cajun spice mix

Preheat the oven to 400°F (200°C, gas mark 6). Line a baking pan with parchment paper.

Place the puff pastry on a floured surface with the long side toward you. Roll the puff pastry until quite thin, being sure to retain its rectangular shape.

Mix the cheese and Cajun spice mix and spread it over the puff pastry, leaving 1 inch (2½ cm) at the far edge uncovered. Moisten this uncovered strip of dough with water and roll the dough away from you to form a long rope. Lightly press the moistened dough against the rolled cylinder to help seal it. Cut the rope into ½-inch (1 cm) wheels and lay them on a the baking sheet.

Bake for 12 to 15 minutes, until golden brown. These are great hot or at room temperature.

YIELD: 6 to 8 servings

NOTE: *If your market does not carry Cajun spice mix, you can approximate it by mixing together 1 tablespoon kosher salt, ½ teaspoon cayenne pepper, 2 tablespoons paprika, 1 teaspoon garlic powder, 1 teaspoon ground thyme, 1 teaspoon dried onion, and 2 teaspoons ground black pepper. Store in a jar with a tight-fitting lid.*

CARIBBEAN CHICKEN WINGS

Look for jarred fresh-packed mango in juice. The mangoes are nice and ripe and already peeled and cut for you. At the Three Stallion Inn, Bob buys mango puree, but this is not an often-seen commodity in the typical market. If you find it, great. It also makes a great dessert sauce.

> 1 pound (450 g) chicken wings
> 1 cup (235 ml) jarred fresh-packed mango pieces,
>   plus 3 tablespoons (45 ml) juice from the jar
> ¼ cup (50 ml) hot sauce, or to taste

Preheat the oven to 350°F (180°C, gas mark 4).

Spread the wings on a baking sheet and cook for 25 to 30 minutes, until just done. In the meantime, put the mango and juice in a food processor fitted with the metal blade and puree. Mix the mango puree and hot sauce, along with salt and pepper to taste, in a large mixing bowl. Add the hot wings and mix to coat them well. Put the wings back on the baking sheet and bake for 5 to 8 minutes more.

You can serve these with traditional accompaniments such as celery sticks and blue cheese dressing.

YIELD: 4 servings

ADD IT!
Spice this up by adding 1 teaspoon ground cumin to the mixing bowl.

CHEESE STRAWS

We've been making these for years, and we have yet to have leftovers. Scatter baskets of them on any convenient surface at a cocktail party, and watch them disappear.

> 2 frozen puff pastry sheets, 9 x 10 inches (23 x 25½ cm)
> 1 cup (100 g) finely grated Parmesan cheese
> 3 tablespoons (10 g) dried oregano

Thaw the puff pastry at room temperature, about 30 minutes. While the pastry is thawing, combine the cheese and oregano.

Preheat the oven to 400°F (200°C, gas mark 6).

Working 1 sheet at a time, gently unfold the puff pastry sheet and roll it with a rolling pin until it increases about half again in size. Sprinkle the pastry with half of the cheese mixture and gently press the mixture into the pastry with the rolling pin.

Fold the pastry sheet in half lengthwise and, once again, gently roll the rolling pin over the folded sheet. Slice the pastry—perpendicular to the fold of the pastry—into ¾-inch (2 cm) strips. Gently twist each strip into a corkscrew.

Repeat this process with the second sheet of pastry and the other half of the cheese mixture.

Place the cheese straws on a baking sheet, an inch or so (2½ cm) apart, and bake for 10 to 15 minutes, until they are golden brown. These are delicious warm or at room temperature.

YIELD: 6 to 8 servings (about 2 dozen straws)

 ADD IT!
You can put just about any herb in these and they are delicious. Chopped rosemary, basil, and tarragon are especially good.

CRAB WONTONS

Packaged wonton wrappers might be one of the best products to hit the market in the past 20 years. You can use them for just about any part of the meal, be it starter, main course, ravioli pasta, or dessert pastry. (See Dessert Wontons, page 461.) Ready-made wonton wrappers are a snap to use and increase your repertoire nicely. And face it, would you make these things if they required you to make wonton wrappers from scratch? No, neither would we.

- ½ cup (65 g) cooked crabmeat
- ½ cup (115 g) Scallion Cream Cheese (see page 36)
- 20 wonton wrappers, about 3 inches (7½ cm) square

Thoroughly mix the crab and the cream cheese. Lay the wonton wrappers out and spoon 1 teaspoon or so of the crab mix onto the center of each. Wet the edges of the wonton wrapper with water and fold to enclose the crab and to form a triangle. Fold the corners from the base of the triangle together, and using a little water, pinch and stick them together.

Heat the oil in a deep fryer or heat 2 inches (5 cm) oil in a heavy-bottomed pot to 350°F (180°C). Fry the wontons in batches, for 4 to 5 minutes, until golden brown. Drain on paper towels and keep warm.

YIELD: 5 servings of 4 wontons per serving

🥫 ADD IT!
These are great served with a sweet-and-sour dipping sauce.

DEVILED EGGS

Our grandmother was very fond of deviled eggs. Like clam chowder, the deviled egg is one of those items that can inspire culinary feuds as to their Proper Preparation. We'll just stay above the fray and say that there are as many variations on the deviled egg as there are grandmothers and church picnics. This is a basic recipe, so feel free to improvise and adorn. The piping of the eggs makes for an elegant presentation, but you can just spoon the yolk mixture into the egg whites.

12 hard-boiled eggs, shelled
½ cup (120 ml) mayonnaise
2 tablespoons (30 g) tarragon-flavored Dijon mustard

Split the eggs and remove the yolks. Mash the yolks in a small mixing bowl with a fork. Add the mayonnaise and the mustard and mix well. Add salt and pepper to taste. Put the yolk mixture in a piping bag fitted with a star tip and pipe into the egg-white halves.

YIELD: 4 to 6 servings

ADD IT!
You can add chopped pickles, curry powder, chopped dill, hot sauce, paprika (traditionally sprinkled on top), capers, chopped chives—we could go on and on.

Duck Liver and Prune Mousse

Bob saves the duck livers from his dinner specials in a resealable plastic bag in the freezer. When he has enough, he makes this wonderful and simple pâté, which is great on crackers or crostini. If—like most of the population at large—you don't happen to have a supply of duck livers in your freezer, feel free to substitute the more easily purchased chicken livers. Even liver haters will like this one!

A note about the seasoning: When you taste for seasoning, remember that salt tastes more pronounced in a hot dish. Since this will be served cold, and you taste it hot, it should taste quite salty. It will not be as salty when cold.

> 2 tablespoons (30 ml) olive oil
> **1 pound (450 g) duck livers (or other livers, such as chicken or rabbit)**
> **3 tablespoons (30 g) minced shallot**
> 2 tablespoons (30 ml) water
> 4 tablespoons (55 g) butter, cut into pieces
> **4 ounces (115 g) pitted prunes**

Heat about 2 tablespoons (30 ml) olive oil in a wide sauté pan or skillet over high heat. Sear the livers and continue cooking until just done—about 5 minutes. Season well with salt and pepper and add shallots. Cook for another minute, stirring. Add 2 tablespoons (30 ml) water and stir to scrape the bits of food off the pan. Scrape everything into a food processor. Add the butter and process until the butter is melted. Add the prunes and process until they are minced and well distributed into the pâté. Scrape into a bowl or mold and chill.

YIELD: 10 to 20 servings

🧂 ADD IT!
Instead of water, deglaze the pan with brandy or cognac to add a distinctive punch to your mousse.

ESCARGOTS IN PUFF PASTRY

Escargots are not just the domain of classic French restaurants. Now you can serve them at home—French waitstaff are optional.

> **1 sheet puff pastry, thawed, 9 x 10 inches (23 x 25½ cm)**
> 4 tablespoons (55 g) butter
> **12 canned escargots, drained**
> **1 tablespoon (10 g) minced garlic**

Preheat the oven to 400°F (200°C, gas mark 6).

Cut 1½-inch (4-cm) rounds from the pastry dough and put them on a baking sheet. Now cut doughnut shapes 1½ inches (4 cm) in diameter, with a 1-inch (2½-cm) hole. Brush a little water on the bottom of the rings and stick them on top of the rounds. Prick the inside of the rounds several times with a fork. Bake for 10 to 12 minutes, until golden brown. The ring should be higher than the center of the rounds; if not, just break the center down with a spoon.

Heat a medium-size sauté pan or skillet over medium heat. Add the butter, and when it melts, add the escargots and garlic. Season with salt and pepper to taste. Sauté 4 to 5 minutes. Put 1 escargot and a bit of the garlic butter in the center of each puff pastry ring.

YIELD: 4 servings

FIGS WITH PROSCIUTTO

Another classic that proves the theory that simple does not mean boring. This would make a fine addition to an antipasto tray. The terrific thing about fresh figs is that you can eat them in their entirety—seeds, skin, and all. The ultimate in efficient packaging!

> **6 fresh figs**
> **6 paper-thin slices prosciutto**
> **½ cup (100 g) whipped cream cheese**

Split each fig in half lengthwise. Cut each prosciutto slice in half. Smear a bit of cream cheese on the cut face of each fig half. Wrap in a piece of prosciutto.

YIELD: 4 servings

GUACAMOLE

Of course we love avocados—with their rich and creamy flavor, avocados are the vegetable that tastes most like butter. It's also a vegetable high in fat, although admittedly the less-bad unsaturated fats. Hass avocados make the best guacamole, as they mush up nicely and aren't at all watery tasting.

If you make this ahead of time, save one of the avocado pits and bury it in your guacamole to help keep it from turning brown.

> **2 ripe avocados (Hass are best)**
> **½ cup (110 g) fresh salsa (in the produce section rather than a jar)**
> **1 lime**

Cut the avocados in half, remove the pits, and scoop out the flesh with a spoon. Put the avocado flesh in a mixing bowl. Add the salsa and squeeze in the juice of the lime. Mash with a fork or potato masher. Adjust seasoning with salt and pepper.

YIELD: 4 to 6 servings

ADD IT!
Try 1 clove of minced garlic; if you want more spice, feel free to finely chop a jalapeño pepper and add it, too.

LIVER CROSTINI AND WATERCRESS

Chicken liver mousse is very easy indeed to make, but you can also buy it at the local supermarket.

> **8 thin slices good-quality baguette bread—stale is fine**
> ¼ cup (60 ml) garlic-infused olive oil
> **1 bunch watercress**
> ¼ **pound (115 g) chicken liver or foie gras mousse**

Preheat the oven to 250°F (120°C, gas mark ½).

Brush bread slices with half of the oil and lightly salt and pepper. Bake on a cookie sheet until crisp. This can be done a day ahead and stored at room temperature, well wrapped.

Remove large stems from the watercress, rinse, and spin dry. Toss the watercress with the remaining oil and salt and pepper. Smear each crostini with some of the mousse. Place 2 or 3 leaves atop each crostini and arrange on a plate.

YIELD: 4 servings

🥫 ADD IT!
Skin and thinly slice a ripe pear; arrange a slice on top of each crostini.

MARINATED MUSHROOMS

> **1 pound (450 g) button mushrooms**
> **1 small onion**
> **2 cups (475 ml) red wine vinaigrette**

Wash the mushrooms and thoroughly pat dry; cut off the bottom of each stem. If the mushrooms are large, cut them in halves or quarters. Put the mushrooms in a mixing bowl. Peel the onion and dice it small. Put the onion in a small saucepan and add the vinaigrette. Cook over medium heat for 6 to 8 minutes, bringing it just to a boil. Pour the hot vinaigrette over the mushrooms and toss to coat well. Refrigerate overnight.

YIELD: 6 to 8 servings

🥫 ADD IT!
Garlic! A clove of minced garlic will spice these up nicely. So will a tablespoon or so of any of your favorite fresh herbs, chopped fine.

Mushroom and Feta Mini-Turnovers

½ pound (225 g) mushrooms
½ cup (75 g) feta cheese
1 sheet puff pastry dough, thawed, 9 x 10 inches (23 x 25½ cm)
2 tablespoons (30 ml) oil

Wash and dry the mushrooms and cut the bottom half-inch (1 cm) off the stems. Put the mushrooms in a food processor fitted with the metal blade and mince.

Heat a medium-size sauté pan or skillet over high heat, pour in the 2 tablespoons (30 ml) oil, then add the mushrooms. Season with salt and pepper and cook, stirring, until the mushrooms give out, then reabsorb, their liquid, 8 to 10 minutes. Remove from heat and add the feta.

Preheat the oven to 400°F (200°C, gas mark 6).

Put the puff pastry on a floured flat surface and roll the dough until quite thin. Cut into 2-inch (5-cm) squares. Put a teaspoon or so of the mushroom mixture on the center of each square, moisten the edges of the dough with water, then fold over to form a triangle. Press the edges of the triangles with the back of the tines of a fork to seal.

Put the triangles on a baking sheet and bake for 10 to 12 minutes, until golden brown.

YIELD: 8 to 10 servings

QUICK PICKLED CAULIFLOWER

Cauliflower, another underutilized vegetable, pickles very nicely and makes a nice switch from the usual cucumber pickle. Also great with cold meats, such as leftover roast beef.

1 small head cauliflower
1 tablespoon (18 g) salt
1 cup (235 ml) red wine vinegar
½ cup (100 g) sugar

Remove the leaves and core from the cauliflower and cut into small florets. Put the florets into a large pot, cover with water, add the salt, and bring to a boil over high heat. Cook for 3 to 4 minutes at a boil, then drain.

While the cauliflower is cooking, combine the vinegar and sugar in a small saucepan. Cook over high heat, stirring occasionally, until the sugar dissolves. Add salt and pepper to taste. As soon as the cauliflower is drained, put it in a mixing bowl and add the vinegar mixture. Toss to coat the cauliflower well. Refrigerate for at least 2 hours, and up to several days.

YIELD: 6 to 8 servings

ADD IT!
Toss a tablespoon of chopped, fresh dill into the vinegar and sugar mixture.

ROAST BEEF ROULADES

We once attended a wedding reception where we watched fisticuffs break out over one particular appetizer, small sliced beef Wellingtons. From this experience, we have since tracked—and can thus confirm—the popularity of appetizers that feature beef.

½ pound (225 g) rare deli roast beef, sliced thin
1 cup (225 g) vegetable cream cheese
1 loaf cocktail rye bread

Lay an 18-inch (45-cm) piece of plastic wrap on a flat surface. On top of the wrap, lay out the roast beef in one layer, slightly overlapping, to form a rectangle. Spread the cream cheese on the beef in a thin layer. Lift the edge of the plastic wrap closest to you. Using the plastic wrap as a starter, starting with one of the long sides, roll the beef into a pinwheel roulade. Keep the plastic on the outside of the roll and use it to encourage the beef to continue rolling. Tightly roll the plastic wrap around the rolled beef and twist the ends of the wrap to tighten the beef. Freeze until firm but not hard.

While the beef is chilling, use a cookie cutter, such as a circle or star, to cut out decorative shapes from the rye bread. (Discard the remains of the bread, or save for another use.) Cut the roast-beef log into ¼-inch (½-cm) rounds. Top each piece of decoratively shaped bread with a beef round.

YIELD: 6 to 8 servings

🧂 ADD IT!
Add a thin layer of washed watercress (stems removed) to the beef-cheese platform and roll that into the roulade as well.

SARAH'S FAVORITE RUMAKI

Bob's wife, Sarah, loves these appetizers.

> 4 strips bacon
> 1 can (8 ounces, or 225 g) water chestnuts, drained
> ½ pound (225 g) chicken livers

You will need 16 toothpicks. Soak the toothpicks in cold water for ½ hour before assembling the rumaki.

Preheat the oven to 400°F (200°C, gas mark 6).

Cut each bacon strip crosswise into 4 pieces. Put the bacon on a work surface; place a bite-size chunk of liver together with a water chestnut in the center. Wrap the bacon around the filling and skewer with a toothpick. Repeat with the rest of the ingredients. Put the rumaki on a baking sheet and bake for 12 to 15 minutes, until the bacon is crisp.

YIELD: 4 servings

 ADD IT!
You can marinate the water chestnuts and the livers for an hour or so in a marinade of soy sauce, chopped fresh ginger, and a little molasses.

SCALLION PANCAKES

These are good dipped in soy sauce.

> 2 cups (250 g) all-purpose flour, plus some for kneading
> 2 tablespoons (30 ml) toasted sesame oil
> 1 cup (100 g) chopped scallions, white and green parts

Put flour, sesame oil, scallions and 1 tablespoon (18 g) salt in a mixing bowl. Add enough water to form dough, about 1 cup (235 ml). Turn dough out onto a floured surface and knead until smooth, about 5 minutes. Cut the dough into pieces about ¼- cup (125 ml) large and roll into long thin ropes, 12 to 14 inches (30 to 40 cm) long. Wrap the dough rope in a pinwheel, pinching the end into the coil to keep it together. Flatten slightly with the palm of your hand to make the pancake stick together.

Heat a wide sauté pan or skillet over medium heat and add ¼ cup (60 ml) of the oil. Fry the pancakes, in batches, for 4 to 5 minutes per side, until golden brown. Drain on paper towels and keep the finished pancakes warm. Cook the rest, adding oil to the pan as needed.

YIELD: 6 to 8 servings

SMOKED SALMON CROSTINI

You can toast the bread a day or two ahead, which makes these starters simple to assemble at the last minute.

12 slices French bread
¼ cup (60 ml) olive oil
½ cup (115 g) Scallion Cream Cheese (see page 36)
12 slices smoked salmon

Preheat the oven to 300°F (150°C, gas mark 2).

Brush the bread slices with olive oil and bake on a baking sheet, turning once, until crisp, about 30 minutes. Cool the bread and spread each slice with cream cheese. Top each with a slice of smoked salmon.

YIELD: 4 servings

🏺 ADD IT!
Sprinkle a handful of capers on each crostini.

SMOKED TROUT MOUSSE

This is great as a dip; it's also excellent piped onto cucumber rounds or into phyllo cups. Smoked bluefish, herring, or even canned sardines will work well if you can't find smoked trout.

>   1 package containing both sides of a smoked trout, about ½ pound (225 g)
>   8 ounces (225 g) cream cheese
>   2 tablespoons (20 g) minced shallot

Put all the ingredients in a food processor fitted with the metal blade and process until smooth. Chill in a bowl, or put in a piping bag.

YIELD: 6-8 servings as a dip

SPICED OLIVES

As a child, Carol once plucked a large kalamata olive from a big barrel in a fancy gourmet shop and took a bite. Revolted by the unexpected pungency, she immediately returned it to the barrel, where to her mother's horror it sank into anonymity. Fortunately, she's since come to her senses about olives, and this is a favorite party recipe.

>   1 pint (250 g) assorted olives
>   2 lemons
>   2 tablespoons (20 g) minced garlic
>   ½ cup (120 ml) extra-virgin olive oil

Put the olives in a mixing bowl. Cut the zest in strips from the lemons and add the zest to the olives. Squeeze one lemon and add the juice. Add the garlic, the olive oil, and pepper to taste. Mix well and marinate for at least 2 hours and preferably overnight.

YIELD: 6 to 8 servings

ADD IT!
Sprinkle an assortment of your favorite fresh herbs, chopped fine. Some good candidates: oregano, thyme, and rosemary.

SOFT PRETZELS

1 tablespoon (12 g) active dry yeast
1 cup (235 ml) warm water
2 tablespoons (30 ml) olive oil
2 cups (250 g) all-purpose flour, plus more for rolling
Kosher salt

Mix the yeast and water in the mixing bowl of a mixer fitted with a dough hook, in a food processor fitted with a plastic blade, or simply in a bowl. Let sit for 5 minutes. Add the oil, then the flour, then 1 tablespoon (18 g) regular salt. Mix, then knead for 8 to 10 minutes, until you have a silky dough.

Lightly oil a large bowl or other container. Put the dough in the bowl, cover in plastic wrap and set it in a warm place until the dough doubles in bulk—about 1½ hours. Punch down the dough and form it into roughly ½-cup (125-ml) balls. Cover and let sit for 10 minutes to let the dough relax.

Lightly spray a baking sheet with pan spray. Take a dough ball and roll it into a rope, 8 to 10 inches long by ½ inch thick (20 to 25 cm by 1 cm). Fold to form a pretzel shape, or whatever shape you want. Place the formed pretzel on a baking sheet. Brush the top with water and sprinkle with kosher salt. Keep the baking sheet covered with a damp towel while you form the rest. Proof the dough, covered with plastic, in the refrigerator for 2 hours.

Preheat the oven to 400°F (200°C, gas mark 6).

Bake for 12 to 15 minutes, until browned, but still chewy. Serve hot.

YIELD: 8 servings

ADD IT!
These are always delicious served with mustard. For a sweet version, brush the uncooked pretzels with melted butter and sprinkle liberally with cinnamon sugar instead of using water and salt.

SPICED PECANS

These nuts are completely addictive, which is why we make them only around the holiday season. Otherwise, we'd never stop eating.

- 2 cups (200 g) shelled pecan halves
- ½ cup (75 g) brown sugar, unpacked
- 2 tablespoons (20 g) Cajun spice mix (see note)
- 4 tablespoons (55g) butter

Preheat the oven to 325°F (170°C, gas mark 3).

Put the pecans in a mixing bowl. Put the brown sugar, the Cajun spice mix, and the butter, along with salt and pepper to taste, in a small saucepan. Cook over low heat, stirring, until the butter and sugar are melted together. Pour in the bowl and mix to coat the nuts well. Spread the nuts on a baking sheet and bake for 20 to 25 minutes, until the coating is caramelized and browned. Cool; you may have to break the nuts apart. Serve at room temperature.

YIELD: 6 to 8 servings

NOTE: *If your market does not carry Cajun spice mix, you can approximate it by mixing together 1 tablespoon salt, ½ teaspoon cayenne pepper, 2 tablespoons paprika, 1 teaspoon garlic powder, 1 teaspoon ground thyme, 1 teaspoon dried onion, and 2 teaspoons ground black pepper. Store in a jar with a tight-fitting lid.*

TUSCAN WHITE BEAN PUREE

We run across this spread fairly frequently as a complement to the bread at local restaurants. It is great with Pita Crisps (page 129).

If you forget to soak the beans, simply put the dried beans into a pot, cover with 4 cups (1 L) water, bring to a boil, remove from heat, and cover. Let them sit for an hour, drain, then proceed as with soaked beans.

> 1 cup (215 g) dried white beans, such as navy or cannellini, soaked overnight in cold water
> 1 tablespoon (10 g) minced garlic
> 1 tablespoon (3 g) minced fresh rosemary
> 2 to 3 tablespoons (20 to 45 ml) extra-virgin olive oil
> 1 teaspoon salt
> 1 teaspoon pepper

Drain the beans and put them in a 1-quart (1-L) pot with 3 cups (700 ml) water. Simmer the beans over medium heat for 45 minutes to an hour, until they are quite soft. Drain the beans, reserving 1 cup (235 ml) of the cooking water, and put them in a food processor. Add garlic, rosemary, olive oil, and salt and pepper. Process until smooth, adding reserved water to make a light puree. Chill for 1 to 2 hours.

YIELD: 4 to 6 servings

ADD IT!
Mix in a tablespoon or so of pesto.

6

Salads

Salads are so much more than the much-maligned bowl of rabbit food that imparts a Calvinistic whiff of virtuous self-denial. In fact, salads can be as self-indulgent or hedonistic as the most decadent dessert. Lobster and Citrus Salad, Seared Tuna and Arugula—these are salads with luxurious ingredients, beautifully presented.

We offer salads in all sizes, to be used as a course for a dinner, or as a lunch or light dinner entrée in their own right. And who says you can't have one for breakfast? Nothing but tradition. The Honeydew and Basil Salad might well be an early-morning sensation.

ARUGULA AND POTATO SALAD

Arugula's peppery yet rich taste lends distinction to any dish it graces.

     1 pound (450 g) Yukon gold potatoes
     2 bunches arugula
     2 lemons
     ¼ cup (60 ml) extra-virgin olive oil

Wash the potatoes in cold water. Place in a pot covered with water; bring to a boil on high heat, then turn heat to low and simmer the potatoes until they are easily pierced by a knife but not falling apart. Drain the potatoes and cool in the fridge. When they're cooled, skin and slice the potatoes. Set aside.

Remove the stems from the arugula, then wash and spin-dry. Squeeze the lemons into a small bowl and whisk together the lemon juice, olive oil, and salt and pepper to taste. In a large bowl, toss the potatoes with half of the dressing. In another bowl toss the arugula with the remaining dressing.

Divide the arugula among 4 plates, top each plate with one-fourth of the potato mixture, and serve.

ADD IT!
Sprinkle crumbled blue cheese over all.

CHICKPEA AND FENNEL SALAD WITH LEMONS

2 lemons
1 can (14 ounces, or 400 g) chickpeas
1 bulb fennel
¼ cup (60 ml) extra-virgin olive oil

Slice the lemons very thin. Bring a 1-quart (1-L) pot of salted water to a boil; immerse the lemon slices for 20 seconds, then immediately remove and drain them. Put the lemon slices in a medium-size nonreactive mixing bowl and set aside.

Cut off the fennel stalks. Reserve a few of the fronds and discard the rest of the top. Split the bulb lengthwise and remove the core, then slice the fennel thin and add to the lemon. Drain the chickpeas and add them to the bowl. Season with salt and pepper and toss with the olive oil. Allow to marinate for 2 to 3 hours. Garnish with the reserved fronds.

YIELD: 6 to 8 servings

CUCUMBER WITH DILL AND SOUR CREAM

If the cucumber is wax coated, always peel it. If it is not, then you may leave the skin on, or peel strips and leave alternating stripes of skin.

2 medium-size cucumbers, or 1 European cucumber
2 tablespoons (4 g) minced fresh dill
1 cup (235 ml) sour cream

Peel the cucumber as desired and slice thinly crosswise. Combine the cucumber, dill, sour cream, and salt and pepper to taste in a large bowl and toss to coat the cucumber well. Allow to sit, chilled, for at least ½ hour and up to overnight.

YIELD: 6 to 8 servings as a side dish

🧂 ADD IT!
Whisk a tablespoon of red wine vinegar and one clove minced garlic into the sour cream.

ENDIVE AND TANGERINE SALAD

Endive and citrus make a great combination. Here, we give it a little twist by using tangerines.

2 heads Belgian endive
2 tangerines
½ cup (120 ml) Italian vinaigrette

Break the endive into individual leaves and put them in a large bowl. Peel the tangerines and break into segments. Add them to the endive. Toss with the vinaigrette.

YIELD: 4 servings

FENNEL AND GRAPEFRUIT SALAD

A great start to a winter meal, when citrus is in high season. The sharp flavor of raw fennel and the bright acidity of grapefruit are perfect foils for each other.

1 bulb fennel
2 ruby-red grapefruit
1 small red onion
3 tablespoons (45 ml) extra-virgin olive oil

Remove and reserve the stalks and fronds from the fennel. Trim off any bruised parts on the outside, halve the fennel bulb lengthwise, core it, and cut into long, thin sticks. Put the sliced fennel in a large bowl. With a sharp knife, cut off the top and bottom of the grapefruit, then cut off all the peel, including the pith and inside membrane. Working over a bowl to catch the juice, use a paring knife to remove each grapefruit segment from the inner membrane. Discard the membrane. Reserve the juice and add the grapefruit to the fennel.

Peel and thinly slice the onion. Mix with the fennel and grapefruit. In a small bowl whisk together the grapefruit juice, oil, and salt and pepper to taste. Toss with the rest of the ingredients and divide among 4 plates. Clip and chop a few of the fennel fronds and sprinkle them over the salad.

YIELD: 4 servings

GRILLED RADICCHIO WITH LEMON-ANCHOVY DRESSING

4 small heads radicchio
4 fillets anchovies
2 lemons
½ cup (120 ml) extra-virgin olive oil

Prepare a grill.

While the grill is heating, cut the radicchio heads into quarters, keeping the core attached. Brush the radicchio with extra-virgin olive oil, sprinkle with salt and pepper, and grill on each side until a bit blackened and wilted. Set aside and let cool to room temperature.

With the side of a knife, mash the anchovies into a paste and scrape into a small bowl. Squeeze the lemon juice into the bowl. Add ½ cup extra-virgin olive oil and pepper and whisk together. Check to see if additional salt is needed (anchovies pack a lot of salt).

Divide radicchio among 4 plates and drizzle the dressing over it.

YIELD: 4 servings

HONEYDEW AND BASIL SALAD

Tequila-lime marinade is readily available at most supermarkets, but if you can't find it, squeeze a lime and add the juice, along with a shot of tequila, to a vinaigrette.

    1 ripe honeydew melon
    1 bunch basil
    ½ cup (120 ml) bottled tequila-lime marinade
    ¼ cup (60 ml) extra-virgin olive oil

Split the melon in half; remove seeds and rind and cut in thin slices. Arrange melon slices on 4 plates.

Pick, wash, and spin-dry the basil. Cut the leaves into feathery-thin slices and sprinkle over the melon.

Whisk together the marinade and olive oil. Drizzle over the melon and basil and serve.

YIELD: 4 servings

JICAMA SALAD

Jicama, a tuber much used in Latin America, is now readily available at most supermarkets. It is juicy and crisp, starchy, and fruity all at the same time. Look for jicama that is firm with tight (not wizened) skin.

> 1 jicama, about 1 pound (450 g)
> 2 limes
> ¼ cup (60 ml) olive oil
> ¼ cup (5 g) chopped fresh cilantro

Peel the jicama and cut into matchsticks. If you have a mandoline, now's the time to break it out, but you can use a sharp chef's knife too. Put the jicama in a serving bowl. Squeeze the lime juice into a small bowl and add the olive oil. Season with salt and pepper and whisk together. Toss the jicama with the dressing. Sprinkle cilantro over and serve.

YIELD: 4 servings

ORANGE AND OLIVE SALAD

> 2 navel oranges
> 1 small red onion
> 1 cup (125 g) pitted kalamata olives
> 3 tablespoons (45 ml) extra-virgin olive oil

With a sharp knife, cut off the crown and base of the oranges, then cut off the skin and pith. Slice the oranges crosswise into wheels, ¼ inch (½ cm) thick. Put the orange slices and any juice into a mixing bowl. Peel the onion and cut into thin rings; break the rings apart into the bowl. Add the olives and olive oil. Season with salt and pepper to taste. Toss well.

YIELD: 4 servings

🧂 ADD IT!
Sprinkle a tablespoon of fresh chopped cilantro into the salad and toss.

WATERCRESS, CITRUS, AND PECAN SALAD

We find fresh citrus salad in jars in the produce section of our market. It's a luxury to have somebody else do all that peeling and segmenting for us.

½ cup (50 g) pecan halves
1 tablespoon (15 ml) vegetable oil
2 bunches watercress
1 jar (24 ounces, or 675 g) mixed fresh citrus salad
3 tablespoons (45 ml) olive oil

Preheat the oven to 300°F (150°C, gas mark 2).

In a small bowl, toss the pecans with the vegetable oil and salt and pepper to taste. Pour onto a baking sheet and bake for 8 to 10 minutes. Allow to cool to room temperature.

Remove large stems from the watercress. Wash and spin-dry. Drain the citrus salad, reserving ½ cup (120 ml) of the liquid. In a small bowl, whisk together the reserved citrus-salad liquid and olive oil, adding salt and pepper to taste.

In a large bowl toss the watercress and citrus fruit with the vinaigrette. Divide among 4 plates, top with pecans, and serve.

YIELD: 4 servings

TOMATOES AND CUCUMBERS WITH SHERRY VINAIGRETTE

This salad is one of the glories of late summer. The aged sherry vinegar adds a wonderful complexity to the flavors of the dish, but if you can't find aged vinegar, regular sherry vinegar will work, too. If you can find a yellow tomato, its low acidity works especially well. Be sure the cucumber does not have a waxed skin, or you will need to peel it.

1 pound (450 g) ripe tomatoes
1 cucumber, or half an English cucumber
3 tablespoons (45 ml) 10-year-old sherry vinegar
½ cup (120 ml) extra-virgin olive oil

Core and slice the tomatoes. Slice the cucumber. Interleaf the vegetables on 4 plates. In a small bowl whisk together the vinegar, olive oil, and salt and pepper to taste. Drizzle over the vegetables and serve.

YIELD: 4 servings

ADD IT!
It's hard to mess with perfection, but a sprinkle of chopped chives on top is also quite delicious.

PANZANELLA

The success of this traditional Italian salad depends on great bread and tomatoes at the peak of their power.

>   1 loaf French or Italian bread, a chewy variety
>   1 pound (450 g) ripe tomatoes
>   1 tablespoon (10 g) minced garlic
>   ¼ cup (60 ml) extra-virgin olive oil

Cut the bread into 1-inch (2½-cm) cubes. Core the tomatoes and cut into ½-inch (1-cm) cubes. Put the tomatoes and garlic in a large mixing bowl and add the olive oil and salt and pepper to taste. Let this mixture sit for about 20 minutes, then add the bread cubes and toss. Allow to sit for another 5 to 20 minutes.

YIELD: 4 to 6 servings

🧂 ADD IT!
Drizzle in 2 tablespoons (30 ml) balsamic vinaigrette with the tomatoes, garlic, and olive oil.

TOMATO RICOTTA SALAD

Despite its name, ricotta salata cheese is not ricotta as you would expect—the soft fresh cheese used in lasagna. Ricotta means "recooked" in Italian and simply refers to the cheese-making process employed. Ricotta salata is a salted firm white cheese similar in texture to feta, and it is wonderful tossed in salad or with vegetables. If you can't find it at your grocer, soak feta cheese in cold water for an hour, drain, and use as a substitute.

> 1 pound (450 g) ripe tomatoes
> ¼ pound (115 g) ricotta salata cheese
> 2 tablespoons (6 g) chopped fresh oregano leaves
> ¼ cup (60 ml) extra-virgin olive oil

Core and slice tomatoes. Divide among 4 plates. Crumble the ricotta salata into small pieces and sprinkle over the tomatoes.

Whisk together the oregano, olive oil, and salt and pepper. Drizzle over the tomatoes and cheese and serve.

YIELD: 4 servings

ADD IT!
Whisk one clove minced garlic and a drizzle of red wine vinegar with the olive oil and oregano.

JAPANESE SOBA NOODLE SALAD

A bowl of simply dressed cold soba noodles—noodles made from buckwheat flour—is a traditional summertime dish in Japan. Look for these noodles packaged in little bundles. If you have any ceramic bowls and chopsticks, break them out, and slurp up this salad with gusto.

   2 bundles (9 ounces, or 255 g, each) soba noodles
   1 cup (235 ml) shiitake-soy dressing (see note)
   ½ cup (50 g) chopped scallions, green and white parts

Heat a 2-quart (2-L) pot of salted water to a boil. Remove the band from the noodles and cook them in the water until al dente, about 10 minutes. Drain and immediately rinse the noodles under cold water. Put the cold noodles in a mixing bowl and toss with the dressing to coat well. Divide the noodles among 4 bowls and sprinkle scallions over them.

YIELD: 4 servings

NOTE: *If you can't find commercial shiitake-soy dressing, whisk ¼ cup (60 ml) soy sauce with ½ cup (50 g) sliced shiitake mushrooms and ¾ cup (175 ml) vegetable-oil-and-vinegar vinaigrette.*

QUICK ASIAN BEAN SPROUT SALAD

This salad works beautifully with simple grilled meats, or as the base for a roll-up sandwich.

> 3 cups fresh mung bean sprouts, about ½ pound (225 g)
> 1 cup (235 ml) sesame-ginger salad dressing
> 3 tablespoons (3 to 4 g) chopped fresh cilantro

Rinse and dry the bean sprouts. Put them in a serving bowl and toss with the dressing. Sprinkle cilantro over the sprouts and serve.

YIELD: 4 servings

> **NOTE:** *If you can't find commercial sesame-ginger dressing, combine 2 tablespoons (30 ml) each dry sherry or sake, rice vinegar, sesame oil, and soy sauce. Add 1 table-spoon (6 g) minced ginger and 2 minced garlic cloves. Process in a food processor until well combined and stir in 2 teaspoons sesame seeds.*

ROASTED BEETS WITH MÂCHE

Mâche, or lamb's lettuce, has very tender leaves and a mild, nutty flavor. If you can't find it, substitute Bibb lettuce.

> 1 pound (450 g) beets
> 2 tablespoons (30 ml) olive oil
> ½ pound (225 g) mâche
> ½ cup (120 ml) raspberry vinaigrette

Preheat the oven to 350°F (180°C, gas mark 4).

Toss the beets with the oil and sprinkle with salt and pepper. Roast beets on a baking pan for about 45 minutes, or until easily pierced by a knife. Allow to cool to room temperature. When the beets are cool, cut off the root and stem ends and slip off the skin with your fingers. Slice the beets and put in a bowl. Toss with half of the vinaigrette.

Wash and spin-dry the mâche and toss with the remaining vinaigrette. Divide among 4 plates and top with beets.

YIELD: 4 servings

ROASTED PEAR, ARUGULA, AND MAYTAG BLUE CHEESE SALAD

4 firm-ripe pears (Bartlett or Anjou is the best choice here)
2 tablespoons (30 ml) extra-virgin olive oil
2 bunches arugula
¼ pound (115 g) Maytag or other firm blue cheese, crumbled

Preheat the oven to 350°F (180°C, gas mark 4).

Peel the pears, nip off the stem, split lengthwise, and remove the core with a melon baller. Toss the pears with half of the olive oil, salt, and pepper. Put the pears on a baking sheet and roast until browned and easily pierced with a knife, about 30 minutes. Remove from the oven and cool to room temperature.

Remove the stems from the arugula, then wash and spin-dry. In a large bowl, toss the arugula with the rest of the olive oil and salt and pepper.

Mold the cheese into the core of the pears, divide among 4 plates, and mound the arugula over them.

YIELD: 4 servings

 ADD IT!
Drizzle a little balsamic vinegar over each salad. Sprinkle chopped walnuts over them for extra crunch.

ROMAINE WITH GRILLED CORN AND GREEN GODDESS DRESSING

In the 1920s, "The Green Goddess" by William Archer was playing in San Francisco. The chef at San Francisco's Palace Hotel created green goddess dressing in honor of the play's star, George Arliss.

2 ears corn with husks
2 heads of hearts of romaine
1 cup (235 ml) Green Goddess Dressing (see note)

Soak the corn, with the husk on, for 30 to 40 minutes in cold water. Meanwhile, prepare a grill.

Remove some of the outer layer of husk from each ear, then peel the husk down halfway and remove the silk. Grill the ears for about 10 minutes, turning so all sides are cooked. Don't worry if the husks char some, or if the kernels get a bit scorched. Cool, remove the remaining husks and slice off the kernels. Put the kernels in a small bowl and set aside.

Remove any damaged outer leaves from the lettuce and snip the tops of the leaves if they are tattered. Cut off the bottom inch (2½ cm) of the lettuce and cut each romaine heart into 4 wedges. Arrange 2 wedges on each plate and spoon the dressing over them. Sprinkle corn over the salad.

YIELD: 4 servings

NOTE: *If you want to make your own "green goddess" dressing, combine the following and mix well: 1 cup (235 ml) mayonnaise, 1 minced garlic clove, 2 well-mashed anchovy fillets, 1 tablespoon (3 g) chopped fresh tarragon, 2 tablespoons (30 ml) tarragon vinegar, 3 tablespoons (10 g) minced parsley, and ¼ cup (25 g) chopped scallions.*

SPINACH AND BACON SALAD WITH POACHED EGG

This classic bistro dish is a snap to put together.

1 bag (10 ounces, or 275 g) spinach leaves
½ cup (120 ml) bottled bacon-Parmesan dressing (see note)
4 eggs

Pick over, wash, and spin-dry the spinach. Put in a large bowl. Heat the dressing over low heat in a small saucepan. In a medium-size sauté pan or skillet bring about 2 inches (5 cm) acidulated water to a simmer. Drop in the eggs and poach until set.

Toss the spinach with hot dressing, divide among 4 bowls, and top each with a poached egg. Serve immediately.

YIELD: 4 servings

 ADD IT!
Cook four slices of bacon and crumble one over each dish. A handful of mushrooms sautéed in red wine vinegar with a pinch of brown sugar would taste good with this salad as well.

NOTE: *You may approximate this dressing by adding 2 or 3 strips of cooked, crumbled bacon and 2 tablespoons (10 g) grated Parmesan cheese to ½ cup (120 ml) bottled balsamic vinaigrette or Italian dressing.*

HEARTS OF PALM SALAD WITH BACON

Hearts of palm were a luxury ingredient on old-style Continental menus, but we don't see them much anymore. We continue to love their subtle flavor.

> 1 can (14 ounces, or 400 g) hearts of palm
> 4 slices bacon, cooked
> ½ cup (120 ml) Italian vinaigrette

Drain the hearts of palm and cut them into 1-inch (2½-cm) pieces. Divide among 4 plates. Chop bacon into small pieces and sprinkle over the hearts of palm. Spoon vinaigrette over the salad.

YIELD: 4 servings

ADD IT!
Before serving, toss the ingredients with a cup (20 g) of cleaned baby spinach.

WARM SALAD OF SCALLOPS AND SUNCHOKES

Sunchokes, also called Jerusalem artichokes, are tuberlike sunflower roots increasingly available at supermarkets. They have a starchy, nutty texture and a flavor reminiscent of artichoke hearts. If you can't find them, try substituting kohlrabi.

1 pound (450 g) sunchokes
1 cup (235 ml) lemon-tarragon salad dressing (see note)
12 large sea scallops, about 1 pound (450 g)

Peel the sunchokes and cut them into ½-inch (1-cm) rounds (they may not be exactly round). Put the sunchokes in a 1-quart (1-L) pot and cover with water. Salt lightly. Bring the sunchokes to a boil, then reduce the heat and simmer until they are soft but firm, about 15 minutes. Drain the sunchokes and put them in a mixing bowl. Toss the sunchokes with the dressing and set aside.

Heat a medium-size sauté pan or skillet over high heat. Remove the side muscle from the scallops and season the scallops with salt and pepper. Heat 2 tablespoons (30 ml) oil in the pan. When the oil begins to smoke, add the scallops carefully, so that they are on end. Allow the scallops to sear for 3 to 4 minutes. Turn them and sear the other end for another 3 to 4 minutes.

While the scallops are cooking, divide the sunchokes among 4 plates. Top each plate of sunchokes with 3 seared scallops and serve.

YIELD: 4 servings

🥫 ADD IT!
This dish looks nice on a bed of romaine lettuce spears.

NOTE: *To make your own dressing, whisk together the juice of 3 lemons (a little more than ¼ cup, or about 60 ml), 3 cloves finely minced garlic, 1 tablespoon (15 g) Dijon mustard, 2 tablespoons (2 to 3 g) minced fresh tarragon, 6 tablespoons (90 ml) olive oil, and salt and pepper to taste.*

ORANGE-SESAME SCALLOP SALAD

Mesclun, otherwise known as field greens, is a variety of young salad greens generally sold by weight in supermarkets. Commercial mixes usually include varieties such as arugula, mizuna, tat soi, frisée, oakleaf, red chard, and radicchio.

> 20 to 40 large sea scallops (2 pounds, or 900 g)
> 1 cup (235 ml) commercial mandarin-orange-ginger-sesame marinade (see note)
> 4 cups (80 g) mesclun

If necessary, clean the scallops by removing the side muscle (discard the muscles). Season with salt and pepper. Heat a wide sauté pan or skillet over high heat. When the pan is very hot, pour in ¼ cup (60 ml) vegetable oil and carefully place the scallops in the pan. Do not crowd the pan; cook the scallops in batches if needed. Cook for 3 to 4 minutes until well browned. Turn the scallops and cook on the other side in the same manner. Do not try to force the scallops off the pan. They will release themselves when they are ready to be turned. When the scallops are cooked, remove the pan from the heat and add the marinade, tossing the scallops to coat.

Divide the mesclun among 4 large, shallow bowls and top with scallops. Spoon the rest of the warm dressing over the salad.

YIELD: 4 servings

NOTE:
If you can't find the dressing, you can make your own by mixing the following:

½ cup (120 ml) crushed canned mandarin oranges
2 tablespoons (30 ml) dry sherry or sake
2 tablespoons (30 ml) red wine vinegar
1 tablespoon (15 ml) dark-roasted sesame oil
1 tablespoon (15 ml) soy sauce
1 tablespoon (6 g) minced fresh ginger
2 cloves garlic, minced

CALAMARI AND ARUGULA SALAD

Calamari, carefully poached, are a tender and delicious addition to a salad or antipasto display. If you have only had tough, rubbery calamari, then try this recipe—attention to poaching and a short cooking time are the keys to success.

> 1 pound (450 g) cleaned calamari, tubes and tentacles
> 1 cup (235 ml) Italian vinaigrette
> 4 cups (80 g) arugula leaves, washed and spun dry, about 2 bunches

Cut the calamari tubes into ½-inch rings. Season the rings and tentacles with salt and pepper. Heat 1 quart (1 L) salted water just to the simmer in a 2-quart (2-L) saucepan. Add the calamari and poach for 5 to 6 minutes, until just done. Be careful to not let the water boil. The calamari are done when they are opaque and firm to the touch. Drain, spread them out on a baking sheet, and chill in the refrigerator for about ½ hour.

Toss the calamari with the vinaigrette and let sit in the refrigerator for 15 minutes. Divide the arugula among 4 plates and spoon the calamari over it.

YIELD: 4 servings

ADD IT!
Slice two ripe tomatoes into chunks and toss with the calamari.

TOMATO AND CALAMARI SALAD

Tomatoes that have been blanched, seeded, and roughly chopped are known as a tomato concassé, and it's a pretty simple preparation.

> 1 pound (450 g) cleaned calamari, tubes and tentacles
> 1 pound (450 g) tomatoes
> 2 tablespoons (20 g) minced garlic
> ¼ cup (60 ml) extra-virgin olive oil

Poach the squid. Cut the calamari tubes into ½-inch rings. Season the rings and tentacles with salt and pepper. Heat 1 quart (1 L) of salted water just to the simmer in a 2 quart saucepan. Add the calamari and poach 5 to 6 minutes, until just done. Be careful to not let the water boil, as calamari will quickly turn tough if overcooked. The calamari are done when they are opaque and firm to the touch. Spread the calamari out on a baking sheet and chill in the refrigerator for about ½ hour.

Prepare the tomatoes: Bring 2 quarts (2 L) water to a boil. Core the tomatoes and cut a shallow X on the bottom of each. Drop in the boiling water for 15 to 30 seconds, or until the skin begins to crack. Remove and plunge them immediately into ice water. Peel the tomatoes—the skin should slip right off. Cut the tomatoes in half and scoop out and discard the inner pulp, leaving just the outer tomato walls. Cut the tomatoes into ¼-inch (½-cm) squares. This is tomato concassé.

Mix the tomato concassé, garlic, and olive oil in a bowl. Season with salt and pepper. Add the cooled calamari and allow to sit, refrigerated, at least ½ hour and up to 2 hours. Serve in bowls with good-quality bread to sop up the juices.

YIELD: 4 servings

🍶 ADD IT!
Toss the salad with 2 tablespoons (6 g) chopped fresh basil and a drizzle of balsamic vinegar.

LOBSTER SALAD

Our grandfather was a lobsterman. Although we never knew him, our mother made sure to pass on the lore of the lobster, leaving us with definite opinions about what should be in a classic lobster salad. For example, onion never belongs in lobster salad. Fortunately, our obstinacy dovetails nicely with the three-ingredient credo.

> 2 lobsters, 1 to 1¼ pounds (450 to 575 g) each
> ½ cup (60 g) minced celery, about 2 stalks
> 1 cup (235 ml) mayonnaise

Bring 4 quarts (4 L) salted water to a boil in an 8-quart pot equipped with a tight-fitting cover. Drop the lobsters into the boiling water, briefly holding their heads in the water to stun them first. Cook for 12 minutes per pound, then drain and chill. When the lobsters are chilled, shell the meat and cut up into bite-sized chunks. Add the celery and mayonnaise, along with salt and pepper to taste.

YIELD: 4 servings

🫙 ADD IT!
Glorious lobster salad is usually served on the plebian toasted hot dog roll, an odd couple combination that works beautifully.

LOBSTER AND CITRUS SALAD

> 4 lobsters, 1 to 1¼ pounds (450 to 575 g) each
> 1 jar (1 pound, or 450 g) fresh citrus salad
> 1 cup (235 ml) mayonnaise

Bring 4 quarts (4 L) salted water to a boil in an 8-quart (8-L) pot that has a tight-fitting cover. Drop the lobsters into the boiling water, briefly holding their heads in the water to stun them first. Cook for 12 minutes per pound, then drain and chill.

When the lobsters are chilled, shell the meat. Cut the tails into medallions and leave the claws as intact as possible.

Drain the fruit salad, reserving ½ cup (120 ml) of the juice. Put the fruit on a plate and arrange the lobster meat attractively on top. In a small mixing bowl, whisk together the mayonnaise and the reserved juice. Spoon on top of the lobster and around the fruit.

YIELD: 4 servings

AVOCADO AND SMOKED TROUT SALAD

We like Hass avocados because they are soft but not watery. With their black, wrinkled skin, it's easy for Hass avocados to bruise and become overripe without anybody noticing, so keep a close eye on them as they ripen. If you can't find this specific commercial dressing, you can add a half cup of kalamata olives and a handful of capers to the Basic Vinaigrette dressing (page 27).

2 ripe Hass avocados
1 package containing both sides of a smoked trout, about ½ pound (225 g)
½ cup (125 ml) kalamata olive and caper salad dressing

Split each avocado in half, remove the seed, and with a tablespoon carefully prise the avocado from its skin, leaving each avocado half intact. Thinly slice each avocado half lengthwise and fan out on 4 plates.

Remove the skin from the smoked trout and break it into chunks about ½-inch square. Divide into fourths and mound on top of avocado. Drizzle the dressing over the salad and serve.

YIELD: 4 servings

ADD IT!
You can pile this salad on a bed of mixed greens for more substance.

Seared Yellowfin Tuna and Arugula Salad

2 bunches arugula
2 tablespoons (30 ml) olive oil
4 small yellowfin tuna steaks, ¾ inch (2 cm) thick, about ¾ pound (340 g) total
¾ cup (175 ml) bottled sesame-orange dressing (see note)

Remove large stems from the arugula; wash, spin-dry, and set aside.

Heat a medium-size sauté pan or skillet over high heat and coat with the oil. Season the tuna with salt and pepper and sear the steaks on both sides until there is about ½ inch (1 cm) of red remaining on the inside of each steak, 4 to 5 minutes per side. Set aside.

While the steaks are cooking, toss the arugula with half of the dressing and divide among 4 plates.

Cut each tuna steak in half diagonally from top to bottom, so that you have 2 triangular wedges of tuna from each piece and can display the rosy middle. Arrange the steaks on top of the arugula and drizzle the remaining dressing over the salad. Serve immediately.

YIELD: 4 servings

ADD IT!
Serve with a little pickled ginger on the side.

NOTE: *You can make a substitute for the dressing by combining 2 tablespoons (30 ml) each dry sherry or sake, rice vinegar, sesame oil, and soy sauce. Add 1 tablespoon (6 g) minced ginger, 1 minced garlic clove and ¼ cup orange juice. Process in a food processor until well combined and stir in 2 teaspoons sesame seeds.*

Squab and Napa Cabbage Salad

If you can't find squab in the supermarket—and you might be surprised at the resources of the meat counter if you ask—then you can use a small Cornish game hen, although you won't need all the meat.

1 squab, about 1 pound (450 g)
1 head napa cabbage
½ cup (120 ml) lemon-tarragon salad dressing

Preheat oven to 300°F (150°C, gas mark 2).

Salt and pepper squab, rub with olive oil, and roast for 30 minutes, or until temperature registers 145°F (60°C) in the thigh. Allow to cool, then take off the skin, remove meat from the bones, and coarsely shred the meat into a bowl.

Remove the core from the cabbage and cut the head into very fine shreds. Toss the cabbage with the dressing, divide among 4 plates, and top each with one-fourth of the squab.

YIELD: 4 servings

ADD IT!
Sauté a cup (150 g) of roasted, shelled chestnuts (you can find bottled chestnuts at the grocery store) in a couple tablespoons (30 ml) olive oil and toss them with the cabbage.

CHICKEN-TABBOULEH SALAD

Raita is a mixture of yogurt, mint, cucumber, and garlic that can be found prepared in many supermarkets, natural food stores, and Middle Eastern, Greek, or Indian markets.

> 2 whole boneless, skinless chicken breasts, about 1¼ pounds (600 g)
> 2 cups (300 g) cooked tabbouleh
> 1 cup (250 g) raita

Heat 1 quart (1 L) water in a 2-quart (2-L) pot over medium heat. Salt and pepper the water and add the chicken. Poach at a simmer for about 20 minutes, until cooked through. Remove from the poaching liquid and chill in the refrigerator.

Divide the tabbouleh among 4 plates. Slice the chicken and arrange on top of the tabbouleh. Spoon the raita over the salad.

YIELD: 4 servings

WARM ARTICHOKE AND CHICKEN SAUSAGE SALAD

2 pounds (900 g) baby artichokes
1 pound (450 g) chicken sausage
1 cup (235 ml) lemon-tarragon dressing (see note)

Prepare the artichokes: Remove the tough outer leaves. Cut off the top third of the artichoke, split it lengthwise, and remove the choke with a melon baller. When all of the artichokes are prepared, put them in a pot of lightly salted water, bring to a boil, and simmer for about 15 minutes, or until they are easily pierced with a knife. Drain the artichokes and put in a large bowl.

While the artichokes are cooking, heat 1 tablespoon (15 ml) olive oil in a large sauté pan or skillet on high heat. Sear the chicken sausage on two sides until browned, 3 to 4 minutes per side. Add 1 cup (235 ml) water, cover, and cook over medium-high heat until the sausages are cooked through, about 10 minutes. (Add more water as needed to complete the cooking.) Slice the sausage and add to the artichokes. Toss with enough of the vinaigrette to coat well and serve.

YIELD: 4 servings as an appetizer

ADD IT!
After you trim the artichokes, you can soak them in aciduated water to prevent browning. Squeeze the juice of one lemon into 2 quarts (2L) water.

NOTE: *To make your own dressing, whisk together the juice of 3 lemons (a little more than ¼ cup, or about 65 ml), 3 cloves finely minced garlic, 1 tablespoon (15 g) Dijon mustard, 2 tablespoons (2 to 3 g) minced fresh tarragon, 6 tablespoons (90 ml) olive oil, and salt and pepper to taste.*

7

Soups

There's an almost infinite elasticity to the concept of soup. It can mean the comforting presence of a simmering pot of stew perfuming the kitchen on a winter's afternoon or the smooth slide of vichyssoise—or, indeed, the clear soothing broth of miso. Soup is also often very forgiving, accepting multiple and disparate ingredients with grace.

While many soups are built on the cleaning-the-fridge principle, that's not to say that more is always better. Here, we offer variations on classics—silky bisques, cold soups, bean soups, and seafood stews. All you need is a spoon. Dig in!

BROCCOLI BISQUE

A great way to use up those broccoli stems, and induce the "Yuck! Broccoli" Brigade to lay down their arms.

> 1 bunch broccoli, about 1½ pounds (675 g)
> 1 medium-size onion
> 1 cup (235 ml) heavy cream

Cut off the broccoli florets and reserve. Cut off and discard the bottom 2 inches (5 cm) of the stems, then cut the stems into 1-inch (2½-cm) pieces. Peel and dice the onion.

Over low heat, cook the onion in a 2-quart (2-L) pot until soft and translucent, about 10 minutes. Add the broccoli stems and add just enough water to cover them. Season with salt and pepper to taste. Over medium-high heat, cook the broccoli for 20 to 25 minutes at a low boil, until quite soft. Puree the broccoli with the water, either using an immersion blender or working in batches with a countertop blender. Push the puree through a medium-mesh strainer back into the pot. Discard the pulp left in the strainer. Add the broccoli florets and heat for 4 to 5 minutes, until they are just cooked. Add the cream and adjust seasoning with salt and pepper.

YIELD: 4 to 6 servings

🫙 ADD IT!
Stir 1 teaspoon red wine vinegar into the bisque to bring out more depth of flavor.

BUTTERNUT SQUASH APPLE CIDER BISQUE

This soup is easy, quick, and delicious—we like to serve it as a starter for winter feasts.

> 1 butternut squash, about 3 pounds (1¼ kg)
> 2 tablespoons (30 ml) oil
> ½ gallon (5½ L) apple cider
> 1 teaspoon Chinese five-spice powder

Preheat the oven to 350°F (180°C, gas mark 4).

Peel, seed, and cube the squash into 1-inch (2½-cm) pieces, saving the seeds.

Rinse the seeds, then toss with a bit of oil, salt, and pepper. Spread the seeds out on a cookie sheet and bake for ½ hour, or until a nice golden brown.

In the meantime, place the squash in a saucepan; add the cider and the spice and bring to a boil. Cook over medium heat until the squash is soft. Puree using an immersion blender, a food processor, or regular blender, adding water if needed to achieve a smooth, thick, but still souplike consistency. Reheat in the saucepan, adding salt and pepper to taste.

Serve soup garnished with some of the toasted seeds.

YIELD: 4 to 6 servings

ADD IT!
1 cup diced onion with the squash and cider; garnish with a dollop of sour cream or plain yogurt if you so desire.

CABBAGE AND BARLEY SOUP

A fairly quick and simple soup that is full of good vitamins. The barley adds a nice thickness to the broth.

- 1 head green cabbage, about 2 pounds (900 g)
- 2 tablespoons (30 ml) oil
- 1 cup (200 g) pearl barley
- 1 can tomato juice (64 ounces, or 2 L)

Core and shred the cabbage, then place in a heavy 4-quart (4-L) pot. Add the oil and cook over low heat, covered, for 15 to 20 minutes, or until the cabbage is wilted. Stir in the barley, add the tomato juice, and turn up the heat to medium. Simmer the soup for 30 minutes, until the barley is al dente. Add salt and pepper to taste and serve.

YIELD: 4 to 6 servings

🧂 ADD IT!
You can dress this soup up with a variety of things. Sauté the cabbage with a little chopped onion and minced garlic, for starters, then sprinkle cooked chopped bacon over the top of each bowl.

Calde Verde

Traditionally, this soup has sliced chorizo or other Portuguese sausage as well.

- 1 bunch kale
- 1 pound (450 g) Yukon gold potatoes
- 2 quarts (2 L) chicken broth

Wash the kale, strip out the stems, and shred the leafy part. Put in a heavy 4-quart (4-L) pot. Peel and slice the potatoes into ¼-inch slices. Add to the pot and add the chicken broth. Cook over medium-high heat until the potatoes and kale are well cooked. Add salt and pepper to taste. The kale should be quite soft—without much resistance to the tooth—and the potatoes falling apart. In fact, some of the potatoes will disappear into the broth, thickening and enriching the soup.

YIELD: 4 to 6 servings

Carrot and Ginger Soup

This is a snap to make, and you will wow your friends with the fresh taste of the ginger and the earthy sweetness of the carrots.

- 2 pounds (900 g) carrots
- 2 tablespoons (12 g) minced fresh ginger
- 1 cup (235 ml) white wine

Peel the carrots, cut them into ½-inch (1-cm) rounds, and put them in a 2-quart (2-L) pot. Cover them with water, add the ginger and wine, and cook at a low boil over medium heat until the carrots are very soft—about 30 minutes. Puree the entire contents of the pot with an immersion blender or in a regular blender. Adjust the seasoning with salt and pepper, and add water to the desired consistency. Heat to a simmer and serve.

YIELD: 4 to 6 servings

🧂 ADD IT!
Drizzle a little crème fraîche over the soup in each bowl when serving.

CORN TARRAGON CHOWDER

A soup for the summer, when the butter and sugar corn comes into high season.

6 ears corn, as fresh as possible
3 tablespoons (10 g) chopped fresh tarragon
2 tablespoons (28 g) butter
2 cups (475 ml) light cream

Husk the corn and remove the silk. Using a sharp paring knife, slice the corn kernels from three ears of corn; put in a small bowl and set aside. Do not discard the corn cobs.

Fill a large sauté pan or skillet with a tight-fitting lid half full of water; place the other three ears of corn, as well as the 3 scraped cobs, in a single layer in the pan, until the water comes to about halfway up the corn. Cover and turn up the heat to high; boil the corn until done, 5 to 7 minutes. Remove the corn and let cool, reserving the cooking liquid.

While the corn is boiling, place a medium-size sauté pan or skillet over medium heat and melt the butter. Add the reserved corn kernels and two-thirds of the tarragon to the pan and sauté until the corn has turned a brighter yellow, about 5 minutes. Remove from heat and set aside.

When the corn on the cob has cooled, slice the kernels from the cobs using a sharp paring knife. Place those corn kernels in a blender, along with 2 cups (475 ml) of the cooking water, and process until smooth.

Put the corn puree, the sautéed corn-tarragon mixture, and the cream in a 2-quart (2-L) saucepan and heat until just heated through; do not boil. Season with salt and pepper. If the mixture is too thick, add more corn water until it's the consistency you prefer. Sprinkle a little chopped tarragon over each bowl as garnish.

YIELD: 4 to 6 servings

ADD IT!
Sauté a few shrimp in butter; chop roughly and sprinkle a handful into each soup bowl.

CURRIED CAULIFLOWER BISQUE

A quick and easy soup with an elegant flavor. Your guests will never guess that the mysterious, evocative ingredient is raisins.

1 head cauliflower
1 tablespoon (7 g) Madras curry powder
¼ cup (40 g) golden raisins

Core the cauliflower and roughly chop the florets. In a heavy 4-quart (4-L) pot combine the cauliflower, curry powder, raisins, and enough water to just cover the cauliflower. Cook over medium heat until the cauliflower is soft, then puree the mixture with an immersion blender, adding water if needed. Season with salt and pepper to taste and serve.

YIELD: 4 to 6 servings

CHESTNUT CREAM SOUP

Rich and earthy—the essence of fall and a perfect and unexpected starter for Thanksgiving.

½ pound (225 g) chestnuts
2 cups (475 ml) apple juice or cider
1 cup (235 ml) heavy cream

Prepare the chestnuts: Put the chestnuts in a 1-quart (1-L) pot and cover with water. Bring to a boil and boil for 7 to 8 minutes. Drain the chestnuts.

Preheat the oven to 350°F (180°C, gas mark 4).

When the chestnuts are cool enough to handle, cut a small X on each one with the point of a paring knife. Put the chestnuts on a baking tray and bake for 12 to 15 minutes, until the X bursts outward a bit. Cool the chestnuts and shell them.

Put the shelled chestnuts in a 2-quart (2-L) pot. Add the apple juice and 1 cup (235 ml) of water. Bring to a boil, lower heat, and simmer for 12 to 15 minutes. Puree the soup with an immersion blender or in a regular blender. Add the cream and season to taste with salt and pepper. Heat to a simmer and serve.

YIELD: 4 to 6 servings

ADD IT!
Sprinkle a handful of cooked, crumbled bacon over each bowl before serving.

CHICKEN TORTELLINI SOUP

You can use any of the wide variety of small filled pastas on the market to vary the flavor of this simple and fast soup.

28 ounces (825 ml) chicken broth
½ pound (225 g) cheese tortellini
2 tablespoons (30 g) pesto sauce

Bring the broth to a boil in a saucepan. Add the tortellini and cook according to package directions, but do not drain when the cooking time is up. Salt and pepper to taste. Divide the soup among 4 bowls and swirl in the pesto.

YIELD: 4 to 6 servings

CHILLED FRUIT AND YOGURT SOUP

Great on a hot summer day. We saw these yogurt smoothies in the supermarket and were intrigued by the possibilities of using them as ingredients.

1 cup (235 ml) white wine
2 pints (1 L) yogurt fruit smoothie, whatever flavor you like
2 tablespoons (6 g) chopped fresh mint

Put the wine in a 2-quart (2-L) pot and cook, over medium heat, until reduced by half. Allow to cool briefly, then stir in the smoothie. Refrigerate until cold. Serve in chilled bowls garnished with mint.

YIELD: 4 to 6 servings

COLD BLUEBERRY SOUP

Wonderful in the summer, as an appetizer or as a dessert.

1 pound (450 g) frozen wild blueberries
1 tablespoon (12 g) minced fresh ginger
1 cup (245 g) plain yogurt

Put the blueberries and the ginger in a 2-quart (2-L) pot and add 2 cups (475 ml) of water. Cook over medium heat for 15 to 20 minutes. Remove from the heat and puree with an immersion blender or in a regular blender. Stir in the yogurt and chill for at least 1 hour. Serve in chilled bowls.

YIELD: 4 to 6 servings

🧂 ADD IT!
Float a small scoop of lemon sorbet in each bowl.

CREAM OF SPINACH SOUP

Full of good vitamins and the subtle flavor of spinach. Popeye would approve!

1 pound (450 g) spinach
1 tablespoon (15 g) tarragon-flavored Dijon mustard
2 cups (475 ml) light cream

Pick through the spinach, removing the large stems and any rotten leaves. Put into a heavy 4-quart (4-L) pot, and add the mustard and 4 cups (1 L) water. Bring to a boil on high heat, then cook for a couple of minutes, until the spinach is wilted. Puree with an immersion blender, or in a regular blender in batches. Return to medium heat and add cream and salt and pepper to taste. Bring to a simmer but do not allow to boil.

YIELD: 4 to 6 servings

🧂 ADD IT!
Sautéing 1 tablespoon (10 g) garlic along with the spinach would make a nice addition.

CREAM OF ASPARAGUS SOUP

The preferred asparagus for this soup is the thicker-stemmed variety, rather than the pencil-thin ones.

> 1 bunch asparagus, about 1 pound (450 g)
> ¼ cup (40 g) chopped shallots
> ½ cup (120 ml) heavy cream

Cut off and reserve the tips of the asparagus. Cut off and discard the bottom 1 to 2 inches (2 to 5 cm), the really woody part of the stalks. (Alternatively, you can peel the stalks and use the whole thing. We are trying to keep the "strings" out.) Cut the stalks into 1-inch (2½-cm) pieces and put them into a 2-quart (2-L) pot along with the shallots. Add 1 quart (1 L) water and bring to a boil over high heat. Reduce to a simmer and cook for 30 to 40 minutes, adding water if needed.

Puree the asparagus and the cooking liquid, then push the resulting puree through a medium-mesh strainer. Return the soup to the pot and heat on medium heat. Add the cream and season with salt and pepper to taste. Add the asparagus tips and cook for a couple of minutes more, then serve.

YIELD: 4 to 6 servings

🥫 ADD IT!
Stir a spoonful of balsamic vinegar into the soup to deepen the flavor.

GREEN BEAN AND BACON SOUP

Usually we hate overcooked green beans, but in this soup they should give up all resistance to the tooth.

> 6 slices bacon, cooked
> ½ pound (225 g) green beans
> 1 quart (1 L) chicken stock or broth

Crumble the bacon and put it into a 2-quart (2-L) pot. Trim the green beans and cut them into 1-inch (2½-cm) pieces. Put the beans and the stock into the pot. Simmer over medium heat until the beans start to break up a bit and are soft, about 45 minutes. Season with salt and pepper to taste.

YIELD: 4 to 6 servings

ADD IT!
Sprinkle finely grated Parmesan cheese on each serving.

HAM AND BEAN SOUP

A classic soup, and for good reason.

> 1 cup (215 g) white navy beans
> 1 quart (1 L) chicken stock or broth
> 1 cup (150 g) diced ham

Put the beans in a 2-quart (2-L) pot and add 1 quart (1 L) water. Bring the beans to a boil over high heat, cover, and remove from heat. Let the beans sit, covered, for 1 hour. Drain the beans and return them to the pot. Add the stock and simmer over medium heat for 30 minutes. Mix in the ham and continue cooking for another 20 to 30 minutes until the beans are tender. Puree 1 cup of the soup in a blender and return it to the pot. Adjust seasoning with salt and pepper. You may have to add a bit of water if the soup has gotten too thick.

YIELD: 4 to 6 servings

ADD IT!
Shred some spinach leaves and add them toward the end of the cooking time.

HONEYDEW MELON PORT WINE SOUP

This is a quick and simple cold soup that is a refreshing start to a summer dinner outdoors. Make sure you have a nice ripe melon. In fact, any kind of melon will do. This soup is perfect for a melon that's too ripe to be served sliced but is still sweet and delicious.

> 1 cup (235 ml) ruby port
> 1 honeydew melon
> 2 limes

In a small saucepan, cook the port over medium-high heat until it is reduced by half. Set aside to cool. Squeeze the juice from one lime and slice the other into thin slices; set aside.

Peel and seed the melon. Coarsely chop it into chunks and place these into a food processor. Add the port and the lime juice. Process until smooth, adding water if needed to make the proper consistency.

Serve in chilled bowls with a slice of lime floating on top.

YIELD: 4 to 6 servings

LENTIL, BACON, AND TOMATO SOUP

V-8 juice can be a great way to add flavor to a soup.

> ½ pound (225 g) bacon
> ½ pound (225 g) lentils
> 1 can V-8 juice, or other vegetable juice cocktail (64 ounces, or 2 L)

Cut the bacon into small cubes and cook over medium heat in a 4-quart (4-L) pot until rendered and crisp. Drain off most of the fat, add the lentils, and briefly sauté with the bacon, allowing fat to coat the lentils. Add the V-8 juice and simmer until the lentils are soft, about 45 minutes. Puree about a quarter of the soup in a blender, mix back in with the rest, adjust the seasoning with salt and pepper, and serve.

YIELD: 4 to 6 servings

🥫 ADD IT!
A hearty soup will deepen in flavor if you sauté minced onion and garlic along with the bacon.

New Mexico Corn and Chicken Soup

This hearty soup will feed a gang. You can make it with canned broth and boneless chicken breast simmered and shredded for a quick weeknight supper, but the homemade stock adds a wonderful richness.

> 1 whole chicken, 2½ to 3 pounds (1 to 1¼ kg)
> 1 quart (1 L) sweet corn soup (see note)
> 1 can (14 ounces, or 400 g) roasted New Mexico green chiles

Place the chicken in a 4-quart (4-L) pot, then add just enough water to cover. Cover the pot, place on high heat, and bring to a boil. Reduce the heat to medium-low and simmer for 45 minutes. Remove the chicken from the pot, reserving the cooking liquid in the pot. Cool the chicken until it can be handled, then remove the meat from the bones. Discard the skin, shred the meat into a bowl, and refrigerate.

Put the bones back in the pot. Cook the stock over medium-high heat for 1 hour. Strain the bones from the stock and let it sit until the fat rises to the top. Remove the fat and discard. (An easy way to degrease stock is to refrigerate it until the fat solidifies and then simply remove the fat with a spoon.)

Put the stock, corn soup, and chicken meat into a heavy pot. Drain the chiles and coarsely chop or briefly process them in a food processor fitted with the metal blade, then add them to the pot. Bring the pot to a boil, add salt and pepper to taste, reduce heat to low, and simmer for ½ hour. The soup is ready to serve.

YIELD: 8 to 10 servings

🥫 ADD IT!
This soup is great with some chopped fresh cilantro and a squeeze of lime.

> **NOTE:** *We find the sweet corn soup in cardboard containers, like juice boxes, at our market and at natural food stores. If you can't find a close approximation, steam 4 ears of corn, remove the kernels, and puree them along with 2 cups (475 ml) cooking water and 1 cup (235 ml) cream.*

PORCINI MUSHROOM BISQUE

4 ounces (115 g) dried porcini mushrooms
½ cup (120 ml) medium-dry sherry
1 cup (235 ml) heavy cream

Place the mushrooms in a mixing bowl. Bring 8 cups of water to a boil and pour over the mushrooms. Let them steep for 15 minutes, until well softened. Drain the mushrooms, reserving the soaking water. Put the mushrooms in a saucepan, add the sherry, and cook over medium heat for 5 minutes, or until the sherry is mostly absorbed. Fit a paper towel into a small sieve and drain the mushroom soaking water through it to filter out the grit. Simmer the mixture for 15 to 20 minutes.

Puree the soup using an immersion blender, or in a regular blender. Return to medium heat, mix in the cream, and add salt and pepper to taste. Serve immediately.

YIELD: 4 to 6 servings

ADD IT!
One trick will make this soup a bit more lively—and indeed most soups benefit from it. Toward the end of the cooking add a dash of vinegar. For this soup we would use sherry vinegar, but any decent one will do. You don't want to add enough so the taste is noticeable, but a dash will add a nice dimension of flavor.

QUICK ESCAROLE SOUP

Escarole in chicken broth is a staple in many Italian households. Long simmering in broth takes a lot of the bitterness out of the escarole.

    1 small head escarole
    1 quart (1 L) chicken stock or broth
    2 tablespoons (30 ml) red wine vinegar

Remove any damaged outer leaves of the escarole. Cut the escarole into ½-inch (1-cm) pieces and wash well under cold water. Heat the stock in a 2-quart (2-L) pot. Add the escarole and vinegar, along with salt and pepper to taste. Simmer for 5 to 10 minutes.

YIELD: 4 to 6 servings

ADD IT!
Drain a can of white beans, such as cannellini, and add them to the soup.

RED PEPPER AND EGGPLANT BISQUE

Rich, delicious, and vegan.

    1 jar (14 ounces, or 400 g) roasted red peppers
    1 medium eggplant, about 1 pound (450 g)
    1 quart (1 L) tomato juice

Drain the peppers, chop them roughly and put them in a 2-quart (2-L) pot. Peel and cube the eggplant into ½-inch (1-cm) pieces and add them to the pot. Add the tomato juice and black pepper to taste. Simmer over medium heat for 35 to 40 minutes. Puree with an immersion blender or in a regular blender until smooth. Adjust seasoning with salt and pepper.

YIELD: 4 to 6 servings

ADD IT!
Add a handful of chopped, sauteed spinach to the pot.

Rich Onion Soup

A long, slow caramelization of the onions is the secret to the rich and sweet flavor of this favorite soup. Homemade beef stock will produce a richer soup, but the canned variety works fine.

3 pounds (1¼ kg) Spanish onions
4 tablespoons (55 g) butter
1 quart (1 L) beef stock or broth
1 cup (235 ml) red wine

Peel the onions and slice them into thin strips. Melt the butter in a heavy 2-quart (2-L) saucepan and add the onions. Cook over low heat, stirring every so often, until the onions are soft and have a rich caramel color. This process will take 45 minutes to 1 hour. Be careful not to let the onions stick and burn, as this will add bitterness to the soup. You can add a bit of water if needed to "unstick" the bottom of the pan.

Next, add the stock and wine, along with salt and pepper to taste. If you are using canned stock, be careful about adding salt, as canned broth is very salty. Bring to a boil, turn down the heat to medium, and simmer for 15 minutes. The soup is now ready to serve, but like most other soups, this will taste even better when reheated tomorrow.

YIELD: 4 to 6 servings

🧂 ADD IT!
Many love this soup with a slice of toasted baguette and Gruyère cheese melted on top.

ROASTED PARSNIP SOUP

This soup is particularly good in the early spring, when you can get parsnips that have spent the winter in the ground. These parsnips have a sweetness and complexity of flavor that is one of the joys of early spring. Look for them at farmers' markets as soon as the ground thaws.

1 pound (450 g) parsnips
¼ cup (60 ml) oil
1 teaspoon grated nutmeg
1 cup (235 ml) heavy cream

Preheat the oven to 350°F (180°C, gas mark 4).

Peel the parsnips and cut into sticks ½ x 2 inches (1 x 5 cm). Toss them in the oil, and lightly season with salt and pepper. Spread the parsnips in a single layer on a baking sheet and bake for about 15 minutes until softened and lightly brown, but not fully cooked through. Be careful not to let them burn. They will add bitterness to the soup if burnt. You can cut a few matchsticks of roasted parsnips to use as a garnish later, if you wish.

Put the parsnips and nutmeg in a 2-quart (2-L) saucepan. Add enough water to cover three-fourths of the way up the parsnips and simmer for 20 minutes, or until the parsnips are quite soft. Puree with an immersion blender or in a regular blender, stir in the cream, adjust the seasoning, and serve.

YIELD: 4 to 6 servings

ROASTED TOMATO TARRAGON SOUP

There is no reason to make this soup unless you can get your hands on real, honest-to-goodness local ripe tomatoes. If you have the goods, though, you can eat this at every meal. You can substitute fresh basil or oregano for the tarragon.

2 pounds (900 g) tomatoes
¼ cup (60 ml) extra-virgin olive oil
1 medium-size Spanish onion
1 tablespoon (15 g) butter
3 tablespoons (10 g) chopped fresh tarragon

Preheat the oven to 300°F (150°C, gas mark 2).

Bring a 4-quart (4-L) pot of water to a boil over high heat. Take the tomatoes and cut a small X on the bottom of each and remove the stem with a paring knife. Dip the tomatoes in the boiling water for 10 to 15 seconds, then run under cold water. Peel the tomatoes and cut in half. Core and squeeze out the seeds into a strainer set over a bowl so you can capture the tomato juice.

Toss the tomatoes with 2 tablespoons (30 ml) oil, season with salt and pepper to taste, and spread them out on a baking sheet. Slowly roast for 30 minutes or so, until they are somewhat collapsed and a bit dried out.

While the tomatoes are roasting, peel and chop the onion into ¼-inch (½-cm) pieces. Put the onion in a 2-quart (2-L) pot with the butter and cook slowly, covered, over low heat, until the onion is soft and translucent. Add the roasted tomatoes, half the tarragon, tomato juice, and enough water to barely cover. Simmer for 15 minutes, then puree the contents of the pot with an immersion blender, or in a regular blender in batches. Add more water if needed and adjust seasoning. When you have just finished cooking, swirl in the other 2 tablespoons (30 ml) olive oil.

This soup can be served hot or cold, garnished with remaining tarragon.

YIELD: 4 to 6 servings

🧂 ADD IT!
A slice of grilled or toasted rustic bread in the bottom of the bowl is a nice addition.

Sorrell Cream Soup

The piquant taste of sorrel is a wonderful spring tonic.

   3 cups (60 g) sorrel leaves
   3 cups (700 ml) chicken stock or broth
   1 cup (235 ml) heavy cream

Rinse the sorrel under cold water and spin-dry; remove the stems and spoiled leaves. Heat the stock in a 2-quart (2-L) pot, and when it boils, add the sorrel. Cook for 1 to 2 minutes, then immediately puree in a blender until smooth. Return to the pot and add the cream. Heat through, but do not boil. Season to taste with salt and pepper.

YIELD: 4 to 6 servings

Sweet Corn and Shrimp Soup

In this recipe, we take a really good commercially prepared product and make it better.

   1 quart (1 L) sweet corn soup (see note)
   ½ pound (225 g) cooked medium shrimp (peeled and deveined)
   3 tablespoons (10 g) chopped chives

Remove the tails from the shrimp and cut the shrimp into small dice. Heat the corn soup, add the shrimp and half the chives, and simmer for 5 minutes. When serving, sprinkle with the remaining chopped chives.

YIELD: 4 to 6 servings

NOTE: We find the sweet corn soup in cardboard containers, like juice boxes, at our market and at natural food stores. If you can't find a close approximation, steam 4 ears of corn, remove the kernels, and puree them along with 2 cups (475 ml) cooking water and 1 cup (235 ml) cream.

THAI GREEN MUSSEL SOUP

This quick and easy soup creates an explosion of flavor. The heat can be scaled up or down to individual taste.

    1 pound (450 g) mussels
    2 tablespoons (30 g) Thai green curry paste
    1 can (14 ounces, or 415 ml) coconut milk

Rinse the mussels and pick them over, discarding any that are not tightly closed or that do not close when tapped on the shell. Pick off any beards—we like using the rope-cultured mussels, as they are much less gritty and don't have much in the way of beards.

Put the mussels in a 2-quart (2-L) pot, add 2 cups (475 ml) water, cover tightly, and cook over high heat until the mussels are opened, 8 to 10 minutes. Drain the mussels, reserving the cooking liquid. Shell the mussels, reserving 12 in the shell.

In a saucepan heat 1 tablespoon (15 ml) oil over medium heat. Add the curry paste and let cook for a minute, stirring. Add the reserved cooking broth (be careful when pouring to avoid the grit that has settled to the bottom) and the coconut milk. Bring to a boil and add salt and pepper to taste.

Divide the mussel meats among 4 wide soup bowls, then ladle the soup and garnish each bowl with 3 mussels still in the shell. Serve immediately.

YIELD: 4 servings

🧂 ADD IT!
This soup can also be garnished with a bit of chopped cilantro and a wedge of lime.

VICHYSSOISE

A classic summer soup served cold, this one is also wonderful served hot. Remember that you need to salt more heavily if serving cold, less if hot. This soup also makes a good base for all manner of additions, from broccoli to chopped cooked bacon and cheddar cheese to sliced mushrooms.

2 pounds (900 g) boiling potatoes
2 large leeks
2 tablespoons (28 g) butter
2 cups (475 ml) half-and-half

Peel the potatoes, cut them into 1-inch (2½-cm) cubes, cover with cold water, and set aside. Trim the root end and remove the dark green portion of the leek. Cut the leeks in half lengthwise, then cut into thin half moons. Place the leeks in a bowl of cold water and swish them around to clean. Remove them from the water by lifting them out with a slotted spoon, leaving any dirt in the water. Leeks are notorious dirt carriers, so you might have to wash them a couple of times.

Next, melt the butter in a 4-quart (4-L) pot over low heat. Add the leeks and cook slowly, covered, for 10 to 15 minutes. When the leeks are softened and somewhat translucent, drain the potatoes and add them to the pot. Pour in enough water to just cover, add salt and pepper to taste, and simmer until the potatoes are quite soft—about ½ hour.

Puree the soup with an immersion blender, or in a regular blender or food processor. Return the pot to the stove, stir in the half-and-half, and adjust seasonings. If you want to serve the soup hot, serve it immediately; otherwise, refrigerate it until cold.

YIELD: 4 to 6 servings

🥫 ADD IT!
This soup is great with a sprinkle of chopped chives as a garnish. If you have chives in bloom, float a big purple blossom on the top of each bowl, too.

WATERCRESS CREAM

A simple soup that brings out a beautiful bright green color and the fresh, peppery flavor of watercress.

    2 bunches watercress
    3 cups (700 ml) chicken stock or broth
    1 cup (235 ml) heavy cream

Rinse the watercress under cold water. Cut off and discard the bottom 2 inches of stems. Heat the stock in a 2-quart (2-L) pot, and when it boils, add the watercress. Cook for 1 to 2 minutes, then immediately puree in a blender until smooth. Return to the pot and stir in the cream. Heat through, but do not boil. Season to taste with salt and pepper.

YIELD: 4 to 6 servings

WHITE GAZPACHO

This is a traditional Spanish version of the classic chilled soup that was in vogue before tomatoes made their way from the New World.

4 slices slightly stale roasted garlic bread
1 cup (125 g) blanched almonds
2 tablespoons (30 ml) extra-virgin olive oil
1 pound (450 g) green grapes

Cut the crusts off the bread and cut the bread into cubes. Put the bread cubes in a small mixing bowl and cover with cold water. Allow this to sit for 10 minutes, then squeeze out the water from the bread. Put the soaked bread, the almonds, the olive oil, and about two-thirds of the grapes into a blender. Add 2 cups (475 ml) cold water. Blend until smooth, adding more cold water if needed. Season with salt and pepper. Allow to sit, refrigerated, for at least 1 hour and preferably overnight. Adjust the seasoning with salt and pepper and serve in chilled bowls. Garnish with the remaining grapes, cut in half.

YIELD: 4 to 6 servings

🥫 ADD IT!
1 clove minced garlic.

8

Breads, Crackers, and Cereals

Bread is the staff of life, so said the ancients. It is great any time of the day and in many societies is considered an essential accompaniment to any meal. Many of us think we don't have time to make our own bread, but the hands-on work is pretty minimal, and you can go about your business while the dough rises quietly under a towel. Keep in mind when making bread that the amount of flour that you use on a given day in a given recipe will vary. You will need less flour during the dry winter than in the humid summer, for example. Flour will hold a surprising amount of moisture.

An equipment note: If you have a stand-type mixer with a dough hook, then breadmaking has just gotten even easier. The kneading, although fun, does take time and effort, and we let the machine do that work for us. If you have a bread machine, you can also use it to mix and knead the dough, then take it out and form it yourself if you want your loaves to look more "homemade."

SEMOLINA BREAD

Semolina flour, made from durum wheat, is generally associated with making pasta, but it makes great bread, too.

> **1 package (¼ ounce, or 7 g) active dry yeast**
> 1½ cups (350 ml) lukewarm water
> **3 cups plus 2 tablespoons (400 g) semolina flour**
> **1 cup (125 g) bread flour**
> 1 tablespoon (18 g) salt
> Flour for kneading

Put the yeast and the water in the mixing bowl of a stand-type mixer fitted with a dough hook. Let the yeast proof for 5 minutes, then add the flours and the salt. Mix and knead, adding flour as needed, for 8 to 10 minutes.

Lightly oil a mixing bowl. Put the dough into the bowl; flip the dough once to coat both sides, cover with plastic wrap, and allow to rise, in a warm place, until doubled in volume. This rise should take 1½ hours or so.

Punch down the dough and form into 2 French-type loaves. Grease a baking sheet and sprinkle with semolina flour. Put the loaves on the sheet and cover with plastic. Again allow to rise until doubled, about 45 minutes.

Preheat the oven to 400°F (200°C, gas mark 6).

When the bread is risen, slash across the top of each loaf diagonally several times. Bake for 25 to 30 minutes until golden brown and the bread sounds hollow when tapped on the bottom. Remove from the baking sheet and cool on racks.

YIELD: 2 loaves, about 1½ pounds each (¾ kg)

Rye Bread

A good basic rye, great with soup or as a sandwich bread.

   1 package (¼ ounce, or 7 g) active dry yeast
   1½ cups (350 ml) lukewarm water
   1 cup (125 g) rye flour
   2 cups (250 g) bread flour
   1 tablespoon (18 g) salt

Put the yeast and the water in the mixing bowl of a stand-type mixer fitted with a dough hook. Let the yeast proof for 5 minutes, then add the flours and the salt. Mix and knead, adding flour as needed, for 8 to 10 minutes.

Lightly oil a mixing bowl. Put the dough into the bowl; flip the dough once to coat both sides, cover with plastic wrap, and allow to rise, in a warm place, until doubled in volume. This rise should take 1½ hours or so.

Grease a baking sheet. Punch down the dough and form into a round loaf. Put the loaf on the baking sheet and cover with plastic. Allow to rise a second time for 30 to 40 minutes, until the dough does not spring back when poked with a finger tip.

While the bread is rising a second time, preheat the oven to 350°F (180°C, gas mark 4). Slash the top of the loaf 3 times with a sharp knife. Bake for 40 to 45 minutes, until browned and the bottom sounds hollow when tapped.

YIELD: 1 loaf, about 2½ pounds (1 kg)

ADD IT!
Jazz up this bread with 1 cup (150 g) dried cherries, or ½ cup (120 ml) molasses (reduce water to 1 cup, or 235 ml), or ¼ cup (30 g) caraway seeds.

BASIL FOCACCIA

Bob's very first cooking job was baking lovely braided baguettes for a local shop when he was about 13, and it was good stuff. As is this. It's great with soups or split as a sandwich bread. You can also use the dough as a pizza crust—just roll it out thinner.

1 package (¼ ounce, or 7 g) active dry yeast
2 cups (475 ml) lukewarm water
½ cup (120 ml) extra-virgin olive oil
4 cups (500 g) all-purpose or bread flour
½ cup (120 ml) basil pesto
2 tablespoons (35 g) salt

In the mixing bowl for a stand mixer, or in a large bowl, combine the yeast and water. Let stand for 5 minutes, then add ¼ cup (60 ml) of the oil, the flour, ¼ cup (60 ml) of the pesto, and the salt. Mix and knead, with either the mixer's dough hook, or by hand, adding a bit of water or flour to adjust the consistency of the dough. Knead for 8 to 10 minutes, until you have a smooth, elastic dough. Grease a large bowl. Put the dough in the bowl, flip the dough once to coat both sides, and cover with plastic wrap. Place the bowl in a warm place until the dough has doubled in volume, about 1½ hours.

Preheat the oven to 400°F (200°C, gas mark 6).

Punch down the dough and roll it out to the size of a baking sheet pan 18 x 12 inches (about 45 x 30 cm), with ½-inch (1-cm) sides. Fit the dough into the pan, stretching the corners to make sure they fully fill the entire pan. Enclose the whole pan in an unused plastic trash bag and allow the dough to rise, in a warm place, for about ½ hour. Remove the trash bag and with your fingertips dimple the surface of the dough. Mix the remaining oil and pesto and liberally brush the surface of the dough. Sprinkle with kosher salt if desired. Bake for 20 to 25 minutes until the bread is lightly browned and sounds hollow when tapped. Remove from the baking pan and cool on a rack.

YIELD: 1 loaf, 18 x 12 inches (45 x 30 cm), about 2 pounds (900 g)

SNOWFLAKE ROLLS

This dough can also be used to make a regular loaf of basic white bread. These are called snowflake rolls because the flour sprinkled over the dough before the second proofing makes the rolls look snow covered.

> 1 package (¼ ounce, or 7 g) active dry yeast
> 2 cups (475 ml) lukewarm water
> ½ cup (175 g) honey
> 4 to 5 cups (500 to 625 g) all-purpose or bread flour
> 1 tablespoon (18 g) salt

Mix the yeast and water in a mixing bowl. Allow to proof for 5 minutes, then add the honey, the flour, and the salt in that order. Mix and then knead, either using the dough hook on a mixer, or by hand, for 10 minutes, until you have a smooth and elastic dough. Lightly oil a mixing bowl, put the dough in, flip the dough once to coat both sides, and cover with plastic wrap. Let the dough rise in a warm place for about 1½ hours, until doubled in bulk. Punch down the dough and divide into roughly 20 pieces. Make balls out of the dough pieces and place them on a baking sheet, close but not touching. Brush each ball of dough with water and sprinkle a little flour on each. Put the whole pan into an unused trash bag and let rise in a warm place for about 20 to 30 minutes. The rolls should be pressing together as they rise.

While the dough rises a second time, preheat the oven to 400°F (200°C, gas mark 6).

Remove the rolls from the bag and bake for 20 minutes, until golden brown and a roll sounds hollow when tapped on the bottom.

YIELD: About 20 rolls

GARLIC BREAD

1 loaf good-quality Italian or French bread
8 tablespoons (115 g) butter, softened
3 cloves garlic, minced
½ cup (40 g) shredded Parmesan cheese

Preheat the oven to 400°F (200°C, gas mark 6).

Split the loaf of bread and put the two halves, cut side up, on a baking sheet. In a small mixing bowl, combine the butter and garlic well. Spread this mixture onto the bread. Sprinkle the Parmesan over both halves. Bake for 10 to 12 minutes, until the cheese and butter are melted and the bread is heated through. Cut into pieces and serve.

YIELD: 6 to 8 servings

HAM AND SWISS POCKETS

These are easier to make than a ham-and-Swiss croissant and are still tasty.

1 tube refrigerator crescent rolls (8 rolls)
8 small, thin ham slices
8 small Swiss cheese slices

Preheat the oven to 350°F (180°C, gas mark 4).

Open the cylinder of dough and lay the dough out on a cutting board. Place a slice of ham and cheese on each roll and fold it over, pinching the edges to make a pocket. Put the pockets on a baking sheet and bake for 12 to 15 minutes.

YIELD: 8 rolls

GARLICKY BAGEL CHIPS

A great way to use up those leftover bagels, and much cheaper than the grocery-store version. These are great with soup, crumbled over a salad, or consumed straight from the oven.

2 bagels
¼ cup (60 ml) olive oil
1 tablespoon (10 g) minced garlic
2 tablespoons (6 g) minced fresh parsley

Preheat oven to 300°F (150°C, gas mark 2). Slice the bagels very thin, so that you have 5 to 6 "O's" from each bagel. Mix the oil, garlic, and parsley along with salt and pepper to taste. Brush the bagel slices on both sides with the mixture and spread out on a baking sheet. Bake for 15 to 20 minutes, until crisp and lightly browned.

YIELD: About 10 chips

PITA CRISPS

You can buy these in the store, but they are easy to make and will save you a lot of bucks. They are great with dips, hummus, or as a snack by themselves.

4 pita bread rounds
½ cup (120 ml) garlic olive oil
1 tablespoon (3 g) dried oregano
1 tablespoon (7 g) paprika

Preheat the oven to 325°F (170°C, gas mark 3).

Cut the pita pockets into 8 wedges, then split apart the 2 sides of the "pocket." Each pita bread round will give you 16 triangles. Put the cut pita in a large mixing bowl. In a small mixing bowl combine the oil, oregano, and paprika; add salt and pepper to taste. Stir well and pour on the pita pieces. Toss gently so that each piece is evenly coated. Spread the pieces on baking sheets in one layer and bake for 25 to 30 minutes, until the pieces are golden brown and crisp.

YIELD: 64 crisps

INDIAN CHAPATI

This is one of the many delicious breads from India. Chapati is a pancakelike bread that is baked on a griddle and used as a scoop for many dishes. You can use a mix of whole wheat and white flours with fine results. This is a great side bread for any curry dish and is terrific alone with raita or chutney.

1 cup (245 g) plain yogurt
3 cups (375 g) all-purpose flour, plus some for kneading
4 tablespoons (35 g) baking powder
1 tablespoon salt

Mix all ingredients except the oil, along with enough water to form a fairly sticky dough. Knead on a lightly floured surface until you have a smooth, pliable dough, about 10 minutes. Cover the dough with plastic and allow to rest for 15 minutes.

Heat the oven to its lowest setting. Cut the rested dough into golfball-size pieces. Flatten, then roll out on a floured surface to about ⅛ inch (⅓ cm) thick. Repeat with the rest of the dough. Heat a wide sauté pan or skillet over medium-high heat and add 3 to 4 tablespoons (45 to 60 ml) oil. When the oil is hot, add 1 or 2 pieces of dough—do not crowd—and cook for 3 to 4 minutes per side. Put the cooked bread in the oven, covered in a clean cloth to stay warm, and continue frying the breads.

YIELD: 8 to 10 breads

WHOLE WHEAT SESAME CRACKERS

2 cups (250 g) whole wheat flour
¼ cup plus 2 tablespoons (45 g) sesame seeds
2 teaspoons black pepper
2 teaspoons salt
½ cup (100 g) shortening
½ cup (120 ml) water

Preheat oven to 350°F (180°C, gas mark 4) and grease a baking sheet.

Mix all ingredients except shortening in a food processor fitted with the metal blade. Add the shortening and process until blended. Add enough of the water, slowly, to bring the dough together. Roll out on a floured surface until very thin. Cut out crackers with a cookie cutter or a water glass. Place on greased baking sheet. Brush with a little water and sprinkle with extra sesame seeds. Bake for 12 to 15 minutes, until crisp and golden brown.

YIELD: About 3 dozen 2-inch (5-cm) crackers

🥫 ADD IT!
You can brush the cracker with olive oil instead of water.

SPICY TORTILLA CHIPS

8 soft corn tortillas, 6 inches (15 cm) in diameter
¼ cup (35 g) dark chile powder
2 tablespoons (12 g) ground cumin

Cut the tortillas into 8 wedges each. Over medium-high heat, heat vegetable oil in a sauté pan or skillet until the oil reaches 350°F (180°C), or to the point at which a test chip bubbles right away. Fry the chips until crisp and golden brown, 3 to 4 minutes. Drain and toss with the spices and salt and pepper to taste.

YIELD: 64 chips

BASIC GRANOLA

Granola, even in bulk at the natural food store, costs the earth. Its ingredients, however, are pretty cheap, so try making it yourself. This is a basic recipe; feel free to add all the bells and whistles that occur to you and your palate.

1 cup (125 g) whole wheat flour
3 cups (250 g) rolled oats
1 cup (225 g) brown sugar, packed
16 tablespoons (½ pound, or 225 g) butter, melted
½ cup (120 ml) water

Preheat the oven to 300°F (150°C, gas mark 2).

Mix the dry ingredients, along with a pinch of salt. Whisk together the melted butter and the water. Pour over the dry ingredients and combine thoroughly. Spread out on baking sheets and bake for 25 to 30 minutes, until crisp and lightly browned. Cool on trays and store in airtight containers.

YIELD: 8 to 10 servings

ADD IT!
Where to start? You could add shredded coconut, raisins, dried cranberries, peanuts, almonds or other nuts, sunflower seeds, and spices such as cinnamon and nutmeg.

Main Dishes

9

Poultry

It wasn't so very long ago that chicken was a luxury item, reserved for Sunday dinner or state and festival occasions. Now, of course, it's so ubiquitous as to evoke eye-rolling at the thought of chicken again, for dinner. In fact, according to the U.S. Department of Agriculture, chicken consumption quintupled—from an annual consumption of 10 pounds to 54 pounds per person—between 1909 and 1999.

Part of that popularity, of course, lies in the fact that the cost of chicken has dropped over the years. But chicken is like Lon Chaney—it has a thousand faces. You can cook chicken with everything from artichokes to zucchini, and chances are, you'll end up with a dish that's perfectly edible if not downright delicious.

Here we offer recipes, such as the classic Roast Chicken with Lemon and Garlic, that riff on a traditional idea or theme. Other times, we use less common flavorings or unusual spices to bring new flair to this hard-working meat. After all, we don't want familiarity to breed contempt.

ROASTED BONED CHICKEN WITH CHESTNUTS AND CABBAGE

Cabbage and chestnuts—two winter staples that in combination seem somehow Dickensian. Savoy cabbage has a milder flavor than regular cabbage and makes an excellent replacement.

A note on the chicken: Before you run screaming into the night at the thought of boning a chicken, please remember that the friendly folks at the butcher shop or meat counter are there to serve. If you call ahead, they'll probably be able to do this for you. However, it's really not that difficult to do yourself, and just think of the bragging rights you'll accrue.

> ½ pound (225 g) chestnuts
> 1 small head savoy cabbage
> 1 roasting chicken, 4 to 5 pounds (1¾ to 2¼ kg)

Preheat the oven to 400°F (200°C, gas mark 6).

Prepare the chestnuts: Put the chestnuts in a small saucepan and cover with water. Bring them to a boil and cook at a low boil for 8 to 10 minutes. Drain the chestnuts and cut a small X on the flat side of each one with a paring knife. Put the chestnuts on a baking sheet and roast them in the oven for 15 minutes or so, until the X bursts outward a bit. Cool the chestnuts and shell them. Don't worry if some of them break.

Lower the heat of the oven to 325°F (170°C, gas mark 3).

Prepare the cabbage: Coarsely shred the cabbage. Heat a wide sauté pan or skillet over high heat and add 3 tablespoons (45 ml) oil. Sauté the cabbage for 8 to 10 minutes, seasoning with salt and pepper. Coarsely chop the chestnuts and stir them into the cabbage. Set aside.

Prepare the chicken: The first step is to bone out the chicken, with the aim of leaving the skin intact, the carcass in one piece, and the bones reserved. To do so, first cut out the backbone. We find kitchen shears to be helpful for this task. Next, remove the first 2 joints of the wings. Working carefully with a boning knife—or other sharp, small knife—remove the ribs and breast bone by scraping along them to release the meat. Lay the chicken on a cutting board, skin down, and cut out the thigh bone by cutting around the head of the bone, cutting a slit right down the bone, scraping the bone free from the flesh with the knife, and cutting through the ball joint at the leg end. Don't worry if the meat gets a bit hacked up. You may choose to remove the leg bone as well, but you don't need to. If you do, cut around the head of the bone at the thigh end to release the meat from the bone, then scrape all around the leg bone down to the end. Turn the leg inside out and pull the bone free, cutting out the end. Turn the boned leg skin-side out again. If you make a hole in the skin, don't worry: when you roll it up and cook it, no one will know.

Put all of your bones in a 2-quart (2-L) pot and cover them with water. Simmer the bones to make a quick broth while the chicken is roasting.

Lay the boned chicken out on a cutting board, skin down. Spread the chestnut-cabbage mixture over the chicken and roll it up, with the seam on the bottom. Tie with butcher twine and place on a rack in a flame-proof roasting pan. Season the chicken with salt and pepper and roast for 1½ to 2 hours, or until the temperature reads 165°F (74°C) at the thickest part. Set the chicken aside to rest for 15 minutes. Put the roasting pan on medium heat and add 2 cups (475 ml) of your stock. Boil, stirring up the brown bits on the bottom of the pan. Reduce the stock to 1 cup (235 ml) and strain.

To serve, cut slices of the chicken so you have a cross section. Moisten with some of the pan sauce.

YIELD: 6 servings

Roast Chicken with Lemon and Garlic

As kids, coming home to the aroma of chicken roasting was a guarantee of a happy stomach come dinner time. Crispy skin, tender moist meat—what more could one want?

We make a special plea not to scorn the dark meat. We may live in a world where the boneless, skinless chicken breast rules the dinner table, but dark meat is nearly always more moist and flavorful.

> 1 roasting chicken, 4 to 6 pounds (1¾ to 2¾ kg)
> 8 cloves garlic
> 3 lemons
> 4 tablespoons (55 g) butter, softened

Preheat the oven to 325°F (170°C, gas mark 3).

Peel the garlic and mince 4 of the cloves. Squeeze the lemons over the butter in a small bowl, reserving the rinds. Mash the juice and the minced garlic into the butter. Rinse the chicken with cold water and sprinkle salt and pepper in the bird's cavity. Stuff the lemon rinds and the remaining garlic into the cavity. Truss the chicken (see page 18 for instructions) and place on a rack on a roasting pan.

Loosen the skin at the top of the breast so that you can get underneath it—you may have to pierce the clear membrane that connects the skin to the flesh. Using a spoon and your fingers, slide the butter under the skin and work it evenly over the breast meat. Salt and pepper the outer skin and roast, basting every so often, for about 20 minutes a pound, or until an instant-read thermometer registers 160°F (70°C) at the thickest part of the thigh. Allow to rest for 15 minutes out of the oven and serve.

YIELD: 6 to 8 servings

ADD IT!
This is classic comfort food, and what better to serve with it but Mashed Potatoes with Cheddar Cheese (page 429) and Green Beans with Dill (page 400).

> **NOTE:** *The juices in the roasting pan, degreased, can be the base for a wonderful sauce or gravy.*

Braised Chicken with Parsley and Lemon

Lemon and chicken is a classic combination generally found in roasting. This recipe brings the duo to the stovetop. It's great served with Grilled Radicchio (page 410) and crusty bread. We specify a cut-up fryer chicken, almost always available at the store, but feel free to substitute your own favorite mix of parts.

1 fryer chicken, cut into 8 serving pieces, about 3 pounds (1¼ kg)
1 bunch flat-leaf parsley
4 lemons
4 tablespoons (55 g) butter, cold
3 tablespoons (45 ml) cooking oil

Season chicken with salt and pepper. Heat 3 tablespoons (45 ml) cooking oil in a medium-size sauté pan or skillet over medium-high heat. Add the chicken and sear until browned on all sides. You may want to do this in batches, as it's important not to crowd the pan.

While the chicken is searing, wash and chop the parsley and slice the lemons into ½-inch (1-cm) slices. Add the parsley and lemon to the pan and 2 cups (475 ml) water. Cover the pan and reduce the heat to a simmer. Cook for 40 to 45 minutes, until the chicken is done and tender. Using a slotted spoon, carefully remove the chicken and lemon from the broth to a platter and keep them warm.

Bring the sauce up to a boil (keep the lid off at this point) and reduce the braising liquid to about 1 cup (235 ml). Whisk in the butter, 1 tablespoon (15 g) at a time. Be sure to monitor the heat and remove as soon as the last butter is melted, to make sure the sauce doesn't break. Adjust the seasoning.

Pour the sauce over the chicken and lemons and serve.

YIELD: 4 servings

ADD IT!
Substitute 2 cups (475 ml) chicken stock for the water, and add a couple of minced shallots to the sauté pan as the last batch of chicken is searing.

CHICKEN BRAISED WITH SHALLOTS AND TARRAGON

To make this recipe we use the entire chicken, as all frugal cooks do. The stock will serve as the braising liquid and the basis for the sauce. This is time-consuming, and you certainly can substitute canned broth; we promise not to tell. (In good conscience, however, we have to say that a real stock is always superior to canned broth.)

> 1 whole fryer chicken, about 3 pounds (1¼ kg)
> 1 pound (450 g) shallots, topped, tailed, and peeled
> ½ cup (120 ml) tarragon vinegar
> 2 tablespoons (30ml) olive oil

Remove the backbone and wing tips from the chicken. Place these and the neck in a pan, cover with water, and bring to a boil. Skim off any froth that rises to the top, reduce to a simmer, and cook for 2 to 3 hours, adding water if needed to keep the bones covered. Strain and discard bones. Chill the stock and remove the fat that rises to the top. This is easiest after the fat has solidified. This step can be done in advance; in fact you can do this step, freeze the stock, and use it in your next dish calling for stock.

Cut the chicken into 8 pieces by splitting the chicken down the breastbone, cutting between the thigh and breast, then cutting the breast in half crosswise (cut right down through the bones) and cutting the drumstick off the thigh.

Preheat the oven to 325°F (170°C, gas mark 3).

In a heavy Dutch oven or ovenproof sauté pan or skillet, heat about 2 tablespoons (30 ml) olive oil over high heat. Season the chicken with salt and pepper, then sear on both sides, turning occasionally, until nicely browned on all sides. You may have to do this in batches—don't crowd the pan, or you won't get a good searing. Remove the chicken and set aside.

Turn the heat down to medium and add the shallots to the pan, stirring occasionally, until slightly caramelized, about 2 to 3 minutes. Add the vinegar, then the chicken. Add enough stock to come up about a third of the way on the chicken. Bring to a boil on the stovetop, then cover and place in the oven. Cook in the oven for about 45 minutes, until the chicken is tender, but not falling off the bones.

Carefully remove the chicken and shallots. Place in a serving dish and keep in a warm place. Degrease the liquid in the pan as well as possible, then bring to a boil on the stovetop and allow to reduce to about 1½ cups (355 ml). Adjust the seasoning, pour half the sauce over the chicken and serve, passing the rest of the sauce in a gravy boat.

YIELD: 4 servings

ADD IT!
Tossing 2 tablespoons (6 g) chopped fresh tarragon into the pan while the shallots are cooking will play up this delicious taste.

OVEN-FRIED CHICKEN DIJON STYLE

Panko, or Japanese bread crumbs, are very coarse white-bread crumbs used to coat foods before frying. They absorb less grease than regular bread crumbs and produce a delectably crunchy, golden brown crust. We find ours at the supermarket, but if you can't dig any up, use fresh bread crumbs.

    1 fryer chicken, cut into 8 serving pieces, about 3 pounds (1¼ kg)
    ½ cup (120 ml) Dijon mustard
    2 cups (100 g) panko

Preheat the oven to 375°F (190°C, gas mark 5).

Wash the chicken in cold water and pat dry. Season with salt and pepper and generously brush the mustard over the meat. In a wide, shallow dish, roll and gently press the chicken into the crumbs. Place on a baking sheet and bake in oven for 35 to 45 minutes, or until the juice runs clear when pierced with a knife.

YIELD: 4 servings

 ADD IT!
Spice up the panko with a tablespoon of dried thyme, a tablespoon of dried basil, and perhaps a couple teaspoons of chile powder.

CHICKEN BROILED WITH HORSERADISH

Here is a sterling opportunity to use that bottle of horseradish in your fridge for more than the occasional Bloody Mary. It adds a nice kick to the midweek chicken dinner. You can ask the folks at the meat counter to perform the backbone surgery on the chicken for you.

1 broiler chicken, backbone removed, about 3 pounds (1¼ kg)
3 tablespoons (45 g) prepared horseradish
1 cup (50 g) fresh bread crumbs
2 tablespoons (28 g) butter, melted

Preheat the broiler. Wash the chicken in cold water and pat dry. Flatten chicken, skin side up, on a broiler pan. Season with salt and pepper.

With the rack set 6 to 8 inches (15 to 20 cm) from the heat, broil the chicken for 10 to 15 minutes, until nicely browned. Be careful not to let it burn. (Remember—a cindery bird is a bitter bird!)

Re-set the oven to 400°F (200°C, gas mark 6) from broil.

Mix the horseradish, bread crumbs, and butter in a bowl. Coat the chicken with this mixture, pressing it gently into the skin, and finish cooking the chicken by baking about 30 minutes, or until the juice runs clear when the chicken is pierced at the thickest point of the thigh.

Cut into serving portions and serve.

YIELD: 4 servings

ADD IT!
If you really want to clean out your sinuses, add ½ teaspoon of cayenne pepper to the bread crumb mixture!

BROILED CHICKEN WITH CHERRY SAUCE

This is a fun and unexpected combination of flavors with a dash of sophistication.

    2 fryer chickens, split, about 5 pounds (2¼ kg)
       (the butcher will split them for you if you can't find them already split)
    1 jar (10 ounces, or 280 g) black cherry preserves
    ½ cup (120 ml) dry white wine
    3 tablespoons (43 g) butter

Preheat the broiler. Wash the chicken in cold water and pat dry. Season with salt and pepper and broil on a broiling pan or rack 8 inches (20 cm) away from the element until well browned on the exposed side. Turn the chicken and continue broiling. Watch out for flare-ups and charring of the skin—a bit of black is OK, but a cindery bird is bitter. The chicken is done when the juices run clear when a knife is inserted into the thickest part of the thigh, or about 10 to 15 minutes a side.

As soon as you slide the chicken under the broiler, combine the preserves and wine in a saucepan over high heat. Bring the mixture to a boil and reduce until thick enough to coat the back of a spoon, approximately 5 minutes. Add salt and pepper to taste and slowly whisk in the butter, 1 tablespoon (15 g) at a time, until the sauce thickens further. Be sure to monitor the heat and remove as soon as the last butter is melted, to make sure the sauce doesn't break.

Place the chickens on a serving plate and pour some of the sauce over them.

YIELD: 4 servings

THAI RED-CURRY CHICKEN

When we were kids, the International Food aisle at the grocery store was a desert of soy sauce, taco shells, and the occasional bag of crunchy chow mein noodles. It's come a long way, baby, as this recipe attests.

 1 fryer chicken, cut into 8 serving pieces, about 3 pounds (1¼ kg)
 1 tablespoon (15 g) Thai red-curry paste—more if you like it hotter, less if not
 1 can (13 ounces, or 385 ml) coconut milk
 2 tablespoons (30ml) olive oil

Wash the chicken in cold water and pat dry. Season with salt and pepper. Select a large sauté pan or skillet with a tight-fitting cover. Cook over high heat, add a couple of tablespoons (30 ml) oil, and sear the chicken in batches, turning until nicely browned on all sides. Remove the chicken and set aside.

Reduce the heat to medium and add the curry paste and coconut milk to the pan; stir to scrape all the yummy chicken bits from the bottom of the pan. Return the chicken to the pan, cover, and simmer for 30 to 40 minutes or until the chicken is tender.

YIELD: 4 servings

ADD IT!
A couple tablespoons (30 ml) Thai fish sauce would always be welcome with a Thai curry.

PRESSED THAI MARINATED CHICKEN

Press cooking, in which you sear a split whole bird under a heavy weight, is a quick way to cook chicken to crispy perfection on the outside and keep the inside moist and delicious. You will need two large cast-iron sauté pans or skillets and a foil-lined brick. This methods works great with other birds as well, such as Cornish hens. To make this dish for more people, or to do ahead, you can cook the chicken up to a day before, store it in the refrigerator, and reheat in a 350°F (180°C, gas mark 4) oven just until heated through, about 12 to 15 minutes.

*A **note about the chicken:** Many grocery stores sell split chickens; if yours doesn't, the folks behind the meat counter will be happy to do it for you.*

> 1 fryer chicken, split, about 2½ pounds (1 kg)
> 1 bottle (12 ounces, or 340 g) Thai ginger marinade (see note)
> ½ cup (120 ml) white wine
> 2 tablespoons (28 g) butter

Marinate chicken with 1 cup (235 ml) marinade for at least 2 hours and for up to a day. We like to use resealable plastic bags for this purpose, as they keep the mess to a minimum and allow for maximum contact of the marinade with the meat. Feel free to turn the bag over periodically to ensure optimal marinade distribution.

Heat about 2 tablespoons (30 ml) vegetable oil in a large cast-iron sauté pan or skillet over medium heat. Place the chicken in the pan, starting with the rib side down and the skin side up. Put the other sauté pan right on top of the chicken and weight it down with a brick. Cook until nicely brown, being careful to turn the heat down if the skin starts to burn. This should take about 10 minutes. Turn the chicken and cook the other side. The cooking should take about 20 minutes, but you can tell the chicken is done when the juice runs clear when pierced in the thickest part of the thigh.

While the chicken is cooking, boil the wine and ½ cup (120 ml) marinade in a saucepan over medium-high heat until the sauce is reduced to about ½ cup (120 ml). Briskly whisk in the butter 1 tablespoon (15 g) at a time. Be sure to monitor the heat and remove as soon as the last butter is melted, to make sure the sauce doesn't break.

Arrange the chicken on a plate and top with some of the sauce.

YIELD: 2 servings

🧂 ADD IT!

Add chopped fresh cilantro and 2 cloves minced garlic to the marinade.

> **NOTE:** *To make your own marinade, combine the following ingredients in a blender and blend until smooth:*
>
> Juice of 3 limes
> ¼ cup (55 g) brown sugar, packed
> 2 tablespoons (30 ml) soy sauce
> 2 tablespoons (30 ml) rice vinegar
> 2 tablespoons (30 g) ketchup
> 1 tablespoon (6 g) minced fresh ginger
>
> 1 tablespoon (10 g) minced garlic
> 2 scallions, chopped
> ¼ cup (45 g) diced fresh mango
> ½ cup (120 ml) water
> Salt and pepper to taste

Chicken Stewed with Orange and Star Anise

When people stew a chicken, the knee-jerk reaction is either to involve vats of canned tomatoes or to opt for a soothing chicken-soup-style bird with lots of chicken broth. Here's a recipe that steps outside those boundaries.

1 fryer chicken, cut into 8 serving pieces, about 3 pounds (1¼ kg)
8 oranges
8 pieces star anise

Using a vegetable peeler, cut wide strips of zest from the oranges, then squeeze the juice from the oranges. Salt and pepper the chicken pieces and place them in a wide, shallow pan with a tight-fitting lid. Add the zest, star anise, and orange juice. (A large resealable plastic bag also works nicely as a container.) Marinate at least 2 hours, or overnight if you have a chance. Turn the meat so that it all has a chance to soak in the citrus flavor.

Remove the chicken from the marinade, and season with salt and pepper. Select a large sauté pan or skillet with a tight-fitting lid. Heat 2 tablespoons (30 ml) oil over high heat and sear the chicken on all sides, in batches if needed, until the skin is nicely browned. The chicken should have plenty of room in the pan. When the chicken is all browned, put all of the chicken in the pan and pour the marinade over the meat, adding water to cover. Cover the pan, turn the heat to medium-low, and simmer for about 30 minutes until the chicken is cooked through. Serve in bowls with some of the broth.

YIELD: 4 servings

 ADD IT!
Sauté a small, diced onion with the last batch of chicken, and substitute chicken stock for water as a braising liquid.

QUICK CHICKEN CACCIATORE

While we call for Chianti mushroom sauce because we wanted to get a taste of wine into the dish, other mushroom sauces work as well. We also have enjoyed this with the likes of mushroom-olive sauce and mushroom-vegetable sauce. Nobody could accuse us of being anti-mushroom.

> 2 sweet peppers, red, green, or yellow as you prefer
> 1 fryer chicken, cut into 8 serving pieces, about 3 pounds (1¼ kg)
> 1 jar (16 ounces, or 450 g) Chianti-mushroom tomato sauce

Split the peppers, remove the core and ribs, and cut into ½-inch (1-cm) strips lengthwise.

Heat the oven to 325°F (190°C, gas mark 5).

Wash the chicken in cold water and pat dry; season with salt and pepper. In an ovenproof sauté pan or skillet with a tight-fitting cover (or a Dutch oven), heat about 2 tablespoons (30 ml) oil and sear the chicken pieces on both sides, being careful to not crowd the pan—you may want to do this in batches. Set the chicken aside and add the peppers to the pan, stirring and allowing them to brown a bit, about 5 minutes.

Put the chicken back in the pan, and add the tomato sauce. Bring to a simmer on the stovetop, then cover and place in the oven for about 45 minutes, or until the chicken is tender but not falling off the bone. Serve.

YIELD: 4 servings

ADD IT!
Of course, a couple cloves of garlic are always welcome in this recipe. A handful of chopped fresh mushrooms sautéed with the peppers wouldn't be amiss, either.

CHICKEN WITH ALE AND ENDIVE

In the States, endive is frequently viewed as a handy shovel for dips, or a useful component in a formal arranged salad, but in Europe, it's also popular as a vegetable in main dishes. Braising is a great way to introduce endive into your everyday cooking.

1 fryer chicken, cut into 8 serving pieces, about 3 pounds (1¼ kg)
2 Belgian endives
1 cup (235 ml) ale (use a brown ale, such as Samuel Smith or Redhook)
2 tablespoons (28 g) butter, cold

Preheat the oven to 350°F (180°C, gas mark 4).

Put the chicken in a roasting pan that can accommodate the chicken in one layer with just a little room to spare. Cut the endive into 4 wedges each and nestle the pieces around the chicken. Season with salt and pepper and pour the ale over all. Bake for 45 minutes, uncovered. The endive should be browned and soft, the chicken cooked through and tender, and the beer partly evaporated. Remove from the oven.

Put the chicken and endive on a platter and keep it warm. Put the roasting pan on medium-heat and stir, making sure to scrape up anything that's stuck to the bottom of the pan. Whisking briskly over low heat, whisk the butter into the pan liquid, 1 tablespoon (15 g) at a time. Be sure to monitor the heat and remove as soon as the last butter is melted, to make sure the sauce doesn't break. Pour the sauce over the chicken and endive, and serve.

YIELD: 4 servings

CHICKEN MARINATED WITH SOY AND GARLIC

Sometimes, clean and understated food is just what we need on a tiring day after work. Serve this with fragrant jasmine rice and steamed veggies, and you'll have the double pleasure of eating well and virtuously.

> 1 fryer chicken, cut into 8 serving pieces, about 3 pounds (1¼ kg)
> ½ cup (120 ml) soy sauce
> 2 tablespoons (20 g) minced garlic, about 3 or 4 large cloves

In a resealable plastic bag combine the chicken, soy sauce, and garlic. Refrigerate, turning every few hours, overnight. Heat the oven to 350°F (180°C, gas mark 4).

Spray a baking sheet with nonstick spray or line with tinfoil. Place the chicken on the sheet and bake until cooked through, about 40 to 50 minutes.

YIELD: 4 servings

🍶 ADD IT!
Add a ½ cup (175 g) honey to the soy-garlic marinade for added sweetness; a tablespoon or 2 of fresh grated ginger is also quite delicious.

ASIAN BOILED CHICKEN

Lemongrass's sour-tangy lemon taste is one of the most prominent flavors associated with Thai cooking; it is used to make herb teas as well as to flavor soups and other dishes. It's generally available at specialty markets and increasingly found in grocery stores.

> 1 fryer chicken, cut into 8 serving pieces, about 3 pounds (1¼ kg)
> ¼ cup (25 g) star anise
> 1 stalk lemongrass

Rinse the chicken with cold water and put into a 2-quart (2-L) pot and cover with water. Add the star anise. Cut the lemongrass into ½-inch (1-cm) lengths. Add to the pot. Season with salt and pepper. Put the pot on medium-high heat and bring to a boil; skim the froth that rises to the top, then reduce heat to a simmer and cook for 30 to 40 minutes, until the chicken is just done. Serve in bowls with some of the cooking liquid.

YIELD: 4 servings

🥫 ADD IT!
Simmer in a handful of chopped fresh cilantro and several minced cloves of garlic for greater depth of flavor. You can also top the bowls with more fresh cilantro or chopped scallions as a garnish.

Barbecued Chicken Breast with Grilled Pineapple

Something about the sweet, sunshiney taste of a pineapple just makes us want to smile. You could pile this dish on a bed of mixed greens for a substantial salad as well.

1 golden pineapple
2½ pounds (1¼ kg) boneless, skinless chicken breasts
1 cup (225 g) barbecue sauce

Prepare a grill.

While the grill is heating, prepare the pineapple by lopping off the leaves, removing the tough outer skin and slicing it into ½-inch (1-cm) rounds. When the grill is ready, season the chicken and grill for 5 to 6 minutes per side. Brush with the barbecue sauce and continue to grill for an additional 1 to 2 minutes on each side. While the chicken is grilling, grill the pineapple for 3 to 4 minutes per side. Serve a couple of pieces of pineapple and a piece of chicken on each plate.

YIELD: 4 servings

CHICKEN BREAST WITH CHANTERELLES AND TOMATOES

The key to this dish is tomatoes at their glory, so we tend to make this in the summer, when our garden is producing. Fresh chanterelles are best here, but you can use also dried ones, rehydrated before you begin, or another type of mushroom, such as cremini.

> 4 ripe tomatoes, about 1½ pounds (675 g)
> 4 bone-in split chicken breasts
> ½ pound (225 g) fresh chanterelles, or 2 ounces (55 g) dried chanterelles, rehydrated

Prepare the tomatoes: Bring 1 quart (1 L) of water to a boil in a 2-quart (2-L) pot. Core the top of the tomato where the stem grew and cut an X at the base of each with a paring knife. Prepare a large bowl of ice water.

Blanch the tomatoes for 10 to 15 seconds, then plunge immediately into the ice water. Using a paring knife, peel off the skin. Halve the tomatoes and squeeze out the seeds and discard them. Coarsely chop the remaining tomato flesh and set aside. (When you have really ripe tomatoes, sometimes you don't need to blanch them to remove the skin, but can just rub the skin with the dull side of a paring knife to loosen it for removal.)

Preheat the oven to 400°F (200°C, gas mark 6).

Put about 2 tablespoons (30 ml) olive oil in a wide sauté pan or skillet and heat over medium-high heat. Season the chicken breasts with salt and pepper. When the oil starts to smoke, sear the chicken, skin side down, for 5 to 6 minutes, until the skin is golden brown. Set the sauté pan aside—do not clean it. Put the chicken in a roasting pan and bake it for 20 to 25 minutes, until the juice runs clear when cut near the bone. Remove the chicken from the oven and keep it warm.

Slice the mushrooms if they are large. Heat the same sauté pan over high heat and add the mushrooms. Cook, stirring frequently, for 4 to 5 minutes. Add the tomato and salt and pepper to taste. Cook, stirring, for 3 to 4 minutes. Put a chicken breast on each of 4 plates and top with some of the mushroom-tomato sauce.

YIELD: 4 servings

🥫 ADD IT!
Add ½ cup (120 ml) white wine to the sauté pan or skillet after the mushrooms and tomatoes have been added.

MADRAS CHICKEN CURRY

This dish is complemented nicely by basmati rice and mango chutney. It also is great with a sprinkle of fresh cilantro just before serving.

    1 medium-size Spanish onion
    2½ pounds (1¼ kg) boneless, skinless chicken breasts
    1 jar (16 ounces, or 450 g) Madras curry sauce

Chop onion into small dice. Heat a large sauté pan or skillet over medium-high heat. Add onion and cook, stirring often, for about 15 minutes, until softened and lightly browned. In the meantime, cut the chicken into bite-size pieces. Add to the onion and sauté until lightly browned. Stir in the curry sauce and simmer for 15 to 20 minutes, adding water if needed.

YIELD: 4 servings

🫙 ADD IT!
Sauté 2 minced cloves of garlic with the onion, and add ¼ cup (60 ml) plain yogurt to the sauce as it simmers.

CHICKEN AND MUSHROOM KEBABS

A simple meal that works; in the summertime, serve with a tarragon potato salad and some sliced tomatoes still warm from the garden. In the winter, opt for the comfort of Cauliflower au Gratin (page 388).

2½ pounds (1¼ kg) boneless, skinless chicken breasts
1 bottle (12 ounces, or 355 ml) lemon-pepper marinade (see note)
16 medium-size white mushrooms, about 1 inch (2½ cm) across

You will need 8 bamboo skewers.

Cut the chicken into 1-inch (2½-cm) pieces and put them in a resealable plastic bag. Add enough marinade to cover them well and refrigerate for at least 2 hours and up to overnight.

Prepare a grill.

Soak skewers in cold water for a half hour, then thread chicken and mushrooms onto each skewer. Grill for 5 to 8 minutes per side and serve.

YIELD: 4 servings

ADD IT!
There's room on those kebabs for more vegetable matter—you can add chunks of red onion and red or yellow peppers for more flavor.

NOTE: *To make 1½ cups of your own marinade, whisk together the following ingredients until the sugar is dissolved:*

½ cup (120 ml) water
2 tablespoons (30 ml) cider or rice vinegar
¼ cup (50 g) sugar
¼ cup (60 ml) lemon juice
¼ cup (60 ml) oil
½ teaspoon garlic powder
½ teaspoon onion powder
1 teaspoon salt
2 teaspoons black pepper

Chicken with Escarole and Bacon

Endive's first cousin, escarole has sturdy leaves and a slightly bitter flavor. Young escarole leaves are tender enough to add to salads, but escarole benefits from cooking—soup is a popular destination for this leaf.

1 head escarole
2½ pounds (1¼ kg) boneless, skinless chicken breasts
8 strips bacon

Remove any damaged outer leaves from the escarole and cut off and discard the top inch or so of the head. Cut the rest of the escarole into squares 1 to 2 inches (up to 5 cm) wide, wash it well, and spin-dry in a salad spinner.

Preheat the oven to 400°F (200°C, gas mark 6).

Heat a wide sauté pan or skillet over medium-high heat and cook the bacon until crisp. Remove bacon to a paper-towel-lined plate to drain. Season the chicken with salt and pepper. Using the pan used to cook the bacon, sauté the chicken on both sides for 4 to 5 minutes a side, until nicely browned. Put the chicken on a baking pan and finish cooking it in the oven for 12 to 15 minutes, until cooked through. While the chicken is in the oven, sauté the escarole in the same pan, adding a tablespoon (15 ml) olive oil first if needed. Sauté the escarole for 6 to 7 minutes, until it browns a bit.

Divide the escarole among 4 plates and top each with a chicken breast. Chop the bacon and sprinkle it over each serving.

YIELD: 4 servings

ADD IT!
Shave Gruyère cheese over each plate for an extra tang.

Sautéed Chicken Breasts with Artichoke Salsa

The name artichoke "salsa" could be misleading. We've seen it as artichoke tapenade and artichoke antipasto as well, but we're basically talking about a jar full of chopped-up artichokes and other tasty ingredients such as roasted red pepper or tomatoes. If you can't find any of the above, send a large jar of marinated artichoke hearts on a trip through the food processor and add a cup of chopped tomatoes.

2½ pounds (1¼ kg) boneless, skinless chicken breasts
1 jar (12 ounces, or 340 g) artichoke salsa
4 ounces (115 g) Monterey Jack cheese, shredded

Heat the oven to 400°F (200°C, gas mark 6).

Wash the chicken with cold water and pat dry; season with salt and pepper. Heat 2 tablespoons (30 ml) olive oil in a sauté pan or skillet over high heat. Sear the chicken, turning occasionally until nicely browned on all sides. Place the chicken in a baking dish, spoon salsa over each breast, and top with cheese. Cover and bake in oven for 20 to 25 minutes; take off the cover for the last 10 minutes if you want the cheese to brown.

YIELD: 4 servings

Chicken Breast Stuffed with Roasted Plums

This dish is great with Zesty Pearl Couscous (page 351) as a side dish.

3 plums
1 medium-size Spanish onion
¼ cup (60 ml) olive oil
2½ pounds (1¼ kg) boneless, skinless chicken breasts, both lobes attached

To roast the plums: Preheat the oven to 350°F (180°C, gas mark 4). Cut the plums in half and remove the pit. Toss the plums with 2 tablespoons (30 ml) of the oil and add salt and pepper to taste. Spread the plums on a baking sheet and roast for 15-20 minutes. Cool the plums and set aside.

Peel and chop the onion into small dice. Heat 2 tablespoons (30 ml) cooking oil in a small, heavy saucepan with a tight-fitting lid. Add the onion, cover, and cook over low heat, stirring occasionally. Roughly chop the plums, add them to the onions, and remove from heat. Set aside to cool.

Preheat the oven to 450°F (230°C, gas mark 8).

Lay plastic film out on a cutting board. Place the chicken breasts on it and cover with another layer of film. With the flat side of a cleaver (or some other heavy flat object, such as a sauté pan or skillet) pound the chicken gently until each breast is of uniform thickness, about ½ inch (1 cm).

Place one-fourth of the plum mixture in a cigar shape in the center of each breast. Fold the ends of the meat over and roll the chicken like a burrito so the plum is inside. Place on a baking sheet, seam side down. Brush with olive oil and sprinkle with salt and pepper. Roast for 20 to 30 minutes, depending on the size of the chicken breasts, until done through.

Allow to rest 5 to 7 minutes, then slice each breast into 4 or 5 rounds and serve.

YIELD: 4 servings

SAUTÉED CHICKEN WITH PESTO WINE SAUCE

A perfect midweek dinner—it's fast, easy, and delicious.

> 2½ pounds (1¼ kg) boneless, skinless chicken breasts
> ½ cup (120 ml) dry white wine
> ¼ cup (60 ml) pesto sauce
> 4 tablespoons (55 g) butter

Season the chicken with salt and pepper and pound it lightly between sheets of waxed paper to flatten to ½ inch (1 cm). Heat a wide sauté pan or skillet over medium-high heat and add about ¼ cup (60 ml) oil. When the oil starts to smoke, add the chicken and sauté for 6 to 7 minutes per side, until just cooked through. Remove the chicken and keep it warm.

Add the wine to the pan and stir to scrape up the savory brown bits on the pan. When the wine has reduced by half, add the pesto, then whisk in the butter, 1 table-spoon (15 g) at a time, to form a smooth sauce. Be sure to monitor the heat and remove as soon as the last butter is melted, to make sure the sauce doesn't break.

Place a chicken breast on each of 4 plates and top with sauce.

YIELD: 4 servings

🥫 ADD IT!
You could sauté a cup or so (100 g) of mushrooms just prior to adding the wine to the pan. This dish would pair well with Broccoli with Lemon and Garlic (page 377), and Barley Risotto (page 352).

SAUTÉED CHICKEN WITH TOMATILLO SAUCE

Tomatillos, also known as ground tomatoes or husk tomatoes, are a pleasantly tart green vegetable that comes wrapped in a papery husk. They're popular in salsa, and we regularly find them at our local supermarket. If you have less luck, you can substitute green tomatoes with a dash of fresh lemon juice, or use canned tomatillos, which are available in many supermarkets, often already ground up.

½ pound (225 g) tomatillos
2½ pounds (1¼ kg) boneless, skinless chicken breasts
4 cloves garlic, minced
4 tablespoons (55 g) butter, cold

Remove the husks from the tomatillos and cut out the stem core. Bring a 2-quart (2-L) pot of salted water to a boil. Blanch the tomatillos by dropping them into the boiling water for 1 to 2 minutes. Drain and process, skin and all, in a food processor until smooth.

Season the chicken with salt and pepper and pound it lightly between sheets of plastic wrap to flatten the breasts to ½ inch (1 cm). Heat ¼ cup (60 ml) oil in a wide sauté pan or skillet over medium-high heat. When the oil starts to smoke, add the chicken and sauté for 6 to 7 minutes per side, until just cooked through. Remove the chicken and keep it warm.

Add the garlic, then the tomatillos to the pan, and stir to scrape up the brown bits of food on the pan. As the sauce bubbles, briskly whisk in the butter, 1 tablespoon (15 g) at a time, to form a smooth sauce. Be sure to monitor the heat and remove as soon as the last of the butter is melted, to make sure the sauce doesn't break. Place a chicken breast on each of 4 plates and top with sauce.

YIELD: 4 servings

Chicken Breast with Sautéed Grapes

This dish is light and elegant, and the ingredients work hard to pull together a wonderful taste combination.

 3 tablespoons (45 ml) olive oil
 2½ pounds (1¼ kg) boneless, skinless chicken breasts
 1 cup (125 g) all-purpose flour
 1 pound (3½ to 4 cups, or 450 g) seedless green grapes, stemmed and rinsed
 4 to 6 tablespoons (55 to 85 g) butter

Preheat oven to 400°F (200°C, gas mark 6).

Wash the chicken with cold water, pat dry, and season with salt and pepper. In a shallow bowl, dredge the chicken in flour. Heat 3 tablespoons (45 ml) olive oil in a sauté pan or skillet over medium-high heat. Sauté the chicken on both sides until it develops a nice crisp, light-brown crust. Remove the chicken to a baking dish and finish cooking in the oven, about 15 to 20 minutes. Set aside the sauté pan—do not clean it.

While the chicken is in the oven, liquefy half of the grapes in a food processor and then squeeze the pulpy juice through a sieve to remove the skin. (We've found a soup ladle to be helpful in pushing the glop through the sieve.) Put the sauté pan back on medium heat and sauté the remaining grapes for a couple of minutes, until the skins brown some. Add the grape juice and salt and pepper to taste. Whisking slowly, add butter 1 tablespoon (15 g) at a time until the sauce thickens. Be sure to monitor the heat and remove as soon as the last butter is melted, to make sure the sauce doesn't break. Place a piece of chicken on each of 4 plates, spoon the grapes and sauce over it, then serve.

YIELD: 4 servings

🍶 ADD IT!
Whisk in a couple tablespoons of cream right before you add the butter for a slightly richer sauce.

CHICKEN WITH FRESH TOMATOES

An "airline" breast, also known as a supreme or Statler breast, is the culinary term for a boned, skin-on breast of chicken with the first joint of the wing attached. We like it because the crispy skin adds depth to the flavor. If you can't find this cut, using split bone-in breasts also works, although you'll need to add about 10 minutes to the baking time.

2 tablespoons (30 ml) olive oil
2½ pounds (1¼ kg) "airline"chicken breasts
2 pounds (900 kg) tomatoes (about 5 cups)
4 cloves garlic, minced
3 tablespoons (43 g) butter

Prepare the tomatoes: Put a 2-quart (2-L) saucepan of water on to boil. When the water boils, immerse each tomato until the skin starts to split and curl, about 1 minute. Remove immediately and peel off the skin—it's very easy. Then split each tomato in half; remove the seeds and chop into ½-inch (1-cm) pieces.

Preheat the oven to 350°F (180°C, gas mark 4).

Season the chicken on both sides. Heat a sauté pan or skillet over high heat and add about 2 tablespoons (30 ml) olive oil. Sear the chicken, skin side down, until well browned—this is a rather spattery procedure, so don't wear your best silk shirt while doing this. Place on a baking sheet, skin side up, and bake for 20 to 25 minutes, or until cooked through. You can tell the chicken is cooked when it is firm to the touch at the thickest point.

While the chicken is baking, return the sauté pan used to sear the chicken to medium heat. Add the garlic and let it sizzle briefly, but do not brown. Add the tomatoes and salt and pepper to taste, then cook for about 5 minutes, until the tomato partially breaks down and some of the juice evaporates. Add the butter, 1 tablespoon (15 g) at a time, whisking slowly until each is melted. Be sure to monitor the heat and remove as soon as the last butter is melted, to make sure the sauce doesn't break.

To serve, place a chicken breast on a plate and spoon the sauce over it.

YIELD: 4 servings

🧂 ADD IT!
Sautéing a handful of chopped fresh basil along with the garlic is not only yummy but will make your nose happy as well.

CHICKEN STUFFED WITH LIVER AND PRUNES

Don't scorn this recipe because it has liver and prunes. You may have hated both as kids, but we promise that their combination of sweet and rich produces a dish to remember. You will need breasts that have both lobes attached. If they are large, you might get 2 servings from each. If they're smaller, then plan on 1 serving per breast.

2 tablespoons (30 ml) olive oil
½ pound (225 g) chicken livers
4 tablespoons (55 g) butter, cold and cut into cubes
2½ pounds (1¼ kg) boneless, skinless chicken breasts with both lobes attached
8 to 12 pitted prunes

Heat about 2 tablespoons (30 ml) olive oil in a medium-size sauté pan or skillet over high heat until it is hot but not smoking. Add the livers and sauté them for 6 to 7 minutes, until they are cooked through. Put the livers in a food processor and add the butter and salt and pepper to taste. Process until smooth.

Preheat the oven to 400°F (200°C, gas mark 6).

Lay the chicken breasts out between 2 sheets of plastic wrap or waxed paper and gently pound them until they are a uniform thickness—about ½ inch (1 cm). With the rib side of the meat up, smear each breast with some of the liver mousse and top with prunes. Roll up each breast, first folding in the wing meat, and finishing with the seam side down. Oil a baking sheet and put the chicken on it. Season the chicken and bake for 20 to 25 minutes, depending on the size of the chicken breasts.

Let sit for a few minutes after removing from the oven, then slice crosswise to make rounds.

YIELD: 4 servings

🍶 ADD IT!
After the livers are almost cooked, add ¼ cup (60 ml) brandy to the pan.

Chicken Breast Stuffed with Feta and Spinach

We can find this pesto near the marinara sauce in the pasta aisle of our supermarket, as well as in the fridge section that houses the fresh pastas and sauces.

10 ounces (280 g) fresh spinach
2½ pounds (1¼ kg) boneless, skinless chicken breasts with both lobes attached
8 ounces (225 g) feta cheese, crumbled
2 tablespoons (28 g) butter

Pick over the spinach, discarding the bad leaves and thick stems, and place in a pot with a cup (235 ml) of water and a bit of salt. Bring to a boil over high heat. Remove from heat when it is just wilted, about 2 minutes. Drain the spinach and refrigerate until cool enough to handle. Squeeze out excess water and chop coarsely. Lightly pound the chicken breasts between two sheets of plastic wrap until it is of uniform thickness—about ½ inch (1 cm). Mix the spinach and feta together. Spread ¼ of the mixture on each chicken breast. Fold in the wing meat on either side, then roll the breast. Place seam side down on the cutting board and tie each roll with white kitchen string.

Preheat the oven to 400°F (200°C, gas mark 6).

Heat a sauté pan or skillet over high heat and add a bit of oil. Season the chicken with salt and pepper and sear each piece, turning occasionally until all sides are nicely browned. Put into a medium-size baking dish and finish in the oven, baking about 20 to 25 minutes.

While the chicken is in the oven, add ½ cup (120 ml) water to the sauté pan and bring to a boil. Stir to remove all the yummy bits that have stuck to the pan. Let the liquid reduce to about ¼ cup (60 ml).

When the chicken is done, remove the twine and slice each breast into 4 or 5 rounds. Fan out on plates. Whisking slowly, add the butter to the reduced sauce, 1 tablespoon (15 g) at a time, until the sauce is nicely thickened. Be sure to monitor the heat and remove as soon as the last butter is melted, to make sure the sauce doesn't break. Pour the sauce over the chicken and serve.

YIELD: 4 servings

CHICKEN STUFFED WITH SWISS AND BACON

This is a slight variation on chicken cordon bleu—you won't even miss the bread crumbs.

2½ pounds (1¼ kg) boneless, skinless chicken breasts with both lobes attached
4 slices Swiss cheese
8 slices bacon, cooked

Preheat the oven to 400°F (200°C, gas mark 6).

Lay the chicken breasts out between 2 sheets of plastic wrap or waxed paper and gently pound them until they are a uniform thickness—about ¼ to ½ inch (½ to 1 cm). With the rib side of the meat up, season each breast with salt and pepper, then lay a slice of cheese and 2 pieces of bacon on each. Roll up, first folding in the wing meat, finishing with the seam side down.

Oil a baking sheet and put the chicken on it. Sprinkle with salt and pepper and bake for 20 to 25 minutes or so, depending on the size of the chicken breasts.

Let sit for a few minutes after removing from the oven, then slice crosswise to make roulades.

YIELD: 4 servings

ADD IT!
This would be lovely served with Mashed Potatoes with Scallions (page 433) and minted Pea Puree (page 409).

CHICKEN BREAST STUFFED WITH ASPARAGUS AND GRUYÈRE

As kids, we had a huge vegetable garden, complete with an asparagus bed that produced shoots of green, tender "sparegrass" year after year. Our youthful taste buds did not consider such reliable production to be a boon, but now we think wistfully of that garden. If you are lucky enough to have a garden full of this yummy vegetable, spring is the perfect time for this dish.

> 2½ pounds (1¼ kg) boneless, skinless chicken breasts with both lobes attached
> 1 pound (450 g) asparagus
> ½ pound (225 g) Gruyère cheese

Place the chicken between two layers of plastic wrap and gently pound with the flat side of a meat cleaver (or a hammer, or a meat mallet or any other heavy blunt object) until the meat is of a uniform thickness—about ½ inch (1 cm)—and roughly rectangular.

Prepare a large bowl of ice water. Fill a 2-quart (2-L) saucepan about half full with lightly salted water and set to boil. Snap off asparagus spears by gently bending each spear until you find the break point. When the water boils, cook the asparagus, uncovered, for about 1 minute, then immediately shock in the ice water, drain, and set aside. Shred the cheese on a box grater or in a food processor.

Heat oven to 400°F (200°C, gas mark 6) and oil a baking sheet.

Season each chicken breast with salt and pepper and arrange on the cutting board with the side that once had skin down, and the longer edge toward you. Divide the cheese and asparagus among the breasts and then roll them up starting from the edge closest to you. Arrange the asparagus spears so that they slightly stick out the end. Place on the oiled baking sheet, seam side down, and bake for about 25 minutes, until firm to the touch. Slice into rounds, arrange on plates, and serve.

YIELD: 4 servings

🧂 ADD IT!
Squeeze a lemon quarter over each serving to add a flavorful citrus kick.

Roasted Chicken Sausage with Grapes and Onion

There are a multitude of fresh sausages at the store these days, so you can choose whatever flavored chicken sausage appeals to you.

> 2 tablespoons (30 ml) olive oil
> **1½ pound (675 g) chicken sausage**
> **1 pound (450 g) Spanish onion**
> **½ pound (225 g) green grapes**

Poach the sausages over low heat in 1 quart (1 L) water until just done, about 20 minutes. Drain the sausages and set aside.

Preheat the oven to 350°F (180°C, gas mark 4).

Peel and cut the onion into julienne. Pick the grapes off the stems and set aside. Heat about 2 tablespoons (30 ml) olive oil in a medium-size sauté pan or skillet over high heat. When the oil begins to smoke, add the onion and cook, tossing, for 4 to 5 minutes, until it softens and browns a bit. Put the onion in a shallow 1-quart (1-L) baking dish and add the sausages and grapes. Roast for 15 to 20 minutes, until the grapes and sausages are browned.

YIELD: 4 servings

SOY-ORANGE ROASTED TURKEY BREAST

The thing about turkeys that keeps people from eating them more often is, of course, their size. We can face the prospect of an annual parade of turkey leftovers with relative equanimity, but upping the frequency meter would cause us to blanch. So the new practice of packaging turkey breasts as a poultry roast of sorts is perfect for those who want to have their turkey more often than Thanksgiving. Hotel-style breasts have whole wings attached and usually include portions of the back, neck, skin, ribs, giblets, and neck. If you can't find one labeled hotel-style, a traditional turkey breast is fine.

    1 cup (235 ml) soy sauce
    2 cups (475 ml) orange juice
    1 hotel-style turkey breast, about 6 pounds (2¾ kg)

Preheat the oven to 325°F (170°C, gas mark 3).

Mix the soy sauce and orange juice. Put the turkey on a rack in a roasting pan and brush liberally with the soy-orange mixture. Season with pepper. Roast for 2 to 2½ hours, basting often with the soy-orange mixture, until either the button on the timer pops, or until a thermometer reads 160°F (71°C) at the thickest part, near the bone. Remove from the oven and let sit for 8 to 10 minutes. Slice and serve.

⬛ ADD IT!
Spice up the basting sauce with sliced fresh ginger.

PANFRIED TURKEY CUTLETS

This fast and easy recipe yields a delicious result when you don't have time for more elaborate preparations.

> 1 pound (450 g) turkey cutlets
> 2 eggs, beaten slightly
> 2 cups (100 g) fresh bread crumbs

Lay plastic wrap out on a cutting board. Place cutlets on the wrap and cover them with another sheet of wrap. With the side of a meat cleaver or other heavy blunt object, pound the turkey until quite thin—about ½ inch (1 cm).

Season the cutlets with salt and pepper. Dip each cutlet first into the egg and then into the crumbs, pressing them gently onto the meat.

Heat ¼ cup (60 ml) olive oil in a sauté pan or skillet over high heat. Sauté the cutlets briefly—3 to 5 minutes per side—until golden. You can cook them in batches, adding oil if needed, as it is important not to crowd the pan.

YIELD: 4 servings

 ADD IT!
Add 3 tablespoons (15 g) freshly grated Parmesan cheese to the bread crumbs, as well as whatever dried spices strike your fancy.

TURKEY PICCATA

Piccata is a classic dish that translates well to the home dinner table. Here, we show a turkey variation.

- **1 pound (450 g) turkey cutlets**
- **1 cup (125 g) all-purpose flour**
- **3 lemons**
- ¼ cup (60 ml) olive oil
- 3 tablespoons (43 g) butter

Lay plastic wrap out on a cutting board. Place the turkey on the wrap and cover it with another sheet of wrap. With the side of a meat cleaver or other heavy blunt object, pound the turkey until quite thin, about ¼ inch (½ cm).

Season the meat with salt and pepper and dip into the flour. Squeeze 2 of the lemons and set the juice aside.

Heat ¼ cup (60 ml) olive oil in a large sauté pan or skillet over high heat. Sauté the turkey briefly—2 or 3 minutes per side—until golden brown. You may have to cook the meat in batches, as it is important not to crowd the pan. Add oil if needed. Put the cooked meat on a plate and set in a warm place.

Keeping the sauté pan on moderately high heat, pour in the lemon juice and bring to a boil, scraping the sides and bottom of the pan to dislodge the brown bits stuck to it. Whisking briskly, whisk in the butter, 1 tablespoon (15 g) at a time, for a smooth sauce. Be sure to monitor the heat and remove as soon as the last butter is melted, to make sure the sauce doesn't break. Arrange the turkey on a plate and spoon the sauce over it. Slice the third lemon thin and use as a garnish.

YIELD: 4 servings

🫙 ADD IT!
Capers are traditionally found in a piccata; you can sauté them briefly before adding the lemon juice.

BRAISED DUCK WITH RHUBARB

When the rhubarb starts popping up in early spring, most people think of strawberry-rhubarb pie, and it's hard to argue with that classic combination. But don't make poor rhubarb into a one-trick pony: it works well in main courses, too, as this recipe attests.

A note on the duck: Most grocery stores sell their ducks in one piece, but it is the work of a moment to ask the kind gentleman behind the meat counter to cut one into 2 breast quarters and 2 leg quarters. With duck the trick is to render the fat that lurks beneath the skin.

    1 cut-up duck, about 4 pounds (1¾ kg)
    1 pound (450 g) rhubarb
    1 pound (450) Spanish onions
    1 tablespoon (15 ml) olive oil

Preheat oven to 300°F (150°C, gas mark 2).

Wash the rhubarb stalks and cut into ½-inch (1-cm) pieces. Peel and slice the onion into long, ½-inch (1-cm) slices.

Heat about 1 tablespoon (15 ml) olive oil in a Dutch oven—or other casserole dish with a tight-fitting lid—over medium heat. Season the duck with salt and pepper and add to the pan. Cook on both sides until each piece is a crispy brown and quite a bit (at least ½ cup, or 120 ml) of fat has been rendered into the pan. Remove the duck and set aside. Drain off the fat and save for future use (for Sinful Roasted Potatoes, on page 434, for example!).

Add the onion, turning down the heat to low and cooking for ½ hour or so, stirring every so often, until the onion is very soft and caramelized. Return the duck to the pot and add the rhubarb. Add ½ cup (120 ml) water, cover tightly, and place in the oven for 1 hour. To serve, place a piece of duck on each plate and ladle the rhubarb and onions over it.

YIELD: 4 servings

🧂 ADD IT!
Substitute chicken stock or orange juice for the water.

BRAISED DUCK WITH TURNIPS AND APPLE CIDER

Here we have a classic autumn dish, with the harvest flavors of cider and turnips. This is delicious served with yams or baked squash. We can almost hear the cold November wind tearing the last leaves from the maples.

Ducks have a fairly thick layer of fat under their skin, and the trick to a good duck recipe is to get rid of that fat. Thus, the rendering part of this recipe.

1 duck, about 4 pounds (1¾ kg)
2 pounds (900 g) yellow turnips or purple-top turnips, or a mix
1 tablespoon (15 ml) olive oil
2 cups (475 ml) apple cider

Cut the duck into 4 serving pieces: 2 breast quarters and 2 leg quarters. (If your store sells ducks already cut up, by all means choose that!) Peel and cut the turnips into 1-inch (2½-cm) cubes.

Preheat the oven to 300°F (150°C, gas mark 2).

Heat about 1 tablespoon (15 ml) olive oil in a large Dutch oven or flameproof casserole dish over medium-low heat. Season the duck with salt and pepper and place in the Dutch oven, skin side down. Cook for about 15 to 20 minutes until the skin is brown and crisp and there's a fair amount of melted fat in the pan. Remove the duck from the oven, pour off the fat, and save for future use (for Sinful Roasted Potatoes, on page 434, for example!).

Return the duck to the pan, add turnips and cider, and bring just to a boil. Cover and braise in the oven for 1½ to 2 hours. If desired, remove the lid for the last 15 minutes or so to further brown the skin. Serve in individual shallow bowls with sauce over all.

YIELD: 4 servings

🥫 ADD IT!
If you have leftovers, grind the meat with the turnips; add soft bread crumbs, fresh rosemary, and an egg, and you have the basis for some delicious duck burgers.

ROAST QUAIL STUFFED WITH PRUNES

If you have never tried quail, now is the time. They have far more flavor than chicken, and none of the "gamey" quality that people tend to worry about with meat or poultry that can be hunted. The quail you buy will be farm-raised, at any rate. Quail can often be found in the grocery store, and the meat counter people can perform the boning as well. "Semi-boneless" quail have the ribs, breastbone, and backbone taken out; the thigh, leg, and wing bones are still in. It might be well to call ahead on this, as it's time consuming.

> 8 semi-boneless quail, 4 to 5 ounces (115 to 140 g) each
> 16 pitted prunes
> 1 cup (235 ml) ruby port wine
> 4 tablespoons (55 g) butter, cold

Preheat the oven to 350°F (180°C, gas mark 4).

Season the quail with salt and pepper, and stuff each with 2 prunes. Place in a roasting pan and roast in the oven until done—about 25 minutes. With quail you want the joints to be still a bit pink—just done. Remove the birds from the pan and keep warm.

Put the roasting pan on the stovetop over medium heat and pour in the port. Let it come to a boil, scraping up the brown bits from the bottom of the pan. Strain into a saucepan over medium heat. Whisking briskly, whisk in the butter, 1 tablespoon (15 g) at a time, until just melted. Be sure to monitor the heat and remove as soon as the last butter is melted, to make sure the sauce doesn't break. Adjust the seasoning. Place 2 quail on each plate for a main course, or 1 for an appetizer. Spoon the sauce over each bird.

YIELD: 4 servings as a main course, 8 as an appetizer

ADD IT!
A risotto studded with pancetta would be a wonderful base for this dish.

ROAST QUAIL WITH GRAPES
AND LAVENDER HONEY

Something about this recipe reminds us of Arthurian princesses and drinking mead. Just us? Okay, then. By the way, don't quail at the thought of hunting for this small bird—we find ours at the local supermarket. You may substitute regular honey if your supermarket doesn't stock lavender honey.

> 8 semi-boneless quail, 4 to 5 ounces (115 to 140 g) each
> 1 pound (about 2½ to 3 cups) seedless green grapes
> ¼ cup (75 g) lavender honey

Heat the oven to 350°F (180°C, gas mark 4).

Season the quail with salt and pepper and place them in a roasting pan. Stem the grapes and toss with a little olive oil, salt, and pepper, then scatter around and over the quail. Roast in the oven for about 30 to 40 minutes, then divide birds and grapes among 4 plates for a main course, or 8 as an appetizer. Drizzle honey over the birds and serve.

YIELD: 4 servings as a main course, 8 as an appetizer

PHEASANT WITH BACON AND APPLE CIDER

Roasting the pheasant before cutting it into serving sizes adds flavor and makes it easier to divide the bird—you can practically pull the pieces apart with your hands.

Celery Root Puree (page 391) is a great accompaniment to this autumnal dish.

1 pheasant, about 3 pounds (1¼ kg)
6 strips bacon
2 cups (475 ml) apple cider
2 tablespoons (30 ml) olive oil
2 tablespoons (28 g) butter, cold

Preheat the oven to 350°F (180°C, gas mark 4).

Rinse the pheasant under cold water, pat dry inside and out, and season inside and out with salt and pepper. Place, breast side up, on a rack in a roasting pan. (Unlike a chicken, a pheasant will try to fall over on its side, so we make a little nest out of foil to hold it upright.)

Place the bacon strips over the breast of the pheasant and roast until an instant-read thermometer reads 160°F (71°C)—about 1½ hours. Allow the pheasant to rest until cool enough to handle. Remove, chop up, and reserve the bacon. Cut the pheasant into serving portions as follows:

• Remove the wishbone, then cut down each side of the breastbone along the ribs and then cut the joint at the base of the wing. This will give you two boneless, skin-on breasts with the wing attached (these are called supremes).

• Remove the thigh and leg by cutting through the joint attaching the thigh to the body. Try to keep the "oyster" with the leg; it's the nugget of meat just beyond the leg joint. This will give you 2 bone-in leg quarters.

You can prepare this dish up to this point up to a day beforehand.

Chop the remaining carcass into 6 to 8 pieces. Heat about 2 tablespoons (30 ml) olive oil in a small saucepan over medium-high heat and brown the leftover pheasant pieces for 8 to 10 minutes. Add the cider and allow to reduce by one-half, then strain the sauce, discarding the bones. Whisking briskly, whisk in the butter, 1 tablespoon (15 g) at a time. Be sure to monitor the heat and remove as soon as the last butter is melted, to make sure the sauce doesn't break. Add the bacon and season to taste with salt and pepper.

Preheat the oven to 400°F (200°C, gas mark 6).

Heat the pheasant in the oven in a shallow baking sheet, with a bit of cider or water in the pan to keep the meat moist until it is just heated through—about 8 to 10 minutes. Place a thigh and a breast on a plate and spoon the sauce over and around them.

YIELD: 2 servings

 ADD IT!
Roast the pheasant with a few chopped sage leaves in the cavity for a deeper flavor and add a tablespoon chopped sage to the sauce when reducing.

BRAISED SQUAB WITH WINE AND TOMATO

Squab, which are very tender young pigeons, have delectable and delicate dark meat and are frequently offered frozen at supermarkets. If you have trouble finding them, Cornish game hens make an acceptable substitute.

> 4 squab, about 1 pound (450 g) each
> 2 cups (475 ml) fruity red wine, such as Beaujolais
> 1 can (14 ounces, or 400 g) diced tomatoes with garlic

Preheat oven to 325°F (170°C, gas mark 3). Heat ¼ cup (60 ml) olive oil in a heavy-bottomed Dutch oven—or similar ovenproof casserole dish with a tight-fitting lid—over medium-high heat. Season the squab with salt and pepper inside and out, then sear on all sides until nicely browned. You may want to do this in batches, so as not to crowd the pan. Add the tomatoes and wine to the pan, cover, and bring to a boil. As soon as it boils, remove from the burner and place in the oven for 1 hour.

Remove the birds from the pan and set aside in a warm place, covered. Put the pan on the stovetop over high heat and reduce the pan liquid to about 2½ cups (570 ml). Place a squab on each of 4 plates and spoon sauce over them.

YIELD: 4 servings

10

Beef and Veal

Most people think of a regal filet mignon or Chateaubriand when they think of beef, which has a reputation of being the sort of thing you order when you dine out for a special occasion. But beef is also the source of an awful lot of the thrifty hamburger-based family casseroles that many of us have consumed with varying degrees of enthusiasm. We remember with horror one particular concoction regularly foisted upon us by our mother (who is actually a notable cook). It involved stuffed peppers, and it was universally reviled by every child in the family. (Our sister had an ingenious removal system that involved the family dog and dropped forks.)

With that in mind, we explore every province of the dominion of beef, from Beef Tournedos with Cognac Cream Sauce to Cajun Burgers. Along the way, we make full use of the huge choices of international spices and dishes that have come along since last we faced the dreaded bell pepper casserole.

We've come a long way, baby. Thank goodness.

Beef Rib Roast with Horseradish and Garlic Crust

It is important to allow a roast to rest after cooking to let the juices redistribute throughout the meat. Roasting at a low temperature lessens shrinkage and results in a roast that is the proper temperature throughout—not just in the center.

A roast like this just screams (or at the very least, asks politely) to be served with Yorkshire pudding or popovers.

> 1 rib roast, about 5 pounds (2¼ kg)
> ¼ cup (60 g) prepared horseradish
> 4 or 5 large cloves garlic, finely minced

Preheat oven to 325°F (170°C, gas mark 3). Wash meat in cold water and pat dry; trim extraneous fat.

In a shallow bowl, mix the garlic and horseradish with 1 tablespoon (18 g) salt and 1 tablespoon (6 g) pepper. Rub the mixture evenly into the top of the roast; place in a roasting pan and roast until desired doneness, as measured with an instant-read thermometer. The meat will continue to rise in temperature after it is taken from the oven, so remove it from the oven when it is about 5 to 10 degrees under the target temperature. For medium rare you will want a temp of 130° (54°C). Figure on about 20 minutes a pound if boneless, or 30 minutes per pound on the bone. Allow meat to rest for 10 to 15 minutes after removing it from the oven. Slice and serve.

YIELD: 6 to 8 servings

🥫 ADD IT!

When you remove the roast from the oven, drain the fat from the roasting pan and place the pan over high heat (assuming the pan is heatproof). Deglaze with red wine, beef broth, and a touch of Worcestershire sauce for a quick pan jus.

Pot Roast with Shallots and Red Wine

The humble pot roast is generally thought of in concert with boiled dinners and other homely fare, but it dresses up nicely, too.

2 tablespoons (30 ml) oil
1 eye of chuck roast, about 4 pounds (1¾ kg)
15 whole shallots, peeled
3 cups (700 ml) dry red wine
4 tablespoons (55 g) butter

Preheat oven to 325°F (170°C, gas mark 3).

Sprinkle meat with salt and pepper. Heat 2 tablespoons (30 ml) oil over high heat in a flameproof Dutch oven, or other casserole dish with a tight-fitting lid. Sear meat on all sides until well browned. Remove the meat and add shallots to the pan and cook for about 5 minutes, also browning them a bit. Place meat back in the pan, pour the wine over it, cover, and cook in oven for 3 hours.

Remove the meat from the pan and keep warm. Over high heat on the stovetop, reduce the cooking liquid to about 1½ cup (355 ml). Whisking slowly, whisk in the butter, 1 tablespoon (15 g) at a time, to thicken sauce. Be sure to monitor the heat and remove as soon as the last butter is melted, to make sure the sauce doesn't break. Slice the meat, add a few shallots to each plate, and pass the sauce on the side.

YIELD: 6 servings

Pot Roast with Guinness and Prunes

The poor prune suffers an undeserved bad reputation. This fruit packs a flavor wallop with its distilled essence of plum, and it pairs with a surprising number of meats and vegetables. Perhaps we should go along with the current trendy name and just call them dried plums.

1 eye of chuck or other pot roast, about 4 pounds (1¾ kg)
16 ounces (475 ml) Guinness or other stout beer
16 ounces (455 g) pitted prunes

Preheat oven to 300°F (150°C, gas mark 2).

Season the beef with salt and pepper. Heat about 2 tablespoons (30 ml) oil in a flame-proof Dutch oven or other similar casserole dish over high heat. Add the beef to the oil and sear on all sides until nicely browned. Add the stout and enough water so that the liquid is one-third to one-half up the side of the meat. Add the prunes, cover, and cook in the oven for about 45 minutes per pound, in this case 3 hours. Be sure that the liquid is not boiling in the oven—we're looking for a nice, gentle simmer here.

Remove the meat from the pot and keep it warm, covered. Take half of the cooking liquid and half of the prunes and process in a food processor or blender until smooth. Stir the mixture into the remaining cooking liquid and adjust the seasoning.

To serve, slice the meat and arrange it on a platter, spoon some of the sauce over it, and pass the rest on the side.

YIELD: 6 servings

GERMAN-STYLE POT ROAST

Pass a tray full of sour pickles and sliced pumpernickel with this one.

1 pot roast, such as chuck eye or bottom round, about 4 pounds (1¾ kg)
3 tablespoons (45 ml) cooking oil
2 cups beer (475 ml), any kind
1 cup (235 ml) sour cream

Preheat the oven to 300°F (150°C, gas mark 2).

Season the meat with salt and pepper. Heat about 3 tablespoons (45 ml) cooking oil in a heavy ovenproof Dutch oven—or some other casserole dish with a tight-fitting lid—and heat over high heat. Add the beef and sear on all sides until browned—about 4 to 5 minutes per side. Add the beer and enough water to come up one-third of the way up the side of the meat. Cover, place in the oven, and cook for 2 to 3 hours. The meat should be quite tender. Remove the meat from the pot and pour the liquid into a 1-quart (1-L) saucepan. Allow to sit for a few minutes, then ladle off and discard as much fat as you can.

On medium heat, reduce the remaining liquid to about 1½ cups (355 ml), then whisk in the sour cream. Slice the meat and pass the sauce on the side.

YIELD: 6 servings

ADD IT!
Spice will add tang to the braising liquid. Try clove, cinnamon stick, or perhaps pickling spice mix.

SWEET GARLIC POT ROAST

Don't be afraid of the hefty amount of garlic in this recipe. Long-cooked garlic loses a lot of its pungency and takes on a sweet, almost nutty flavor.

> **3 heads of garlic**
> **1 pot roast, such as chuck eye or bottom round, about 4 pounds (1¾ kg)**
> **3 tablespoons (45 ml) cooking oil**
> **1 cup (235 ml) Oloroso or golden sherry**

Preheat the oven to 300°F (150°C, gas mark 2).

Break the heads of garlic apart and peel the cloves; set aside. Season the meat with salt and pepper. Heat about 3 tablespoons (45 ml) cooking oil in a heavy ovenproof Dutch oven—or other casserole dish with a tight-fitting lid—over high heat. Add the beef and sear on all sides until browned—about 4 to 5 minutes per side. Add the garlic, the sherry, and enough water to come up about one-third of the way up the side of the meat. Bring the liquid to a boil, then remove from the heat. Cover, place the pot in the oven, and cook for 2 to 3 hours, until the meat is quite tender.

Remove the meat from the pot and place on a platter; set in a warm place. Pour the pot liquid into a 1-quart (1-L) saucepan. Allow to sit for a few minutes, then ladle off and discard as much fat as you can. Reduce the remaining liquid to about 1½ cups (355 g). The garlic cloves should break down; if they don't, you can mush them with a spoon. Slice the meat and pass the cooking-liquid gravy on the side.

YIELD: 6 servings

🧂 ADD IT!
Peel a few parsnips, cut them into chunks, and add them to the pot.

COMPOUND BUTTERS AND STEAKS

Steaks, grilled or pan broiled, are great with a variety of compound butters as their only embellishment. Here the quality of the beef is important—usually a rib, loin, or tenderloin cut is used.

In addition to the steak, and butter—one of our "free" ingredients—these compound butters have two ingredients each. Making a compound butter couldn't be easier, and it can be made ahead and stored in the freezer or refrigerator for several weeks. Be sure to wrap it tightly, as butter likes to pick up smells in the fridge. Simply combine all the ingredients, plus pepper and salt as desired, and whip together in a food processor.

Lay a sheet of plastic wrap on a counter with the long side toward you and mold the butter into a cylinder on the wrap. Roll into a tight log and chill. To use, simply slice off rounds, remove the plastic, and place on the cooked steaks just prior to serving.

We like to make these flavored butters::
+ Butter, shallot, and anchovy
+ Butter, garlic, and lemon juice and zest
+ Butter, shallot, and horseradish
+ Butter, basil, and garlic

Pepper-Encrusted Beef Tournedos with Cognac Cream Sauce

A variation on a classic continental dish. Don't forget your martini with this one!

¼ cup (20 g) whole black peppercorns, crushed into a coarse grind
4 filet mignon steaks, 8 ounces (225 g) each
¼ cup (60 ml) cognac
½ cup (120 ml) heavy cream
2 tablespoons (28 g) butter, room temperature

Preheat oven to 450°F (230°C, gas mark 8). Season the steaks with salt and lightly dredge the top and bottom in the pepper.

Heat 2 tablespoons (30 ml) oil in a sauté pan or skillet over high heat. Sear the steaks on both sides until well browned—about 3 minutes per side. Do not wash the sauté pan. Place the steaks on a baking sheet and cook in oven until the desired doneness; we generally allow about 10 minutes for a medium steak.

While the steak is in the oven, heat the cognac in the sauté pan used to sear the steaks over medium heat until it boils, stirring to scrape up the savory bits that have stuck to the bottom of the pan. Add the cream and reduce, stirring occasionally, until dime-size bubbles appear in the sauce. Slowly whisk in the butter, 1 tablespoon (15 g) at a time, to form a smooth sauce. Be sure to monitor the heat and remove as soon as the last of the butter is melted, to make sure the sauce doesn't break. Remove the meat from the oven and allow to rest for a couple of minutes; then place each filet on a plate. Adjust the seasoning, pour the sauce over the steak, and serve.

YIELD: 4 servings

🧂 ADD IT!
Add a cup of sliced mushrooms to the sauce along with the cognac.

GRILLED FILET MIGNON WITH MAYTAG BLUE CHEESE AND PORT WINE SAUCE

We're not talking washing machines, but the Maytag name is no coincidence—the cheese was developed in 1941 by the grandsons of washing-machine inventor Frederick Maytag. One of the first artisan cheeses created in the United States, Maytag Blue's tangy, almost lemony flavor and crumbly texture have made it a darling in the foodie world. Of course, you can substitute another blue cheese in this recipe.

4 filet mignon steaks, 8 ounces (225 g) each
4 ounces (115 g) Maytag Blue cheese, crumbled
½ cup (120 ml) ruby port
4 tablespoons (55 g) butter, room temperature

Get the grill going, particularly if using charcoal.

Season the steaks with salt and pepper and grill to the desired degree of doneness. While the steak is cooking, heat the wine over high heat in a medium-size sauté pan or skillet; let boil, stirring occasionally, until the liquid is reduced by half, about 4 to 5 minutes. Stir in half of the cheese; when it's partially melted, whisk in the butter, 1 tablespoon (15 g) at a time. Adjust the seasoning—be careful, as the cheese is quite salty. Place the steaks on plates; crumble the remaining cheese over each steak and spoon sauce over the entirety.

YIELD: 4 servings

 ADD IT!
Grill asparagus alongside the filet and serve with perfectly ripe sliced summer tomatoes drizzled with oil and vinegar. Heaven.

CARPETBAG STEAK
(FILET MIGNON STUFFED WITH OYSTERS)

Carpetbag steak is a dish that's been around for many years—in fact, some say that it originated in San Francisco during the Gold Rush. Named after the capacious valises carried in the 1800s, this is a great way to serve surf and turf.

8 oysters, or 12 if small
4 filet mignon steaks, 8 ounces (225 g) each
2 tablespoons (30 ml) olive oil
¼ cup (60 ml) Oloroso or golden sherry
4 tablespoons (55 g) butter, room temperature

Preheat oven to 400°F (200°C, gas mark 6).

Shuck the oysters and set them aside in a bowl, discarding the shells. Reserve the oyster liquor. Turning each steak on its side, cut a slit in the side of the filets with a sharp knife to form a pocket; be careful not to cut through the steak. Stuff 2 oysters (3 if small) into the pocket of each steak and secure with a toothpick.

Heat about 2 tablespoons (30 ml) olive oil in a sauté pan or skillet over high heat. Season the steaks with salt and pepper and sear them on each side until nicely browned. Remove the steaks to a metal baking tray and finish them in the oven to desired temperature—we like about 10 minutes for a medium steak.

When the steaks are done, allow them to rest a few minutes. While they're resting, heat the sauté pan and add the sherry and oyster liquor. Reduce the sauce by half, stirring to remove brown bits from the bottom of the pan. Whisking slowly, add the butter 1 tablespoon (15 g) at a time, to form a smooth sauce. Be sure to monitor the heat and remove as soon as the last of the butter is melted, to make sure the sauce doesn't break.

To serve, place a steak on each plate and top with the sauce.

YIELD: 4 servings

ADD IT!
Sauté a tablespoon (10 g) minced shallots before adding the sherry and oyster liquor to deepen the flavor of the sauce.

Hazelnut-Crusted Sirloin Steak with Balsamic Syrup

This is the essence of cooking that is both fine and simple. Serve with Very Simple Risotto (page 358) and Braised Leeks with Tomato and Blue Cheese (page 403).

1 cup (235 ml) balsamic vinegar
1 cup (150 g) blanched hazelnuts
4 strip sirloin steaks, about 2½ pounds (1 kg)
2 to 3 tablespoons (30 to 45 ml) oil

Put the balsamic vinegar in a small saucepan and cook over medium heat until it is reduced to about ¼ cup (60 ml) and has the consistency of syrup. Set aside.

In a food processor, whirl the hazelnuts until they are finely chopped.

Preheat the oven to 450°F (230°C, gas mark 8).

Season the steaks with salt and pepper, then put the hazelnuts in a pie pan or similar flat pan and press the steaks into the hazelnuts on both sides. Heat 2 to 3 tablespoons (30 to 45 ml) oil in a wide sauté pan or skillet over medium-high heat. When the oil begins to smoke, add the steaks and sear them for 4 to 5 minutes per side, then put the pan in the oven for 7 to 8 minutes for medium-rare meat. You may cook them for more or less time, according to your preference. Place each steak on a plate and drizzle the balsamic syrup over them.

YIELD: 4 servings

STRIP STEAK WITH PORCINI CRUST AND MADEIRA SAUCE

We find dried mushrooms at our grocery store, another item in the amazing influx of great foods that have hit the shelves in the past decade.

> **4 ounces (115 g) dried porcini mushrooms**
> ¼ cup (60 ml) cooking oil
> **4 New York strip steaks, trimmed of all fat and silverskin,**
>   **about 2½ pounds (1 kg) total**
> **¼ cup (60 ml) Madeira**
> 4 tablespoons (55 g) butter

Using a blender or food processor, grind the mushrooms to a fine powder. Put the powder in a pie plate.

Preheat the oven to 450°F (230°C, gas mark 8).

In a large sauté pan or skillet, heat about ¼ cup (60 ml) cooking oil over high heat. While the oil is heating, season the steaks with salt and pepper and dredge them thoroughly in the porcini powder. Place the steaks in the sauté pan and sear until nicely browned on both sides. Take care not to overcrowd the pan—you may need to do the steaks in batches. Set the pan aside—do not clean it.

Put the steaks on a cooking sheet and finish to the desired degree of doneness in the oven—about 10 minutes for a medium steak. Allow to rest for a couple of minutes after cooking.

While the steaks are in the oven, add the Madeira to the sauté pan or skillet and bring to a boil, scraping up all the brown bits in the pan. When the wine has been reduced by one-half, slowly whisk in the butter, 1 tablespoon (15 g) at a time, to form a smooth sauce. Be sure to monitor the heat and remove as soon as the last of the butter is melted, to make sure the sauce doesn't break.

Arrange the steaks on serving plates and pour the sauce over them.

YIELD: 4 to 6 servings

FLANK STEAK WITH PEPPERS AND ONIONS

Everybody always wants to stuff the poor flank steak; its long, flat construction seems to invite such treatment. It's a pity, because flank steaks really shine when grilled.

2 pounds (900 g) flank steak
4 tablespoons (60 ml) olive oil
1 pound (450 g) red and yellow peppers
1 pound (450 g) Spanish onions

Season the steak with salt and pepper and drizzle with about 2 tablespoons (30 ml) olive oil. Refrigerate, covered, for 2 to 3 hours.

Get the grill going. While grill is heating, cut the onions and peppers into long strips ½ inch (1 cm) wide.

Grill the steak to the desired degree of doneness—about 8 minutes per side for medium. While the meat is grilling, heat the remaining 2 tablespoons (30 ml) olive oil in a large sauté pan or skillet over high heat. Sauté the onions and peppers, adding salt and pepper to taste.

Remove the steak from the grill and allow to rest for 5 minutes. Slice the steak thin across the grain and place on a platter. Top with sautéed vegetables.

YIELD: 4 servings

 ADD IT!
Vinegar, chopped garlic, and chopped fresh cilantro would spice up the steak marinade nicely.

ROUND STEAK WITH CHIANTI MUSHROOM SAUCE

Steak and mushrooms is a classic combination, and with good reason. This recipe adds a twist with tomatoes. If you can't find Chianti mushroom sauce, add ½ cup (120 ml) red wine to a jar of tomato mushroom sauce.

> 1 thin-cut round steak, 2 pounds (900 g)
> 1 cup (125 g) all-purpose flour
> 1 jar (16 ounces, or 450 g) Chianti mushroom sauce

Cut the steak into 4 even-sized pieces. Place each piece on a cutting board and pound with the square-edged side of a meat tenderizer or other heavy blunt object until about it is about ½ inch (1 cm) thick. Season with salt and pepper. Dredge each piece of steak in flour. Heat 3 tablespoons (45 ml) cooking oil in a sauté pan or skillet over high heat. Sauté the steaks, in batches, until a nice brown crust develops on each side—about 4 to 5 minutes per side.

Put the steaks in a warm place to rest and add the sauce to the sauté pan. When the sauce is heated through, place the steaks on plates and pour the sauce over them.

YIELD: 4 servings

 ADD IT!
When it comes to fungi, there's no such thing as too much, so sauté a cup of mushrooms before adding the tomato sauce.

SWISS STEAK

Weekday cookery doesn't have to be boring. Try serving this over some wide buttered noodles, with Sautéed Rapini with Garlic and Red Pepper Flakes (page 411) on the side.

   1 top round steak, about 1½ pounds (675 g)
   ½ cup (60 g) all-purpose flour
   1 can (14 ounces, or 400 g) diced tomatoes with onion and pepper

Gently pound the steak with a meat tenderizer, using the large cube side. Season with salt and pepper, then dredge in the flour. Heat 3 tablespoons (45 ml) cooking oil in a wide sauté pan or skillet with a tight-fitting cover over medium-high heat. When the oil begins to smoke, sear the steak on both sides until browned—about 3 to 4 minutes per side.

Pour off as much oil as you can, add the tomatoes, and cover, stirring to scrape up the savory brown bits from the bottom of the pan. Reduce the heat to a simmer and cook for 45 minutes. Serve the meat with the sauce.

YIELD: 4 servings

🥫 ADD IT!
Sauté 1 cup (100 g) sliced mushrooms in the pan just prior to adding the tomato sauce.

BRACIOLA

If there is a decent-sized Italian population around where you live, it is likely you will find top round steak cut thin for braciola all ready to go in the meat department. If you can find this cut, skip the butterflying part of the directions and proceed from there. There are tomato braising sauces on the market now that work as well as marinara sauce.

> 1 top round steak, about 1½ pounds (675 g)
> 1 15-oz bag of stuffing such as Pepperidge Farm
> 2 cups (500 g) marinara or other prepared tomato sauce

Lay the steak on a cutting board and carefully butterfly it so that you have one large, very thin, rectangle of meat. Cover with plastic wrap and gently pound the meat with the flat side of a cleaver or meat tenderizer, to make it of even thickness. Prepare the stuffing per package directions and spread it out on the steak. Roll the steak up, starting with one of the longer sides and tucking in the ends like a burrito, finishing with the seam side down. Tie with butcher twine.

Preheat the oven to 325°F (170°C, gas mark 3).

Season the meat with salt and pepper. Put the oil in an ovenproof Dutch oven that has a tight-fitting lid, and heat over high heat. When the oil begins to smoke, sear the meat on all sides, 4 to 5 minutes per side. Add the marinara sauce, cover, and put the dish in the oven. Braise for 1½ hours. Remove the steak from the pot and allow it to rest for 10 minutes, then slice it into rounds. Skim as much fat as possible from the marinara sauce and pour over the meat rounds.

YIELD: 4 servings

🫙 ADD IT!
Mince a small onion and several cloves of garlic and add it to the stuffing.

SZECHUAN STIR-FRIED TENDERLOIN WITH TANGERINE PEEL

The bitterness of the tangerine peel cuts the rich beef flavor beautifully. This would be great spooned over fragrant jasmine rice, with Sautéed Snap Peas (page 408) as a side dish.

2 tangerines
1 pound (450 g) tenderloin tips, cut into 1-inch to 2-inch (2½-cm to 5-cm) cubes
1 cup (235 ml) Szechuan cooking sauce (see note)

Peel the tangerines and cut the peels into ½-inch (1-cm) strips. Squeeze the juice from the tangerines into a small container. Set the peel and the juice aside. Heat ¼ cup (60 ml) cooking oil in a wide sauté pan or skillet, or a wok, over high heat. When the oil is hot but not smoking, sear the tenderloin tips for 7 to 8 minutes, until nicely browned. Remove the meat and keep it warm.

Add a bit more oil if needed and sauté the tangerine peel for 4 to 5 minutes. Return the meat to the pan and continue cooking for 4 to 5 minutes. Add the tangerine juice and the cooking sauce and cook, tossing to coat the meat, for 2 to 3 minutes.

Divide among 4 plates.

YIELD: 4 servings

 ADD IT!
For more bite, cook 1 cup (130 g) diced onion with the tangerine peel.

NOTE: *To make your own Szechuan cooking sauce, combine the following ingredients in a small saucepan:*

¼ cup (60 ml) soy sauce
¼ cup (60 ml) medium-dry sherry
¼ cup (50 g) sugar
2 tablespoons (30 ml) rice vinegar
2 tablespoons (30 g) hoisin sauce
1 tablespoon (15 ml) toasted sesame oil

1 tablespoon (5 to 10 g) ground
  Asian red chiles, such as sambal
1 teaspoon minced garlic
1 teaspoon salt
1 teaspoon pepper

Whisk in 2 tablespoons (15 g) cornstarch. Put the pot on medium heat and bring to a simmer until the sauce thickens and loses its cloudiness. Makes about 1½ cups.

BEEF FONDUE

This was a great favorite in our house during the 1970s—the heyday for fondue in America. It is still a lot of fun, and fondue pots are kitschy collectibles these days.

> 1½ pounds (675 g) beef tenderloin
> 2 tablespoons (30 g) prepared horseradish
> 1 cup (235 ml) sour cream

You will need a fondue pot and 1 quart (1 L) cooking oil.

Cut the beef into 1-inch (2½-cm) cubes. Season with salt and pepper. Mix the horseradish and sour cream together and season with salt and pepper. Set aside.

Heat the oil on the stovetop to 325°F (170°C), then transfer to the fondue pot, or just heat it in the fondue pot, using the flame. The oil is ready when adding a piece of meat makes it bubble and sizzle. Everybody chooses a fondue fork and spears a piece of meat. Fry it in the oil for 3 to 4 minutes, until it is done to your liking. Spoon some sauce onto your plate and dip the meat in it. Enjoy.

YIELD: 4 servings

SMOKED BRISKET

In Oklahoma and Texas, "barbecue" means smoked brisket—and a magnificent contribution to the cuisine it is! You will need a smoker for this recipe, which you can pick up pretty cheap at just about any department store.

The classic combo platter here calls for beans, coleslaw, and cornbread.

> 1 flat-cut fresh brisket, about 3 pounds (1¼ kg)
> 1 cup (100 g) barbecue or steak spice dry rub
> 2 cups (500 g) barbecue sauce—we recommend a tomato-
> and molasses-based sauce

Prepare the smoker. Rub the brisket with the spice dry rub. Place the brisket in the smoker and smoke for 2 to 3 hours. Remove from the smoker.

Preheat the oven to 300°F (150°C, gas mark 2).

Put the brisket in a roasting pan, brush with the barbecue sauce, and loosely cover with foil. Bake in the oven for 2 to 3 hours. Slice thin and serve with additional barbecue sauce.

YIELD: 6 to 8 servings

CHICKEN-FRIED STEAK

Yes, we know: Heart attack on a plate. But boy, these things are good. They must be, or truck stops nationwide would shrivel and die.

> 4 cube steaks, about 1½ pounds (675 g)
> 1 egg
> 1 cup (125 g) all-purpose flour

Season the steaks with salt and pepper. Whisk the egg in a bowl with a bit of water. Season the flour with salt and pepper and put it into a pie plate. Heat about 4 tablespoons (60 ml) oil in a wide sauté pan or skillet over medium-high heat. Dip the steaks into the flour, then the egg, then the flour again. Pan-fry 5 to 6 minutes per side, until golden brown.

YIELD: 4 servings

ADD IT!
If you really want to mount a no-holds-barred assault on your arteries, make cream gravy to pour over the top of the steaks. Just melt 3 tablespoons (43 g) butter in the pan you fried the steaks in and stir in a couple tablespoons (15 g) flour until it makes a thick paste. Be sure to scrape up all the meat leavings to turn the paste brown. Gradually add a cup or two (up to 475 ml) of milk, and cook, stirring, over medium heat until thickened.

GRILLED MOJO BEEF TIPS WITH POTATOES

For those unfamiliar with it, mojo criollo marinade is a tangy blend of orange and lemon juices accented with garlic and spices. It's generally found in the Hispanic food section of many supermarkets and is made by a variety of manufacturers, such as La Lechonera, Badia and Goya. It's an excellent medium for grilling. Serve this with Lime-Garlic Roasted Corn (page 393).

2 cups (475 ml) mojo criollo marinade
1½ pounds (675 g) beef sirloin tips
4 medium-size boiling potatoes such as white or Yukon gold,
   about 1½ pounds (675 g)

Put the marinade in a mixing bowl or resealable plastic bag. If the beef is in long strips, cut it into 2-inch (5-cm) chunks. Add the beef to the marinade, mix well, and marinate the beef for at least 3 hours and preferably overnight.

Prepare a grill.

Peel the potatoes and slice thin—about ¼ inch (½ cm) thick . Season the potatoes with salt and pepper and toss them with 3 tablespoons (45 ml) cooking oil. When the grill is ready, remove the meat from the marinade and grill for 7 to 8 minutes for medium rare—more or less according to your taste—turning to mark all sides. At the same time, lay the potatoes on the grill and cook them for 2 to 3 minutes per side, until grill-marked and cooked through. Put the meat on a platter and surround with the potatoes.

YIELD: 4 servings

BEEF TIPS BRAISED WITH KIMCHI

Kimchi, a spicy, pungent condiment of pickled vegetables—particularly cabbage—is a Korean staple. These days, it's also pretty easy to find in the supermarket, thanks to the amazing pro-liferation of packaged international foods.

   2 pounds (900 g) sirloin tips, cut into 2-inch (5-cm) cubes
   1 jar (16 ounces, or 455 g) kimchi
   ¼ cup (60 ml) soy sauce

Season the meat with salt and pepper. Select a sauté pan or skillet with a tight-fitting cover. Heat 2 tablespoons (30 ml) olive oil to the sauté pan and heat over high heat. Sear the meat in batches, turning occasionally, until browned on all sides. Reduce the heat to medium and add the kimchi and soy sauce to the pan. Stir in the meat, cover, and simmer for 10 minutes.

YIELD: 4 servings

Beef Stew with Fire-Roasted Chiles and Oranges

Fire-roasted salsa, widely available in supermarkets, gives this dish a earthy, smoky flavor. Choose your heat level among the salsas available. Serve with steamed flour tortillas to roll the meat in and to sop up the juices.

2 pounds (900 g) beef stew meat
1 jar (12 ounces, or 340 g) fire-roasted salsa
4 oranges

Preheat oven to 300°F (150°C, gas mark 2).

Using a vegetable peeler, cut wide strips of zest from the oranges, then squeeze the juice. Set zest and juice aside.

Heat about ¼ cup (60 ml) olive oil to a heavy flameproof Dutch oven (or other flameproof casserole dish) over high heat. Season the beef with salt and pepper and sear in batches until well browned on all sides.

When the searing is finished, return all the beef to the pot and add the salsa, orange zest, and juice, along with enough water to almost cover the meat. Put the cover on the pot and braise in the oven for 2 to 3 hours, being careful not to let it boil vigorously. Add water if it is getting too dry. When done, adjust the seasonings and serve.

YIELD: 4 servings

OVEN-BARBECUED BEEF RIBS

Big, meaty beef ribs—the kind that are cut off a rib roast—are sometimes tough to find. Ask your butcher—if he has some, this recipe will have you putting in a standing order.

> 4 pounds (1¾ kg) beef ribs
> 1 cup (235 ml) beer
> 2 cups (500 g) barbecue sauce, your choice

Preheat the oven to 300°F (150°C, gas mark 2).

Put the ribs in a shallow roasting pan. Mix the beer and barbecue sauce together and thoroughly douse the ribs with the sauce. Cover the pan with foil and bake for 2 to 3 hours. Baste every so often with more sauce mix. The ribs should be caramelized with the sauce and falling-off-the-bone tender.

YIELD: 4 servings

Short Ribs, Braised and Glazed

This is the kind of sticky-fingered, messy-mouthed meal that kids love to dig into. Serve with steamed rice and Sautéed Snap Peas (page 408).

> 3 to 4 pounds (1¼ to 1¾ kg) short ribs, trimmed of fat
> 2 cups (475 ml) teriyaki sauce
> 1 cup (250 g) hoisin sauce

Combine all the ingredients, along with some black pepper, in a resealable plastic bag and marinate for at least 4 hours or, even better, overnight.

Preheat oven to 325°F (170°C, gas mark 3).

Put the ribs and marinade in a Dutch oven or other casserole dish with a tight-fitting lid. Add enough water to come one-third of the way up the ribs, cover, and braise in oven for about 2 hours. Remove the lid and continue to cook until the sauce is mostly evaporated and has formed a glaze on the meat—about 45 minutes or so. Remove the ribs and arrange them on a platter. Serve with many napkins.

YIELD: 4 servings

🍶 ADD IT!
You could spike the marinade with a couple minced cloves of garlic and some diced chiles for extra zip.

BASIC MEATBALLS

If you have a batch of these in the freezer, you're a pot of pasta and a can of tomato puree away from having a quick meal on the table. Of course, a salad to accompany the meal wouldn't hurt, either.

1 pound (450 g) ground beef
1 egg
1 cup (115 g) seasoned dried bread crumbs
2 tablespoons (30 ml) oil

Combine all the ingredients in a mixing bowl, along with salt and pepper to taste. Mix well, using your fingers. Form into meatballs about 1-inch (2½-cm) wide. Heat about 2 tablespoons (30 ml) oil in a sauté pan or skillet over medium-high heat. When the oil starts to smoke, add the meatballs and brown them on all sides—this can be a spattery operation, so an apron might be a good idea. Remove the meatballs from the pan and place them on a plate with a couple thicknesses of paper towels to absorb excess oil.

At this point, you can put them in resealable plastic bags and freeze them until you are ready to take them out and submerse them in any of a variety of sauces: marinara, brown gravy, or mushroom gravy with sour cream added at the last minute.

Gently stew them in whatever sauce you like. You can also bake the thawed meatballs at 350°F (180°C, gas mark 4) for 15 minutes or so, until cooked through. Bake for a half hour if the meatballs are still frozen.

YIELD: 4 servings of 2 meatballs apiece

ADD IT!
We like to add a half cup (50 g) finely grated Parmesan cheese to the mix when we have it on hand.

BURGER AND OLIVE SIMMER

It just goes to show: Sloppy Joes don't have to feature tomato sauce. Ladle this on crusty rolls and serve with a salad.

  1 pound (450 g) ground beef
  ½ cup (60 g) green olives, sliced
  2 cups (500 g) barbecue sauce

Heat a wide sauté pan or skillet over medium heat and add the ground beef. Cook, breaking it up with a spoon, until the pink is gone. Add the olives and barbecue sauce and continue cooking at a simmer for 15 to 20 minutes.

YIELD: 4 servings

🥫 ADD IT!
Sauté half a minced onion and a half cup (50 g) sliced mushrooms along with the meat.

BURGER AND SPINACH SAUTÉ

This is great with rice or mashed potatoes.

> 10 ounces (280 g) spinach
> 1 pound (450 g) ground beef
> 1 can (14 ounces, or 400 g) diced tomatoes with onions and peppers

Pick over the spinach, discarding wilted or yellow leaves and snipping off large stems, then wash and spin-dry it. Tear into small pieces. Heat a wide sauté pan or skillet over medium-high heat. Add the ground beef and cook, breaking it up with a spoon, until it is no longer pink. Add the spinach to the pan and stir until the spinach wilts. Add the diced tomatoes and season with salt and pepper to taste. Reduce the heat to low and simmer for 10 minutes.

YIELD: 4 servings

ADD IT!
It's embarrassing, really, how addicted we are to garlic. That said, we would be remiss if we didn't point out that sautéing 2 minced cloves of garlic with the hamburger would deepen the flavor of this dish.

WORCESTERSHIRE BURGERS

> 1 small onion
> 1 pound (450 g) ground beef
> 2 tablespoons (30 ml) Worcestershire sauce

Peel the onion and cut it into small dice. In a small sauté pan or skillet over medium heat, sauté the onion in 1 tablespoon (15 ml) cooking oil for 5 to 6 minutes, until the onion softens. Set aside and let cool. Mix together the meat, onion, and Worcestershire sauce. Season with salt and pepper.

Form 4 patties and grill or fry them as you prefer.

YIELD: 4 servings

ADD IT!
This is a classic burger, and the additions come with the toppings. Try topping with a meaty slice of tomato and crumbled blue cheese; serve on a crusty Kaiser roll.

CAJUN BURGERS

Serve with Dirty Rice (page 355).

> 1 pound (450 g) ground beef
> 1 tablespoon (7 g) Cajun spice mix (see note)
> 1 tablespoon (10 g) minced garlic

Mix together the meat, spice mix, and garlic. Season with salt and pepper. Form 4 patties and grill or fry them as you prefer.

YIELD: 4 servings

 ADD IT!
You can up the spiciness quotient by adding a few squirts of your favorite hot sauce, such as Tabasco.

NOTE: *If your market does not carry Cajun spice mix, you can approximate it by mixing together 1 tablespoon salt, ½ teaspoon cayenne pepper, 2 tablespoons paprika, 1 teaspoon garlic powder, 1 teaspoon ground thyme, 1 teaspoon dried onion, and 2 teaspoons ground black pepper. Store in a jar with a tight-fitting lid.*

BEER BURGERS

The best bet for this recipe is to choose your favorite beer, carefully measure out the amount needed, and set aside the rest to savor with the burger!

- 1 pound (450 g) ground beef
- 1 tablespoon (7 g) steak rub spice mix (see note)
- ½ cup (120 ml) beer

Mix together the meat, spice mix, and beer. Season with salt and pepper. Form 4 patties and grill or fry them as you prefer.

YIELD: 4 servings

NOTE: *If your market does not carry steak rub spice mix, you can approximate it by mixing together 1 tablespoon salt, ¼ teaspoon cayenne pepper, 1 tablespoon paprika, 1 teaspoon garlic powder, 1 teaspoon dried onion, and 1 tablespoon ground black pepper.*

TERIYAKI BURGERS

As all the carb counters know, burgers don't have to be served on a bun. Accompany this one with a salad of sliced cucumbers and bean sprouts tossed in a vinaigrette made of sesame oil, rice vinegar, 1 small clove minced garlic, and 1 teaspoon minced pickled ginger.

- 1 pound (450 g) ground beef
- ¼ cup (60 ml) teriyaki sauce
- 2 stalks scallion

Mix together the meat and the teriyaki sauce in a bowl. Mince the scallion, both the green and white parts, and add to the bowl. Season with salt and pepper. Form 4 patties and grill or fry them as you prefer.

YIELD: 4 servings

TAMALE PIE

Tamale pie has been around since the 1920s, as housewives started cooking with more packaged products. It's proven to be a dinner staple for a reason: It's yummy.

> **1 pound (450 g) ground beef**
> **2 cups (500 g) fire-roasted tomato and corn salsa, whatever spice level you prefer**
> **1 box (8½ ounces, or 240 g) corn muffin mix**

Heat a medium-size sauté pan or skillet over medium-high heat and add the burger, breaking it up into small bits and cooking until no longer pink. Add the salsa and cook for 10 minutes at a simmer.

Preheat the oven to 350°F (180°C, gas mark 4).

Make the muffin batter following the instructions on the box.

Grease a deep pie pan or 9-inch-square (23-cm-square) baking dish. Pour the burger mix into the baking pan. Top with the muffin batter, spreading it out to cover the beef. Bake for 12 to 15 minutes.

YIELD: 4 to 6 servings

ADD IT!
Tamale pie is an easily expandable dish. You can add chopped green pepper, minced garlic, and sliced olives to the beef mixture, and stir shredded cheddar cheese into the corn muffin batter, just for starters.

BRAISED AND BAKED CORNED BEEF

This is the perfect dish for a cold winter's night. It takes time to cook, but the preparation is a snap. Just leave it simmering and go about your business. For a twist on the traditional side dishes, try serving it with Braised Red Cabbage (page 382) and Orange Carrots (Page 385)

    1 corned beef, about 3 to 4 pounds (1¼ to 1¾ kg)
    2 tablespoons (15 g) pickling spice mix
    1 cup (235 ml) honey mustard

Put the corned beef and the pickling spice mix into a large pot and cover with water. Heat almost to a boil, turn down the heat to low, and simmer for 2 hours.

Preheat the oven to 325°F (170°C, gas mark 3).

Remove the corned beef from the pot and put it on a rack in a roasting pan. Slather the mustard all over the corned beef and bake for 1 hour.

YIELD: 6 to 8 servings

CORNED BEEF HASH

Our dad has an unseemly addiction to hash. For most people, a perfectly done roast beef is a treasure in and of itself. Not for Dad, however. For him, a roast beef is the tedious but necessary first step in the weary journey of leftovers that must end with the Glory That Is Hash. This one is for you, Dad.

    1 pound (450 g) cooked corned beef
    1 pound (450 g) potatoes, peeled and chopped large
    2 medium-size onions, peeled and roughly chopped

Using a food processor or meat grinder, coarsely grind the meat, potatoes, and onions. Mix all of the ingredients together. Heat about ¼ cup (60 ml) oil in a medium-size sauté pan or skillet over medium-high heat. Add the hash ingredients. Flatten into a pancake shape and cook for 10 to 15 minutes. Turn with a spatula and cook for another 15 to 20 minutes. The potatoes should be cooked through and the hash nicely crusted. Cut into wedges and serve.

YIELD: 4 to 6 servings

NOTE: *This is great with a poached egg on top at any time of the day.*

GRILLED ITALIAN SAUSAGE WITH ONIONS AND PEPPERS

Poaching sausages before grilling has the lovely advantage of ensuring that you don't have to turn the sausages into charred little tubes just to ensure they're done. It also makes for a much juicier finished product. The heck with peanuts and Cracker Jack—this is the meal we associate with baseball games, particularly if the sausage and veggies are stuffed into a crusty submarine sandwich roll.

> 1½ pounds (675 g) Italian sausage, hot or sweet
> 1 pound (450 g) Spanish onion
> 1 pound (450 g) sweet peppers

If you are using charcoal, get the grill going.

Poach the sausages over low heat in 1 quart (1 L) of water until just done, about 20 minutes; drain the sausages and set aside. Core and seed the peppers and peel the onions. Slice the peppers and onions into strips ½-inch (1-cm) wide.

When the grill is ready, grill the sausages about 5 minutes per side. While sausages are grilling, heat 2 tablespoons (30 ml) olive oil in a large sauté pan or skillet over medium-high heat. Sauté the peppers and onions for 8 to 10 minutes, seasoning to taste with salt and pepper. Place the sausages on a platter and top with vegetables.

YIELD: 4 servings

ADD IT!
Adding 1 or 2 large minced cloves of garlic to the veggies ups the "yum" factor even more.

VEAL

Veal has also been known as a high-end dish, but over the years it's become controversial as claims of inhumane treatment of veal calves swirl through the court of public opinion. Fortunately, veal lovers do have a choice—many markets offer free-range veal, from animals that have not been improperly penned or raised. If you remain uncomfortable with the idea of serving veal, you can substitute chicken or pork in most of these dishes.

VEAL ROAST WITH ROSEMARY AND PEARS

Pears are a perfect foil for the mildness of veal; here, look for pears that aren't crunchy-hard, but not so ripe that they'll bruise if you look at them cross-eyed.

> 1 veal top round roast, about 4 pounds (1¾ kg)
> ¼ cup (7 g) chopped fresh rosemary
> 8 firm-ripe Bartlett or Anjou pears

Preheat the oven to 350°F (180°C, gas mark 4).

Rub the roast with extra-virgin olive oil, season with salt and pepper, and place on a rack in a roasting pan. Peel, halve, and core the pears. Nestle the pears around the veal and sprinkle the rosemary over all.

Roast for about 30 minutes per pound—until an instant-read thermometer reads 145°F (63°C) for medium rare. Allow to rest 15 minutes and carve.

Arrange a couple of roasted pear halves on each plate with the meat.

YIELD: Serves 8.

 ADD IT!
Deglaze the roasting pan with a cup of wine, apple juice, or chicken stock. Whisk in a few tablespoons (about 50 g) butter, a pat at a time, just until they melt. Strain. The result: A quick and delicious sauce.

BRIE-STUFFED VEAL CHOP WITH CRUMB CRUST

Here's a variation on the breaded baked chicken or pork chops, the staple of many work-aday dinners. It's different, but not scary enough to set off the Strange Food Radar found on many children.

> 4 veal rib chops, ¾ inch (1½ cm) thick
> 4 ounces (115 g) Brie cheese
> 4 tablespoons (55 g) butter
> ½ loaf Herb Basil Focaccia (see note)

Cut a pocket in the meaty part of each chop and stuff with 1 ounce of the Brie; fasten with a toothpick. Break the focaccia into small pieces and process in a food processor until you have coarse crumbs. In a medium saucepan, melt the butter over low heat. Combine the butter and crumbs. Season the chops with salt and pepper and press the crumbs firmly onto both sides of each chop. Lay on a baking sheet covered with wax paper and chill at least one hour, or up to overnight.

Preheat the oven to 450°F (230°C, gas mark 8).

Heat about ¼ cup (60 ml) olive oil in a medium-size sauté pan or skillet over medium-high heat. Sear each chop for 4 to 5 minutes per side, until the crumbs form a nice golden crust. You will need to do this one, maybe two at a time, as it's important not to crowd the meat. Be careful to work your spatula gently under the chops when turning so as to keep the crumb crust in place.

Place the chops on a baking sheet and finish cooking in the oven for about 15 minutes for medium.

YIELD: 4 servings

🧂 ADD IT!
Add a tablespoon of chopped fresh rosemary to the crumb-butter mix.

> *NOTE: See page 125 for the recipe. If you wish to purchase a herbed focaccia, you will need a 1-pound (450 g) loaf.*

VEAL PICCATA

Veal piccata is a warhorse of restaurant menus, and many foodies view it as an uninspired choice. But there's a reason it's such a staple: the stuff is good. Who can really argue with success? Certainly not us.

1 pound (450 g) veal cutlets
1 cup (125 g) all-purpose flour
3 lemons
3 tablespoons (43 g) butter

Lay a sheet of plastic wrap on a cutting board. Lay the veal on the wrap and cover with another sheet of wrap. With the side of a meat cleaver or other heavy blunt object, pound the veal until quite thin, about ⅛ inch (¼ cm).

Season the meat with salt and pepper and dip into the flour. Squeeze 2 of the lemons and set the juice aside.

Heat ¼ cup (60 ml) olive oil in a large sauté pan or skillet over high heat. Sauté the veal briefly—2 or 3 minutes per side—until golden brown. You may have to cook the meat in batches, as it is important not to crowd the pan. Add more oil if needed. Put the cooked meat on a plate and set in a warm place.

Keeping the sauté pan on moderately high heat, pour in the lemon juice, and bring to a boil, scraping the sides and bottom of the pan to dislodge the brown bits stuck to it. Briskly whisk in the butter, 1 tablespoon (15 g) at a time, to form a smooth sauce. Be sure to monitor the heat and remove as soon as the last of the butter is melted, to make sure the sauce doesn't break.

Arrange the veal on a serving plate and spoon the sauce over it. Slice the third lemon thin and use as a garnish.

YIELD: 4 servings

🧂 ADD IT!
Capers are traditionally found in a piccata; you can sauté them briefly before adding the lemon juice to the pan.

Veal Scaloppini with Artichoke-Tomato Sauce

The name artichoke "salsa" could be misleading. We've seen it as artichoke tapenade and artichoke antipasto as well, but we're basically talking about a jar full of chopped-up artichokes and other tasty ingredients such as roasted red pepper or tomatoes. If you can't find any of the above, send a large jar of marinated artichoke hearts on a trip through the food processor and add a cup of chopped tomatoes.

> 1 pound (450 g) veal cutlets
> 1 cup (125 g) all-purpose flour
> 10 ounces (280 g) artichoke salsa

Lay a sheet of plastic wrap on your cutting board and lay the veal on top of that. Cover with another sheet of wrap. Pound with the side of a meat cleaver or other heavy blunt object until the veal is quite thin—about ½ inch (1 cm) thick.

Mix the flour with salt and pepper to taste. Dredge the veal in the flour. Heat ¼ cup (60 ml) olive oil in a sauté pan or skillet over high heat. Sauté the veal briefly—about 1 to 2 minutes per side. Set the meat aside in a warm place. Warm the salsa in the pan.

Arrange the veal cutlets on a plate and spoon the salsa over them.

YIELD: 4 servings

ADD IT!
Mince 2 cloves garlic and sauté briefly before adding the artichoke sauce to the pan.

VEAL SCALLOPS WITH SAUTÉED SPINACH AND LEMON-TARRAGON SAUCE

Strangely enough, one of the few vegetables universally loved in our family was spinach. (We guess the Popeye Indoctrination Program was successful.) In our ongoing quest to Share the Spinach Love, we offer the following recipe—spinach and lemon is a classic combination. Serve it with Wild Rice Pilaf (page 360).

10 ounces (280 g) spinach
1 pound (450 g) veal cutlets
1 cup (235 ml) fat-free lemon-tarragon salad dressing (see note)
4 tablespoons (55 g) butter, cold

Lay a sheet of plastic wrap on your cutting board and lay the veal on top of that. Cover with another sheet of wrap and pound with the side of a meat cleaver or other heavy blunt object until the veal is quite thin, about ⅛ inch (¼ cm).

Pick over the spinach, discarding wilted leaves and snipping off large stems. Wash and spin-dry the spinach.

Set the oven on its lowest setting.

Season the meat with salt and pepper. Heat 2 tablespoons (30 ml) olive oil in a sauté pan or skillet over high heat. Sear the meat until nicely browned on both sides, about 2 minutes per side. You may need to do this in batches, as crowding the pan is not a good thing. Place the meat on a plate and keep it warm in the oven.

While the meat is in the oven, sauté the spinach in the sauté pan, seasoning with salt and pepper, until just wilted. Divide among 4 plates.

Add the dressing to the pan and heat until bubbling. Briskly whisk in the butter, 1 table-spoon (15 g) at a time, to form a smooth sauce. Be sure to monitor the heat and remove as soon as the last of the butter is melted, to make sure the sauce doesn't break.

Place the veal on the spinach and spoon the sauce over and around it.

YIELD: 4 servings

NOTE: *Fat-free dressing works best in this recipe, because it is less likely to break in the sauce and become greasy. To make 1½ cups (355 ml) of your own dressing, combine the following ingredients in a blender and blend on high speed until smooth:*

Juice of 1 lemon
½ cup (120 ml) water
2 tablespoons (40 g) honey
3 tablespoons (45 ml) cider vinegar
1 tablespoon (12 g) sugar
1 tablespoon (15 g) Dijon mustard
2 tablespoons (2 g) minced fresh tarragon
½ teaspoon minced garlic
Salt and pepper to taste

Put the dressing in a small saucepan and whisk in 1 tablespoon (8 g) cornstarch. Bring to a simmer over medium heat, stirring until the dressing thickens slightly and clarifies. Chill.

VEAL SCALOPPINI WITH PORCINI MUSHROOMS

1 pound (450 g) veal cutlets
1 cup (125 g) all-purpose flour
2 ounces (55 g) dried porcini mushrooms
4 tablespoons (55 g) butter, cold

Put the mushrooms in a bowl and cover with 2 cups boiling water. Allow to steep for 15 minutes. Using a slotted spoon, remove the mushrooms; roughly chop them and set aside. Pour the mushroom liquid through a layer of cheesecloth or paper towel fitted in a sieve. Set the liquid aside.

Lay a sheet of plastic wrap on your cutting board and lay the veal on top of that. Cover the meat with another sheet of wrap. Pound with the side of a meat cleaver or other heavy blunt object until the veal is quite thin—about ½ inch (1 cm).

Mix the flour with salt and pepper to taste. Dredge the veal in the flour. Heat ¼ cup (60 ml) olive oil in a sauté pan or skillet over high heat. Sauté the veal briefly, 1 to 2 minutes per side. Set the meat aside in a warm place. Add the mushrooms and 1 cup (235 ml) of the steeping liquid to the sauté pan and heat over high heat until the liquid is reduced by two-thirds. Briskly whisk in the butter, 1 tablespoon (15 g) at a time, to form a smooth sauce. Be sure to monitor the heat and remove as soon as the last of the butter is melted, to make sure the sauce doesn't break. Adjust the seasoning, arrange the veal on serving plate, and spoon the sauce over it.

YIELD: 4 servings

ADD IT!
Whisk in ¼ cup (60 ml) heavy cream as the sauce is reducing.

218

Veal Schnitzel

1 pound (450 g) veal cutlets
2 eggs, beaten slightly
2 cups (100 g) fresh bread crumbs

Lay a sheet of plastic wrap on a cutting board, place the veal on the wrap, and cover the veal with another sheet. With the side of a meat cleaver or other heavy blunt object, pound the veal until quite thin—about ½ inch (1cm).

Season the meat with salt and pepper and dip first into the egg and then into the crumbs, pressing them gently onto the meat.

Heat ¼ cup (60 ml) olive oil in a sauté pan or skillet over high heat. Sauté the schnitzels briefly—2 or 3 minutes per side—until golden. You can cook them in batches, adding oil if needed, as it is important not to crowd the pan.

YIELD: 4 servings

ADD IT!
This is a good basic recipe that is fine to eat unadorned, but classic additions are fried capers and a fried egg on top.

VEAL STEW WITH OLIVES

The produce section of our supermarket has several bins of gourmet olives to choose from. If you can't find garlic-cured olives, an assortment of regular cured olives will work as well.

> 2 pounds (900 g) veal stew meat, in 1-inch (2½-cm) cubes
> ½ pound (225 g) garlic-cured olives
> 2 cups (475 ml) dry white wine

Heat ¼ cup (60 ml) olive oil in a heavy-bottomed sauté pan or skillet over medium-high heat. Season the meat and sear it in batches—being careful not to crowd the pan—until well browned. Put all the veal back in the pan and add the olives and wine.

Cover, reduce heat to low, and simmer, covered, for 1 hour. If you don't have a cover for your sauté pan or skillet, foil will do just fine. Bob notes that at the Inn, he doesn't have a proper cover for 90 percent of his pots and pans.

YIELD: 6 servings

 ADD IT!
Whisk ¼ cup (60 g) sour cream in the dish and serve over wide buttered noodles sprinkled with sesame seeds.

VEAL STEW WITH PEPPERS

The tomato-sauce choices in the supermarket these days are truly dizzying, so naturally no market can stock everything. If you can't find Chianti mushroom sauce, just use regular mushroom tomato sauce and add ½ cup (120 ml) red wine. This stew is great with rice, buttered noodles, a pasta such as farfalle, or spaetzle.

2 pounds (900 g) veal stew meat, in 1-inch (2½-cm) cubes
1 jar (16 ounces, or 450 g) Chianti mushroom sauce
1 pound (450 g) assorted bell peppers, red, yellow, or green

Core the peppers and cut them into bite-size cubes. Heat ¼ cup (60 ml) olive oil over medium-high heat in a heavy-bottomed sauté pan or skillet with a tight-fitting cover. Season the meat with salt and pepper and sear it in batches—being careful not to crowd the pan—until well browned. Sauté the peppers in the same pan for 5 minutes, until slightly softened. Put all the veal in the pan and add the sauce. Cover, reduce heat to low, and simmer for 1 hour.

YIELD: 6 servings

11

Pork

Erik, the sous chef at the Three Stallion Inn, recently returned from a trip to Bali. The highlight of the trip (and he had photos to prove it) was the discovery of a 12-foot-tall religious statue he saw in a temple—made entirely out of pork! Now these folks get it—the same way large swaths of Americans (especially in the South) get it—pork is versatile, economical and delicious in its many forms and uses. We even know of several vegetarians who make "the bacon exception." While we have little experience using pork as a building material, we do know that fresh or smoked, barbecued or braised, ground for sausage or carved as a roast, pork is the foundation of many a good meal.

Today's pork is much leaner than that of even 50 years ago. "The other white meat" is an all-around star performer that can stand in ably for veal or chicken in many dishes. Another chef who works with Bob, Levi, has a sticker on his knife box that says it all—"Praise the Lard."

PORK SHOULDER WITH FENNEL AND CIDER

Braising, then roasting, gives pork a succulent flavor, and fennel and cider play off each other beautifully. Try serving this with Rosemary Couscous (page 354).

> 1 pork shoulder roast, about 4 to 5 pounds (1¾ to 2¼ kg)
> 2 bulbs fennel
> 3 cups (700ml) apple cider

Heat the oven to 325°F (170°C, gas mark 3).

Put the roast in a Dutch oven with a tight-fitting cover. Season with salt and pepper. Cut off and discard the fennel tops and cut each bulb into 8 wedges. In a small pan bring the cider to a boil and pour it over the meat. Cover and bake for about 2 hours, remove the cover, and scatter the fennel wedges around the roast. Roast for another hour with the cover off.

Remove the roast and fennel from the pan and keep warm. Degrease the cooking liquid and reduce it to about 2 cups (475 ml). Slice the roast, spoon the sauce over it, and serve with the roasted fennel on the side.

YIELD: 6 to 8 servings

SMOKED SHOULDER WITH CABBAGE

We're sneaky, getting orphan foods like cabbage and prunes into dishes. But if you haven't tried cabbage since you sampled a sad little watery portion last St. Patrick's Day, put aside your suspicion. Cabbage can be good stuff.

1 boneless smoked shoulder roll, about 2 pounds (900 g)
1 small head green cabbage
1 cup (235 ml) heavy cream

Heat the oven to 350°F (180°C, gas mark 4).

Cut the smoked shoulder into 1-inch (2½-cm) cubes. Core the cabbage and cut it into ½-inch (1-cm) strips. You should have about 4 cups (300 g). Put the cabbage in a 2-quart (2-L) pot and cover with water. Cook for 10 to 15 minutes over high heat, until the cabbage is soft. Drain the cabbage. Combine the shoulder, cabbage, and cream in a casserole dish. Bake, uncovered, in the oven for 30 minutes, until the mixture is golden brown on top and bubbling.

YIELD: 4 servings

ADD IT!
Sprinkle the top with a cup (80 g) of cooked chopped bacon and shredded Gruyère for a crispy crust.

VINDALOO PORK CURRY

Our friend Michael Brown, an aficionado of all things spicy, looks upon a good vindaloo as a fine opportunity to work up a healthy sweat. Vindaloo, a specialty of central and southern India, is certainly one of the most sinus-clearing and spicy curries available. It's based on a complicated and varying blend of spices—fortunately, premade sauces are now widely available.

This dish goes great with steamed basmati rice and chutney on the side.

> 3 pounds (1¼ kg) boneless pork butt or shoulder
> 1 pound (450 g) Spanish onions
> 1 container (10 ounces, or 285 ml) Vindaloo curry sauce

Cut the pork into 1-inch (2½-cm) cubes. Peel and chop the onions into medium dice. Heat a large sauté pan or skillet over medium-high heat and add about 3 tablespoons (45 ml) olive oil. Fry the onions until softened and lightly browned, about 8 to 10 minutes. Add the pork and allow to brown. Add the curry sauce and 1 cup (235 ml) water. Reduce heat and simmer for 30 to 45 minutes, until meat is tender.

YIELD: 4 to 6 servings

PORK AND BLACK BEAN STEW

This is a delicious stew that is also high in protein and fiber. It's great over rice.

> 1 fresh pork shoulder, about 4 pounds (1¾ kg)
> 2 cans (14 ounces, or 400 g, each) black beans, drained and rinsed
> 2 jars (12 ounces, or 340 g, each) green salsa

Trim the pork off the bones and then cut the meat into 2-inch (5-cm) cubes. Season the meat with salt and pepper. Heat a flameproof Dutch oven over high heat and add 2 to 3 tablespoons (30 to 45 ml) oil. When the oil is hot but not yet smoking, add the meat and sear until well browned on all sides. It's important not to crowd the pan, so you may have to do this in batches. Reduce the heat to low. Return all of the seared meat (and any collected juices) to the pot and add the black beans and the salsa, plus 1 cup (235 ml) of water. Cover and simmer for 1½ to 2 hours.

YIELD: 6 to 8 servings

🫙 ADD IT!
Add a cup of chopped fresh tomatoes and a cup of frozen corn kernels to the stew as it simmers.

ROAST PORK WITH SAGE AND ROSEMARY

Sometimes simple is what you want, even what you need. These flavors go well together and allow you to savor the flavor of each element of the dish.

    1 bone-in pork rib roast, about 4 pounds (1¾ kg)
    2 tablespoons (3 to 4 g) chopped fresh rosemary
    2 tablespoons (3 to 4 g) chopped fresh sage

Preheat oven to 325°F (170°C, gas mark 3). Place the pork on a rack in a roasting pan. Mix together the herbs. Salt and pepper the roast thoroughly and press the herb mixture firmly onto the surface of the meat. Roast to the desired doneness, about 2 hours for medium well. Your instant-read meat thermometer should read 150°F (66°C). Let the meat rest for 15 minutes before carving.

YIELD: 6 to 8 servings

 ADD IT!
Many fruits pair well with pork, but we particularly like the way that apples play with the sharp, smoky rosemary flavor in this recipe. Make a fragrant applesauce or just peel and core the apples and bake them in the oven with the pork roast for the last hour or so. Simple perfection.

ROAST PORK AND PEARS

A toothsome twist on the usual pork-and-apple combination. Truly, pork was made to cook with fruit.

> 6 pears, firm but ripe (we like the Bartlett or Anjou varieties for this)
> 1 pork loin roast, bone-in, about 3 pounds (1¼ kg)
> 3 tablespoons (5 g) chopped fresh rosemary

Peel the pears, split them in half, and, using a melon baller, remove the cores. Put the pears in a 1-quart (1-L) saucepan and just barely cover them with water. Poach over medium heat for 20 to 25 minutes, until soft but still firm. Drain the pears.

Heat the oven to 325°F (170°C, gas mark 3).

Put the pork in a roasting pan and season with salt and pepper. Sprinkle the rosemary over the meat. Arrange the pears around the pork. Cook for about 30 minutes per pound, until a thermometer inserted near the bone reads 150°F (66°C). Slice the meat and serve with the roasted pears.

YIELD: 6 servings

 ADD IT!
Mix a couple cloves of finely minced garlic into the chopped rosemary and rub the mixture firmly into the roast before cooking.

HONEY AND GARLIC PORK ROAST

Honey is one of those perfect foods that you can do just about anything with. It pairs beautifully with many fruits and meats, and makes a delightful sauce all on its own. Mashed Potatoes with Roasted Garlic (page 432) and Maple-Glazed Carrots (page 384) would be good accompaniments for this dish.

> 4 cloves garlic, minced
> 1 cup (350 g) honey
> 1 boneless center-cut pork loin roast, about 3 pounds (1¼ kg)

Preheat the oven to 325°F (170°C, gas mark 3).

Combine the garlic and honey in a small mixing bowl. Put the pork on a rack in a roasting pan and brush well with the honey mixture. Season with salt and pepper. Roast for 20 to 25 minutes per pound, basting every 15 minutes with more of the honey, until a meat thermometer reads 150°F (66°C). Remove from the oven and allow to sit for 10 minutes, then carve.

YIELD: 6 servings

🫙 ADD IT!
This would be even more delicious with 2 to 3 teaspoons minced fresh rosemary mixed into the honey.

Pork Loin Stuffed with Spinach and Sun-Dried Tomato Pesto

This is a dressy meal that's surprisingly easy to prepare. Roast a pan of chopped celery root and parsnips for a lovely side dish.

> 2 pounds (900 g) fresh spinach
> 1 boneless center-cut pork loin roast, about 4 pounds (1¾ kg)
> 1 jar (8 ounces, or 225 g) sun-dried tomato and garlic pesto

Pick through the spinach, discarding the bad leaves and pinching off large stems as needed. Rinse and place in a steamer in a 2-quart (2-L) saucepan with about 2 inches (5 cm) water in it. Steam the spinach a few minutes until just well wilted. Allow to cool, squeeze out as much moisture as possible, and chop fine. Set spinach aside.

Place the pork on a cutting board with the long side of the pork loin parallel to the edge of the counter. Hold the knife blade flat and parallel to the cutting board, with the edge facing away from you. Starting about a third of the way up the front edge of the roast, cut horizontally along the length of the meat almost all the way through to the back, leaving about a ½-inch (1-cm) "hinge" of meat. Fold the top two-thirds of the roast back on this "hinge" so that it is lying flat on the cutting board. Now, starting at the base of the hinge, cut the top two-thirds of the roast into halves in the same manner, again not cutting all the way through, but leaving another hinge in the back. Fold this piece out, so that you now have 1 flat rectangle of pork.

Place the meat between two layers of plastic wrap and gently pound with the side of a meat cleaver (or some other solid blunt object, like a heavy pan) until the meat is of uniform thickness, about ½ to ¾ inch (1 to 1½ cm) thick. Remove top plastic wrap. Season the meat with salt and pepper and spread evenly with the pesto. Now spread the spinach evenly over the meat, leaving ½ inch (1 cm) at one of the long edges of the meat uncovered. Using the bottom layer of plastic wrap, starting with the long side of the rectangle facing you, roll the meat jelly-roll fashion, leaving the seam side down. Tie the meat with butcher twine. The meat can be prepared to this step up to two days in advance.

Preheat the oven to 350°F (180°C, gas mark 4).

Place the roast on a rack in a roasting pan, season the roast well with salt and pepper, and cook for approximately 1½ hours, until your meat thermometer reads 165°F (74°C). Allow to rest for 15 minutes and cut slices showing the pinwheel of pesto and spinach.

YIELD: 6 to 8 servings

ROAST PORK LOIN WITH APRICOT-GINGER GLAZE

If you can't find apricot preserves, a good jar of marmalade will also work just fine. We've served this with Roasted Acorn Squash (page 367) and Mashed Potatoes with Scallions (page 433).

1 boneless center-cut pork loin, about 3 pounds (1¼ kg)
1 jar (10 ounces, or 280 g) apricot preserves
2 tablespoons (12 g) minced fresh ginger
2 tablespoons (28 g) butter

Preheat the oven to 350°F (180°C, gas mark 4).

Place the pork in roasting pan, season with salt and pepper, and place in preheated oven. While pork is cooking, melt the preserves in a small saucepan and mix in the ginger. Allow to simmer briefly, then set aside. After the meat has cooked for about 45 minutes, brush liberally with the apricot mixture. Continue to cook until a meat thermometer registers 150°F (66°C), about 1¼ hours for a roast of this size.

Allow the meat to rest for 10 minutes before carving. While the meat is resting, reheat the apricot glaze. Whisking slowly, whisk in the butter 1 tablespoon (15 g) at a time. Pass on the side as a sauce.

YIELD: 4 to 6 servings

Brined Pork Roast
with Sweet-Hot Pepper Sauce

Brining pork is a serious snap to do, and it results in an outstandingly moist and flavorful piece of meat.

> 1 boneless center-cut pork loin roast, about 4 pounds (1¾ kg)
> 2 quarts (2 L) All-Purpose Pork Brine (page 32)
> 1 jar (10 ounces, or 280 g) pepper jelly
> 4 tablespoons (55 g) butter

Brine the pork for a few hours or more according to the instructions in the brine recipe.

Preheat oven to 350°F (180°C, gas mark 4).

Place roast on a rack in a roasting pan, season with salt and pepper, and roast for about 1½ hours, or until a thermometer reads 150°F (66°C) Remove from oven and allow to rest in a warm place about 10 to 15 minutes.

Melt the pepper jelly in a saucepan. Whisking briskly, whisk in the butter 1 tablespoon (15 g) at a time until it is just melted and the sauce is smooth and glossy. Slice the roast and pass the sauce on the side.

YIELD: 6 servings

ROAST FRESH HAM WITH CIDER-SAGE SAUCE

Full disclosure: We love this sauce. It's sweet, crisp, and absolutely satisfying to make and eat. And it tastes as if you went to much more trouble than you really did.

This ham is the round meat (top part of the leg) of the pig, usually cured and smoked, but it also makes a terrific roast when fresh. If your meat counter doesn't carry it, you may substitute a pork loin roast instead. We've also made this sauce with a regular ham with delightful results. Instead of mashed potatoes, try the ham with Potato Pancakes (page 439) and Brussels Sprouts with Cream and Chestnuts (page 379).

1 fresh ham, about 6 pounds (2¾ kg)
1 quart (1 L) apple cider
1 bunch fresh sage
4 tablespoons (55 g) butter

Preheat oven to 325°F (170°C, gas mark 3).

Place the ham on a rack in a roasting pan. Season well with salt and pepper. Mince half of the sage and sprinkle over the meat. Pour 2 cups (475 ml) cider into the pan. Roast for about 40 minutes per pound, or until a meat thermometer reads 150°F (66°C). Remove from the oven; transfer the ham to a platter and allow to rest for 15 minutes.

While the ham is resting, pour off the roasting liquid and skim off as much fat as possible. Add the rest of the cider to the pan and bring to a boil on the stovetop, stirring to scrape up the brown bits on the bottom of the pan. Add the degreased cooking liquid and the rest of the sage, finely chopped. Reduce the liquid by half. Whisking briskly, whisk in the butter 1 tablespoon (15 g) at a time it is until just melted and the sauce is smooth and glossy. Adjust the seasoning and serve the sauce on the side after carving the ham.

YIELD: 8 to 10 servings

PORK SIRLOIN CUTLET WITH MUSTARD AND BREAD CRUMBS

This is comfort food kicked up a notch. Add some oven-roasted potatoes and a salad of bitter greens, and you've got yourself a meal.

4 slices home-style white bread, crusts removed
2 pounds (900 g) pork sirloin cutlets
½ cup (120 ml) Dijon mustard

Put the bread into a food processor fitted with the metal blade and pulse a few times until you have bread crumbs.

Place the cutlets between two sheets of plastic wrap and pound gently with the flat side of a meat cleaver (or iron sauté pan or skillet, or meat tenderizer—think heavy blunt object) until the meat is a uniform ¼ inch (½ cm) thick. You may want to cut the meat into smaller serving portions once it is pounded.

Next, heat a heavy sauté pan or skillet over medium heat and add about ¼ cup (60 ml) oil. While the sauté pan is heating, season the pork with salt and pepper and brush mustard liberally over each piece. Dredge in the crumbs, pressing them on to ensure complete coverage. Shake off the excess crumbs and sauté the cutlets until nicely browned on each side and a crisp crumb crust has formed, about 5 to 7 minutes a side. You may need to cook the meat in batches—don't crowd the pan—and add oil as needed. Remove the cutlets from the pan and fan out on plates.

YIELD: 4 servings

ADD IT!
Add ¼ cup (25 g) finely grated Parmesan and 2 to 3 teaspoons dried oregano to the bread-crumb mixture.

GRILLED PORK TENDERLOIN WITH MANGO-PEACH SALSA

Pork and apples, pork and peaches, pork and mangoes, pork and oranges, is there any fruit that pork doesn't pair well with?

2 pork tenderloins, about 2 pounds (900 g)
1 bottle (12 ounces, or 355 ml) tequila-lime marinade
1 jar (12 ounces, or 340 g) mango-peach salsa

Trim silver skin (the shiny thin membrane that frequently covers a tenderloin) from pork and marinate, refrigerated, in the tequila-lime marinade for at least 2 hours and up to overnight.

Prepare a grill.

When it is ready, grill the pork for 7 to 10 minutes per side. Remove from the heat and allow to rest for 3 to 4 minutes. In a sauté pan or skillet, heat the salsa over low heat. Slice the meat into medallions. Fan out on plates and spoon the salsa over it.

YIELD: 4 servings

NOTE: *If you cannot find the marinade in your grocer's, you can make your own by blending the following ingredients until smooth:*

Juice of 3 limes
1 ounce (28 ml) tequila
¼ cup (50 g) sugar
2 tablespoons (30 ml) red wine vinegar
1 teaspoon minced garlic
1 tablespoon (1 to 2 g) chopped fresh cilantro
1 small jalapeño chile
¼ cup (60 ml) oil
Salt and pepper to taste

Can't find the salsa either? Here's a recipe that yields about 3 cups (750 g):

2 medium-size tomatoes, about ¾ pound (340 g) total
2 peaches, about ½ pound (225 g) total
1 cup (175 g) fresh-pack mango, or fresh mango, cut into ½ -inch (1-cm) dice
1 tablespoon (15 ml) red wine vinegar
1 small jalapeño or serrano chile, or to taste
1 tablespoon (10 g) minced garlic
½ cup (80 g) small-diced onion
2 tablespoons (2 g) minced fresh cilantro

Bring 4 cups (1 L) water to a boil in a saucepan. Meanwhile, prepare a large bowl of ice water. Cut out the core of the tomatoes and mark a small X in the base of each with a paring knife. Drop the tomatoes in the boiling water for 15 to 20 seconds, remove them with a slotted spoon, and plunge them into the cold water. Blanch the peaches in same boiling water for 20 seconds, also shocking them in the cold water.

Peel the tomatoes, squeeze out the seeds, and chop them roughly. Split the peaches, remove the stones, and chop the flesh into ¼-inch (½-cm) dice. Put the tomatoes and peaches in a mixing bowl. Put the mango, vinegar, chile, and garlic in a blender and blend until smooth. Add to the bowl along with the remaining ingredients and salt and pepper to taste. Allow to sit, refrigerated, for 2 hours and up to a day, so the flavors mingle.

Orange-Glazed Pork Tenderloin Stuffed with Caramelized Onion

1 pound (450 g) Spanish onions
4 tablespoons (55 g) butter, room temperature
2 pork tenderloins, about 2 pounds (900 g)
10 ounces (280 g) Seville orange marmalade

Peel and slice the onion into long strips, ½-inch (1-cm) thick and put in a heavy-bottomed pan with half of the butter. Cook over low heat, stirring occasionally, until the onions are very soft and caramelized. Be careful not to let the onions burn. This process should take 45 minutes to an hour. Allow to cool.

Trim off any silverskin—the shiny membrane that often covers a tenderloin—and cut each tenderloin in half crosswise. Holding the knife blade flat and parallel to the cutting board, cut each piece horizontally, beginning at one long side. Do not cut all the way through—leave a "hinge" of meat about ½-inch (1-cm) thick at the other long side. Fold out the meat to form a flat, roughly rectangular piece. Lay plastic wrap on your cutting board, lay the meat out on it, and cover with another layer of wrap. With the side of a meat cleaver, pound the meat gently until it is a uniform thickness—about ¼ inch (½ cm).

Season the meat with salt and pepper, then put a couple of tablespoons of the caramelized onion in a row along the center of the meat, lengthwise. Roll up the meat, tucking in the ends like a burrito, leaving the seam side down. Tie the rolls with butcher twine.

Preheat oven to 400°F (200°C, gas mark 6).

Put about 2 tablespoons (30 ml) oil in a sauté pan or skillet and heat over medium-high heat. Sear the meat on all sides until well browned. Set the sauté pan aside; do not wash. Place the meat rolls on a baking sheet and roast for 15 to 20 minutes until cooked through. Allow to rest for 4 to 5 minutes, remove the twine, and slice crossways into rounds.

While the meat is roasting, add ¼ cup (60 ml) water to the sauté pan and bring to a boil, scraping up the brown bits on the bottom. Add the marmalade and let it melt. Whisking slowly, add the rest of the butter 1 tablespoon (15 g) at a time. Adjust the seasoning to taste.

To serve, fan out the slices of meat on each of 4 plates and spoon the sauce over it.

YIELD: 4 servings

BONELESS PORK CHOPS WITH CHERRY SAUCE

4 boneless loin pork chops, about 1½ pounds (675 g)
8 ounces (225 g) cherry jam
2 tablespoons (30 ml) balsamic vinegar
3 tablespoons (43 g) butter

Heat the oven to 400°F (200°C, gas mark 6).

Season the pork chops with salt and pepper. Heat a medium-size sauté pan or skillet over high heat. Add about 2 tablespoons (30 ml) oil. When the oil starts to smoke, add the pork chops, searing them for 3 to 4 minutes per side. Put the chops on a baking sheet and bake them for 10 to 12 minutes, until just cooked through.

While the chops are in the oven, combine the jam and vinegar in a small saucepan over medium heat. When the jam melts, briskly whisk in the butter, 1 tablespoon (15 g) at a time, until it is just melted and the sauce is smooth and glossy. Season with salt and pepper. To serve, put a pork chop on each of 4 plates and spoon some sauce over it.

YIELD: 4 servings

PORK CHOPS WITH LEEKS AND CREAM

Leeks have a lovely creamy flavor that pairs well with a multitude of foods, but there is no denying that they are masters at concealing dirt within their many layers. Be very thorough with the washing if you want to avoid the dreaded gritty crunch when you bite.

2 leeks
4 center-cut pork chops, about 2 pounds (900 g)
1 cup (235 ml) heavy cream

Trim the root end and remove the dark green portion of each leek. Cut the leeks in half lengthwise, then cut into thin half moons. Place the leeks in a bowl of cold water and swish them around to clean. Remove them from the water by lifting them out with a slotted spoon, leaving any dirt in the water. Heat a sauté pan or skillet over high heat and add about 2 tablespoons (30 ml) olive oil. Season the pork chops with salt and pepper, then sear them on both sides until golden brown. Remove the chops and set them aside. Reduce the heat to medium, and cook the leeks for 5 to 8 minutes until they are softened. Put the chops back in the pan and add the cream. Cover the pan and simmer over low heat until the pork chops are cooked through, about 30 minutes.

To serve, place a chop on each of 4 plates. Adjust the seasoning for the sauce, then spoon the sauce over the chops.

YIELD: 4 servings

🥫 ADD IT!
A few tablespoons (5 g) chopped fresh thyme, rosemary, chervil, or chives (any or all) added during the last few minutes of cooking will further enliven this dish.

Ancho-Marinated Pork Chops

Ancho chiles are dried poblano peppers—a common ingredient in Mexican cookery.

3 medium ancho chiles, about 3 ounces (85 g)
4 center-cut pork chops, about 2 pounds (900 g)
¼ cup (5 g) chopped fresh cilantro

Remove the stems from the chiles. (If they break, don't worry about it.) Put the chiles in a 1-quart (1-L) saucepan and cover with water. Cook over medium heat at a simmer for 15 to 20 minutes, until the anchos are soft. Put the chiles and 1 cup (235 ml) of the cooking water in a food processor and process with the metal blade until smooth. Season the pork chops with salt and pepper and put them in a resealable plastic bag or a shallow dish. Add the chile puree and coat the chops well. Marinate for at least 3 hours, refrigerated, and up to overnight.

Prepare a grill.

When it is ready, remove the chops from the marinade and grill for 10 to 12 minutes per side. Scatter the cilantro over the chops and serve.

YIELD: 4 servings

 ADD IT!
You can spice up the marinade with vinegar, garlic, or fruit juice such as pineapple or orange. Serve with a black bean salad and posole.

Pork Chops with Peppers

We love the way the acerbic sting of vinegar adds richness and life to peppers.

> 3 medium-size sweet peppers, whatever color you like
> 4 center-cut pork chops, about 2 pounds (900 g)
> ¼ cup (60 ml) apple cider vinegar

Core the peppers and cut them into strips ½-inch (1-cm) wide. Season the chops with salt and pepper. Heat a wide sauté pan or skillet over medium-high heat. Add about 2 tablespoons (30 ml) oil to the pan. When the oil begins to smoke, add the pork chops. Sear them for 4 to 5 minutes per side, until browned. Remove the chops from the pan and set aside. Cook the peppers for 6 to 8 minutes, until they begin to soften. Turn the heat down to medium. Put the chops back in the pan, nestling them down into the peppers. Pour the vinegar into the pan. Season to taste with salt and pepper. Cook for 15 to 20 minutes.

YIELD: 4 servings

 ADD IT!
Substitute a medium onion, sliced in ½-inch rings, for one of the peppers.

ORANGE-CORIANDER PORK CHOPS

Coriander seeds are a common ingredient in many cuisines, such as those of India, the Middle East, and Southeast Asia. Cilantro, that delightful leafy herb so popular in Mexican and Thai cuisine, comes from the same plant, but the leaf and the seeds impart two very different flavors. Coriander is available both ground and in seeds, but you'll get better flavor if you take a minute to grind the seeds yourself.

4 center-cut pork chops
¼ cup (20 g) ground coriander
1 cup (235 ml) orange juice
4 tablespoons (55 g) butter

Season pork chops with salt and pepper. Thoroughly rub coriander into the meat on both sides of the chops, covering them as completely as possible. (Don't be afraid to put some elbow grease into it.) Heat 2 to 3 tablespoons (30 to 45 ml) olive oil in a medium-size sauté pan or skillet over medium heat until the oil is hot but not smoking. Add the pork chops. Cook for 8 to 10 minutes per side. Remove the chops and keep them warm. Add the orange juice to the pan and bring to a boil, stirring to scrape up the brown bits at the bottom of the pan. Allow the sauce to reduce by one-half. Briskly whisk in the butter, 1 tablespoon (15 g) at a time, until it is just melted and the sauce is smooth and glossy. Season the sauce with salt and pepper. Serve the chops with the sauce spooned over.

YIELD: 4 servings

ADD IT!
Add a small minced shallot to the pan drippings and sauté until soft before adding the orange juice. Serve with Dirty Rice (page 355) and Garlicky Spinach (page 415).

Smoked Pork Chops with Braised Sauerkraut

Smokers aren't expensive, but they do take up space, which can be an issue for the storage-strapped among us. Alternatively, you can buy presmoked chops. Inquire at the meat counter.

Boiled potatoes, dark and dense pumpernickel bread, and a good mustard are natural accompaniments to this dish.

> 4 center-cut pork chops, bone in
> 1 pound (450 g) fresh sauerkraut
> 2 cups (475 ml) Riesling wine

Heat a smoker and place pork chops on a rack. Put damp wood chips such as applewood into the smoking pan and smoke the chops for about ½ hour. Remove from the smoker. This step can be done up to 2 days in advance—the chops can be refrigerated in the interim.

When you are ready to cook, put the chops in a sauté pan or skillet large enough to accommodate them. Rinse the sauerkraut well in cold water and drain. Place over the chops, pour wine over all, and simmer, covered, for about 45 minutes.

YIELD: 4 servings

CHINESE BLACK BEAN SPARERIBS

These black beans are not the same ones you find in a South American soup, or the pork shoulder recipe in this chapter. They are fermented, salted soybeans popular in Chinese cuisine. You can buy just the fermented black beans and make your own sauce, or you can buy ready-made sauce. This recipe is for the latter.

2 racks baby-back pork ribs, about 4 pounds (1¾ kg)
2 jars (10 ounces, or 280 g each) Chinese black bean sauce
½ cup (8 g) chopped fresh cilantro

Heat the oven to 300°F (150°C, gas mark 2).

Put the ribs in a roasting pan and add 2 cups (475 ml) water. Cover the pan with foil and roast for 2 hours. Remove the pan from the oven and drain out all liquid. Cut the rib racks into individual ribs. Pour the black bean sauce over the ribs, making sure to cover them thoroughly. Bake in the oven, uncovered, for 30 minutes. Chop the cilantro and sprinkle over the ribs.

YIELD: 4 to 6 servings

Ham Steak with Red Eye Gravy

Red-eye gravy is a Southern favorite, but isn't as well known in the rest of the States. According to legend, red-eye gravy got its name from Andrew Jackson, at the time a general (and the future seventh president of the United States). Jackson, who was speaking with his cook about the next meal, took a look at the cook's eyes—red-rimmed from a night of drinking—and told him to bring him country ham with gravy as red as his eyes. Cheese grits and maybe a couple of fried eggs make this a great breakfast, lunch, or dinner.

1 fully cooked ham steak, about 1½ pounds (675 g)
2 tablespoons (15 g) all-purpose flour
1 cup (235 ml) black coffee

Heat a sauté pan or skillet over high heat. Add 1 tablespoon (15 ml) oil. When the oil smokes, add the ham. Cook the ham for 5 to 6 minutes per side, until it is browned and heated through. Remove the ham steak and keep it warm. Add the flour to the pan and mix it in with the drippings, stirring to make a paste. Add the coffee and stir in well to make a gravy. Season with pepper to taste. Serve the gravy over the ham.

YIELD: 4 servings

BRATWURST WITH SAUERKRAUT AND JUNIPER BERRIES

1 pound (450 g) fresh sauerkraut
8 dried juniper berries
4 bratwurst (fully cooked), about 1 pound (450 g)

Preheat oven to 350°F (180°C, gas mark 4).

Put the sauerkraut in a colander and rinse it well under cold water. Put the sauerkraut and 1 cup (235 ml) water into a baking dish 9 inches (22¾ cm) square, or other 2-quart (2-L) shallow baking dish. Slightly crush the juniper berries with the side of a knife and add them to the sauerkraut. Cover the dish with foil and bake for 45 minutes.

Meanwhile, heat a medium-size sauté pan or skillet over medium-high heat. Sear the bratwurst on 2 sides. After the sauerkraut has been in the oven for 45 minutes, add the bratwurst and re-cover with the foil. Bake for an additional 15 minutes.

YIELD: 4 servings

SAUSAGE IN CREAM GRAVY

The American South would not be able to get started in the morning without sausage gravy—you can even get it at McDonald's. Traditionally served over biscuits, this is also good over toast or crackers. It is a belly buster, but every so often we say, "Go for it!"

1 pound (450 g) bulk breakfast sausage meat, the kind in a tube, not links
¼ cup (30 g) all-purpose flour
1½ cups (355 ml) milk

Heat a medium-size sauté pan or skillet over medium heat. Add the sausage meat and cook, breaking it up with a spoon, until it is no longer pink, about 10 to 12 minutes. Add the flour and stir in well, so that it forms a thick paste in concert with the sausage fat. Add the milk, stirring as you pour it in. Cook, stirring, until the mixture boils and the sauce thickens. Reduce the heat to low and cook for another 10 minutes at a simmer. Season with salt to taste and with plenty of black pepper.

YIELD: 4 servings

Breakfast Sausage with Fried Apples and Onions

A little different for breakfast, also great for supper.

- **1 medium onion**
- **2 tart apples, such as Granny Smith**
- **1 pound (450 g) breakfast sausage links**
- 1 tablespoon (30 ml) oil

Preheat the oven to 375°F (190°C, gas mark 5).

Peel the onion and cut it into rings. Peel and core the apples and cut them into 12 wedges each. Put the sausage in a shallow baking dish and bake until cooked through, about 25 minutes. While the sausage is baking, heat a medium-size sauté pan or skillet over medium-high heat. Add the oil. When it begins to smoke, add the onions and apple. Season with salt and pepper to taste and sauté, allowing the apples and onion to brown a bit, for 10 minutes. The apples should be cooked but still firm, and the onions soft. Divide the apple and onion mixture among 4 plates and top with sausages.

YIELD: 4 servings

12

Lamb

Lamb is sometimes the forgotten stepchild of meats—Americans eat a lot more chicken, beef, and even pork. Many people tell us that lamb tastes too gamey; in fact, some of these same people admit that lamb has never passed their lips.

The indifference to lamb leaves us feeling like the world is upside down, because when we were growing up, a roast leg of lamb with a crust (see page 252) was a great favorite of the whole family—despite our mother's cooking the bejeezus out of it. Fortunately, the cycle of abuse has been broken with our generation. Lamb is now served rosy red and succulent (and our dear mother has even reformed her ways).

Lamb available in U.S. supermarkets comes from the western United States, or from Australia and New Zealand. We doubt many will find American commercial lamb too gamey. In fact, in Bob's restaurant, customers have accused him of serving them beef when it is Colorado lamb—it has become that mild. The stuff from Down Under has a slightly more pronounced flavor, but it's still not overwhelming.

MARGERY'S ROAST LEG OF LAMB WITH A CRUST

This was a great favorite in our house when we were growing up. Back in the day, we always got the lamb cooked to a uniform grayness. We know better now and usually go for medium lamb. The crust works to seal in the juices and is a wonderful, crunchy thing in its own right, rich with the flavor of the meat juices. This recipe won't work well for rare lamb—the crust needs some time in the oven to get crispy. Lamb leg is often sold semi-boneless, that is, with the aitch bone (the hip bone) removed for easier carving. You can get the butcher to do this for you as well.

> 1½ cups (185 g) all-purpose flour
> 2 tablespoons (about 2 g) chopped fresh thyme (or oregano, or rosemary)
> 1 leg of lamb, aitch bone removed, 4 to 5 pounds (1¾ to 2¼ kg)

Preheat the oven to 325°F (170°C, gas mark 3).

In a small mixing bowl combine the flour, thyme, about a teaspoon of pepper, and a tablespoon (18 g) salt. Mix in enough water to form a paste—about ¾ cup (175 ml). Put the lamb leg on a roasting rack in a roasting pan and spread the flour paste all over it. Roast the lamb for about 30 minutes per pound for medium—your instant-read thermometer will read 145°F (63°C) at the bone. Let the meat rest for 10 to 15 minutes after removing it from the oven. Take off the crust in pieces fit for serving, slice the lamb, and serve with pieces of the crust.

YIELD: 6 to 8 servings

🧂 ADD IT!
We're sure that you will be shocked to hear that we usually also mix in a couple of minced garlic cloves into this crust, or at the very least a liberal sprinkling of garlic powder.

GRILLED BUTTERFLIED LEG OF LAMB

This is classic festive fare for our clan, where lamb is nearly universally regarded as a prince of meats. There's something about the alchemy of lamb and a grill that adds an extra tang. (Just don't let our brother get to the lamb ahead of you.) We like to serve this with saffron couscous and grilled vegetables.

Although it's fairly simple to bone and butterfly a leg of lamb, the kind folks at the meat counter will do it for you, too.

> **1 leg of lamb, boned and butterflied**
> **¼ cup (60 ml) basil pesto**
> **1 cup (245 g) plain yogurt**

Mix the yogurt and pesto in a large bowl and combine with salt and pepper to taste. Place the lamb and yogurt mixture in a large resealable plastic bag and coat the meat well. Refrigerate for at least 6 hours and preferably overnight, turning the bag over every few hours. (Well, except for the middle of night shift. No turning necessary there.)

Prepare a grill.

When it is ready, remove the lamb from the bag and grill for about 15 minutes per side, or to the desired degree of doneness. Although butterflying the meat will make it somewhat the same thickness, there is enough of a thickness variation to yield meat of varying degrees of doneness. Use our finger-prod method to test for doneness (see page 16).

Remove the lamb from the grill to a platter. Allow the meat to rest for 10 minutes and slice into thin slices across the grain.

YIELD: 6 to 10 servings, depending on the size of the leg. Figure about 6–8 ounces (170–225 g) of boneless lamb per person.

LAMB STUFFED WITH FENNEL AND LEMON SAUCE

Fennel is sadly underutilized in cookery today, which is a shame, as the versatile vegetable pairs nicely with everything from salads to sauces. In this recipe, fennel's crisp sweetness is a wonderful foil for the richness of lamb. It's widely available in the produce aisle at most supermarkets.

3 bulbs fennel
4 lemons
1 leg of lamb, boneless, 4 to 5 pounds (1¾ to 2¼ kg)
8 tablespoons (115 g) butter

Cut off the tops of the fennel, halve the bulbs lengthwise, and remove the core at the root end. Slice the bulbs into thin strips, ½-inch (1-cm) thick. Heat about 2 tablespoons (30 ml) olive oil in a medium-size sauté pan or skillet over medium heat until the oil is hot but not smoking. Add the fennel and cook, stirring occasionally, until it is softened and partly caramelized, about 15 minutes. While the fennel is cooking, remove the zest from 2 lemons. Mince the zest finely and stir into the fennel; season the mixture with salt and pepper to taste and set aside to cool.

Preheat oven to 325°F (170°C, gas mark 3).

Lay the leg of lamb out on a cutting board and as best you can cut into it and rearrange pieces so there is a roughly rectangular and evenly thick piece of meat. Season the meat with salt and pepper and spread the fennel mixture over it, leaving a 1-inch (2½-cm) gap at the top. Roll the lamb jelly-roll fashion, starting along the longer side, finishing with the seam down. Tie the meat with butcher twine.

Place the lamb on a rack in a roasting pan and roast for about 20 minutes per pound, or to the desired degree of doneness—your meat thermometer will read 145°F (63°C) for medium lamb. Remove from the oven and allow it to rest in a warm place for 15 minutes, covered.

Squeeze the juice from the lemons. While the roast is resting, pour the juices from the roasting pan into a measuring cup and skim the grease from the top. Pour the remaining juice back into the pan, along with the lemon juice and half of the butter. Bring to a boil over medium heat, stirring to scrape the brown bits from the bottom of the pan. If you are low on liquid here, add ¼ cup (60 ml) water. Allow the sauce to reduce a little and whisk in the remaining butter 1 tablespoon (15 g) at a time. Adjust the seasoning with salt and pepper.

To serve, slice the meat across and top with some of the sauce.

YIELD: 8 to 10 servings

ADD IT!
Sauté 2 large cloves minced garlic with the fennel. You can also add ½ cup (120 ml) white wine to the sauce as you deglaze the pan.

Lamb Stuffed with Sun-Dried Tomato Pesto and Spinach

1 pound (450 g) fresh spinach
1 leg of lamb, boneless, 3 to 4 pounds (1¼ to 1¾ kg)
1 jar (8 ounces, or 225 g) sun-dried tomato pesto

Wash spinach and pick through, removing questionable leaves and snipping the extra-thick stems. Put the spinach in a steamer and steam in a 2-quart (2-L) pot until just done, about 5 minutes. Drain and cool. When cool, squeeze out as much water as possible and chop coarsely.

Preheat the oven to 325°F (170°C, gas mark 3).

Lay the leg of lamb out on a cutting board and as best you can, cut into it and rearrange pieces so there is a roughly rectangular and evenly thick piece of meat. Season the meat with salt and pepper and spread the pesto over it, leaving a 1-inch (2½-cm) gap at the top. Now spread the spinach over the pesto evenly. Roll the lamb jelly-roll fashion, starting along the longer side, finishing with the seam down. Tie the meat about three times with butcher twine.

Place the lamb on a rack in a roasting pan, and roast, uncovered, for about 20 minutes per pound, or to the desired degree of doneness—your meat thermometer will read 145°F (63°C) for medium lamb. Remove from the oven and allow to rest for 15 minutes, covered in a warm place.

Slice the meat and fan a couple of slices out on each plate.

YIELD: 6 to 8 servings

Rack of Lamb with Pine Nut and Rosemary Crust

"Frenching" a rack refers to the practice of cutting the meat away from the end of a rib or chop, so that part of the bone is exposed. We are seeing Frenched lamb racks—1 or 2 per package—at our supermarkets on a regular basis. If you can't find the product already prepared, the butcher at the supermarket will do it for you if you find it intimidating.

- ¼ cup (35 g) toasted pine nuts
- 2 tablespoons (3 g) minced fresh rosemary
- 3 tablespoons (45 ml) extra-virgin olive oil
- 1 frenched lamb rack, 8 bones, about 1 pound (450 g)

To toast the pine nuts: Preheat the oven to 350°F (180°C, gas mark 4). Spread the nuts on a baking sheet and bake for 7 to 10 minutes, or until the nuts look toasty brown.

Adjust the oven to 450°F (230°C, gas mark 8).

In a blender or food processor, grate the pine nuts and rosemary together with the olive oil. Sprinkle salt and pepper on meat and coat the top of the rack with the nut-herb mixture.

Place the meat on a rack in a roasting pan and roast for about 15 to 20 minutes for medium rare. The best way to test for doneness is to press the end of the eye of the meat with your finger (see page 16). The firmer the meat, the more done it is.

Allow the meat to rest for 5 minutes and slice between the bones. Place 4 pieces on each plate and serve.

YIELD: 2 servings

ADD IT!
Garlic always adds spice, so whirl a couple of chopped cloves in the blender with the nuts and rosemary.

LAMB KEBAB WITH PEPPERS

Grilling used to be a strictly summer activity, but the popularity of gas grills has made it easy to grill year-round—we've been out in blizzards, turning the meat.

These kabobs are great on couscous or rice pilaf.

> 2 pounds (900 g) lamb leg meat, cut into 1½-inch (3½-cm) squares
> 1 bottle (12 ounces, 355 ml) honey-Dijon marinade (see note)
> 2 bell peppers, red or yellow

You will need 8 bamboo or metal skewers.

In a large resealable plastic bag, combine the meat and marinade and refrigerate for at least 2 hours and preferably overnight, turning the bag over every few hours (during your waking hours, that is.)

If you're using bamboo skewers, be sure to soak them in cold water for ½ hour before loading them.

Cut the peppers in half, clean out the core, and cut into squares 1 to 2 inches (up to 5 cm) wide. Thread the skewers alternately with meat and peppers.

Prepare a grill.

When it is ready, grill the skewers for about 5 minutes a side for a medium kebab.

YIELD: 4 servings

NOTE: *To make your own honey-Dijon marinade, blend the following ingredients in a blender until smooth:*

½ cup (120 ml) water
2 tablespoons (30 g) Dijon mustard
¼ cup (80 g) honey
1 tablespoon (15 ml) red wine vinegar
1 tablespoon (10 g) minced garlic
2 tablespoons (30 ml) olive oil
1 teaspoon chopped fresh thyme
Salt and pepper to taste

MADRAS LAMB CURRY

The increased availability of bottled curry sauces makes it relatively simple to make a curry without having to wrestle with a drawerful of new spices. Great accompaniments are raita and chutney.

> 1 pound (450 g) Spanish onions
> 2 pounds (900 g) lamb leg meat, cut into 1-inch (2½-cm) cubes
> 1 can (10 ounces, or 280 g) Madras curry sauce

Peel and cut onions into ¼-inch (½-cm) dice. Season lamb with salt and pepper. Heat about 3 tablespoons (45 ml) olive oil in a heavy flameproof Dutch oven over high heat. Sear the meat in batches until browned and set aside. Reduce the heat to medium and sauté the onion until soft and a bit browned. Add the meat, the curry sauce, and ½ cup (120 ml) water. Cover pan tightly and reduce the heat to low. Simmer for about 1 hour. Serve in wide shallow bowls, ladled over basmati rice.

YIELD: 4 servings

 ADD IT!
Simmer 2 large cloves of chopped garlic and ¼ cup (60 g) plain yogurt in the sauce for a deeper flavor.

RACK OF LAMB WITH HOISIN AND GARLIC

Rack of lamb has a reputation as one of those high-falutin' foods that you can order only at restaurants, but the truth is that they are remarkably easy to cook. If you're looking for a dish with a high Impress the Guests factor, you can't beat a rack of lamb. This would be great with Wild Rice Pancakes (page 359) and Broccoli with Orange Glaze (page 378).

> 1 Frenched lamb rack, 8 bones, about 1 pound (450 g)
> 2 tablespoons (30 g) hoisin sauce
> 2 cloves minced garlic

Preheat the oven to 450°F (230°C, gas mark 8).

Sprinkle salt and pepper on meat. Mix the hoisin sauce and the garlic together in a small bowl and coat the lamb meat with it, rubbing it in vigorously with your fingers.

Place the meat on a rack in a roasting pan and roast for about 20 minutes for medium rare. The best way to test for doneness is to press the end of the eye of the meat with your finger (see page 16). The firmer the meat, the more done it is.

Allow the meat to rest for 5 minutes, then slice between the bones.

YIELD: 2 servings

BONELESS LAMB LOIN WITH TAPENADE WRAPPED IN PHYLLO

Tapenade is very easy to make yourself, but it's also available in the fresh-food and produce section at many supermarkets.

> 1 boneless lamb loin, about 12 ounces (340 g)
> 3 tablespoons (45 g) black olive tapenade
> 3 sheets phyllo dough, thawed
> 3 tablespoons (43 g) butter

Heat oven to 400°F (200°C, gas mark 6).

Season lamb with salt and pepper. Heat a sauté pan or skillet over high heat. Add a couple teaspoons olive oil and sear the lamb until it's nicely brown on all sides. Set aside.

Melt the butter over low heat. Lay out a phyllo sheet and brush with the butter. Lay another sheet on top of the first, brush with more butter, then repeat the process with the third sheet.

Place the lamb on the dough with the long side facing toward you. The phyllo will be larger than needed, so you should cut off the excess, leaving 2 inches (5 cm) on either end of the loin, which you will tuck in when you roll up the meat. Spread the meat evenly with the tapenade. Roll up the meat in the phyllo, tucking in the ends, and place it on a baking sheet seam side down.

Roast for 20 minutes, until the phyllo is nicely browned and the meat registers 130° (54°C) on an instant-read meat thermometer. This will give you medium-rare lamb—you may choose your own preferred degree of doneness. If you want medium-well or well-done meat we recommend cooking it longer at a lower oven temperature, so as to not burn the phyllo.

Allow the lamb to rest for 5 minutes and cut into 6 slices.

YIELD: 2 servings

BRAISED LAMB SHANKS

This dish is great served on top of tender simmered white beans.

> 4 lamb shanks, preferably hind shanks, about 1 pound (450 g) each
> ½ cup (130 g) sun-dried-tomato garlic pesto (see note)
> 2 cups (475 ml) dry red wine
> 4 tablespoons (55 g) butter, room temperature

Preheat oven to 325°F (170°C, gas mark 3).

Wash lamb shanks, pat dry and trim as much fat as possible. Season each shank with salt and pepper. Heat about 3 tablespoons (45 ml) olive oil on high heat in a heavy flameproof Dutch oven or other flameproof casserole dish. Sear the meat until nicely browned on all sides. You can do this step in batches if need be—the trick is to give each piece plenty of room to sizzle or it will not sear properly.

Set the meat aside. Add the pesto to the pan and stir around for a minute, making sure to scrape the cooked bits off the bottom of the pan. Add the wine and stir again. Return the shanks to the pot, cover tightly, and simmer in the oven for about 2 hours.

Remove the meat and keep it covered in a warm place. Put the baking dish back on the stovetop on high heat and reduce the cooking liquid by one-half. Reduce the heat to low and whisk in the butter, 1 tablespoon (15 g) at a time, just until the butter has melted. Be careful, too much heat can break the butter emulsion. Adjust the seasoning. Place a shank on each of 4 plates and spoon the sauce over.

YIELD: 4 servings

NOTE: *To make a cup of your own pesto, pour 2 cups (475 ml) boiling water over 1 cup (50 g) sun-dried tomatoes and allow to steep until softened, about 15 minutes. Drain the tomatoes and place in a food processor fitted with the metal blade. Add ½ cup (120 ml) olive oil and 2 tablespoons (20 g) minced garlic, along with salt and pepper to taste, and process until smooth.*

Braised Lamb Shanks with Tomatoes and Tapenade

Tapenade, that delightful spread made of olives, capers, and garlic, is generally found with the fresh salsas, hummus, and fresh pasta sauces in the refrigerated specialties section of your grocery store. We like to serve this meat in a shallow bowl filled with garlic mashed potatoes. Spoon the sauce over and enjoy.

4 lamb shanks, about 1 pound (450 g) apiece, preferably hind shanks
1 tub (7 ounces, or 200 g) tapenade
2 cans (15 ounces, or 425 g, each) diced tomatoes with garlic and spices

Preheat oven to 325°F (170°C, gas mark 3).

Wash lamb shanks in cold water, pat dry, and trim as much fat as possible. Season with salt and pepper. Heat about 3 tablespoons (45 ml) olive oil on high heat in a heavy flameproof Dutch oven or other flameproof casserole dish. Sear the meat until nicely browned on all sides. You can do this step in batches if need be—the trick is to give each piece plenty of room to sizzle or it will not sear properly. Remove shanks from pan and keep warm.

Puree half of the tomatoes and add to the pan, stirring to remove the tasty brown bits stuck to the bottom. Add the tapenade and stir until mixed. Return the shanks to the pot and pour the remaining tomatoes over the meat. Cover tightly and simmer in the oven for about 2 hours.

To serve: Place a shank in a shallow bowl and generously ladle the sauce over it.

YIELD: 4 servings

ADD IT!
Add 2 to 3 sprigs of rosemary to the braising mixture.

BROILED LAMB CHOPS WITH TOMATOES

Sometimes, simple is better, and in that case, the broiler can be your best friend. No fussing about with deglazing a pan or building a sauce; broiling really lets the native flavors shine.

    8 loin lamb chops, about 2½ pounds (1 kg)
    4 cloves garlic
    4 ripe tomatoes

Heat broiler. Wash lamb chops and pat dry; trim fat off the chops as necessary. Mince the garlic fine and rub over the lamb; don't be afraid to get your hands good and garlicky at this task. Season the lamb with salt and pepper. Place the lamb on the broiling rack. Cut off the top quarter of the tomatoes and discard. Season the tomatoes with salt and pepper.

With the oven rack 4 to 6 inches (10 to 15 cm) from the broiler element, broil the chops for 5 to 7 minutes per side for medium rare, or to the desired degree of doneness. When you turn the chops, add the tomatoes to the broiling pan.

Place 2 chops and a tomato on each plate.

YIELD: 4 servings

 ADD IT!
Brush minced garlic and olive oil on sliced crusty bread and grill the slices for a minute or so; it'll make a great extra spoon for shoveling in the lamb and tomatoes!

Cumin-Dusted Lamb Chops with Pomegranate Molasses

Pomegranate molasses, a delightful condiment that manages to be both sweet and sour, has been hailed as the new balsamic vinegar. Originally from the Middle East, this thick syrup made from concentrated pomegranate juice is great for grilling, salads, and here, as a sauce in its own right. As its popularity rises, pomegranate molasses has been migrating steadily from gourmet and specialty shops to the local supermarket.

> 8 loin lamb chops, about 2½ pounds (1 kg)
> 2 tablespoons (15 g) ground cumin
> ¼ cup (60 ml) pomegranate molasses

Preheat the oven to 400°F (200°C, gas mark 6).

Season the chops with salt and pepper and rub on both sides with cumin. Heat 2 tablespoons cooking oil in a large sauté pan or skillet over high heat. Sear the chops on both sides. Place on a baking sheet and bake, about 10 minutes for medium. The best way to test for doneness is to press the meat with your finger (see page 16). Remove from the oven and let rest for a few minutes.

To serve: Place 2 chops on each plate and drizzle pomegranate molasses over them.

YIELD: 4 servings

GRILLED LAMB CHOPS ON BLACK BEANS WITH SALSA VERDE

Serve this with corn muffins and a plate of sliced summer tomatoes sprinkled with minced onions and chopped fresh cilantro.

> 8 loin lamb chops, about 2½ pounds (1 kg)
> 1 can (12 ounces, or 340 g) black beans
> 1 jar (10 ounces, or 280 g) green salsa, room temperature

Prepare a grill.

Sprinkle the chops with salt and pepper and grill for about 7 minutes per side for a medium-rare chop. (You can leave on the grill longer if you'd like it cooked more thoroughly.) While the meat is grilling, heat the beans in a saucepan. Place the beans on a plate, top with lamb chops, and ladle a hearty spoonful of salsa over all.

YIELD: 4 servings

13

Game

We have included a few game recipes in the book because we thought it might be fun to see what we could do with more exotic fare. However, we tried not to go off the deep end and used just rabbit and venison. Rabbit can be found in the frozen section of many supermarkets. Venison is a little harder to find, but there is a growing supply of farm-raised meat out there.

Both farm-raised rabbit and venison are lean meats with a subtle flavor. Wild versions will have a more pronounced gaminess, which many people cherish and others revile. Venison, in particular, is a healthy alternative to beef. You can, however, feel free to substitute chicken for rabbit and beef for venison in these recipes.

So whether there is a hunter in your family or you just want to try something different, here are some ideas—if you're game to try them, that is.

DIJON FRIED RABBIT

1 fryer rabbit, about 3 pounds (1¼ kg)
1 cup (235 ml) Dijon mustard
2 cups fresh bread crumbs from a home-style white bread
½ cup (120 ml) olive oil

Cut the rabbit into 8 serving pieces: the legs, 2 pieces from the loin, and 2 from the ribs. Season the rabbit with salt and pepper; then, using a pastry brush, coat each piece with mustard. Roll the rabbit pieces in the bread crumbs to coat well.

Heat the olive oil in a wide sauté pan or skillet over medium heat. Fry the rabbit until golden brown and cooked through, about 10 minutes per side. Drain the meat on paper towels for a minute and serve.

YIELD: 4 servings

GRILLED RABBIT WITH GARLIC AND ROSEMARY

1 fryer rabbit, about 3 pounds (1¼ kg)
¼ cup (60 ml) olive oil
4 cloves garlic
2 sprigs rosemary

Cut the rabbit into 8 serving pieces: the legs, 2 pieces from the loin, and 2 from the ribs. Place them in a bowl or a resealable plastic bag and add the olive oil. Mince the garlic and chop the rosemary; add to the rabbit, mixing together to coat well. Season with salt and pepper. Allow to marinate for at least 2 hours and up to overnight.

Prepare a grill.

When it is ready, grill the rabbit for 8 to 10 minutes per side.

YIELD: 4 servings

Rabbit Braised with Olives

1 fryer rabbit, about 3 pounds (1¼ kg)
3 tablespoons (45 ml) olive oil
1 cup (125 g) assorted olives
1 cup (235 ml) white wine

Preheat the oven to 300°F (150°C, gas mark 2).

Cut rabbit into 8 serving pieces: the legs, 2 pieces from the loin, and 2 from the ribs. Season the rabbit with salt and pepper. Heat a heavy ovenproof Dutch oven on the stovetop over high heat and add the olive oil. Sear the rabbit on all sides, add the olives and wine, cover tightly, and braise in the oven for 1 to 1½ hours.

YIELD: 4 servings

Rabbit Braised with Porcini Mushrooms

If you can't find a rabbit all cut up, your butcher will do it for you.

1 fryer rabbit, about 3 pounds (1¼ kg)
2 ounces (55 g) dried porcini
2 tablespoons (20 g) minced garlic

Pour 2 cups (475 ml) boiling water over the porcini and allow to steep for 15 minutes. Drain, reserving the liquid, and set both aside.

Preheat the oven to 300°F (150°C, gas mark 2).

Cut the rabbit into eight serving pieces: the legs, 2 pieces from the loin, and 2 from the ribs. Season the rabbit with salt and pepper. Heat a heavy ovenproof Dutch oven on the stovetop over high heat and add enough olive oil for frying, about 3 tablespoons (45 ml). Sear the rabbit on all sides, then add the porcini and the garlic.

Fit a paper towel into a small sieve and drain the porcini broth through it to filter out the grit. Add 1½ cups (355 ml) of the broth to the Dutch oven. Cover tightly and braise in the oven for 1½ hours.

YIELD: 4 servings

VENISON WITH CHESTNUT PUREE AND MOLE

Mole refers to a group of many Mexican sauces based on, among other things, chiles, pumpkin seeds, and bitter chocolate ground together.

> **2 pounds (900 g) venison loin or top round**
> **¼ cup (50 g) unsweetened chestnut puree**
> **1 jar (8 ounces, 250 g) Mexican mole**

Heat the oven to 400°F (200°C, gas mark 6).

Cut the venison into medallions about 4 ounces (115 g) each if using top round, or into 8-ounce (225-g) steaks if using loin. Heat a sauté pan or skillet over high heat and add 2 tablespoons (30 ml) olive oil. Season the meat and sear on both sides.

Put the venison on a baking sheet, spread the chestnut paste over the top of each and finish cooking in the oven, about 10 minutes for medium. While the venison is cooking, heat the mole in a small saucepan. To serve, place a pool of mole on each of 4 plates and top with the venison.

YIELD: 4 servings

Venison with Goat Cheese and Corn Sauce

2 pounds (900 g) venison loin or top round
4 ounces (115 g) soft goat cheese
2 cups (475 ml) sweet corn soup (see note)

Preheat the oven to 400°F (200°C, gas mark 6).

Cut the venison into medallions about 4 ounces (115 g) each if using top round, or into 8-ounce (225-g) steaks if using loin. Heat a sauté pan or skillet over high heat and add 2 tablespoons (30 ml) olive oil. Season the meat with salt and pepper and sear on both sides.

Put the venison on a baking pan, spread the goat cheese over the top of each, and finish cooking in the oven, about 10 minutes for medium. While the venison is cooking, heat the soup in a small saucepan. To serve, place a pool of soup on each of 4 plates and top with venison.

YIELD: 4 servings

NOTE: *We find the sweet corn soup in cardboard containers, like juice boxes, at our market and at natural food stores. If you can't find a close approximation, steam 2 ears of corn, remove the kernels, and puree them along with 1 cup (235 ml) cooking water and a half cup (120 ml) cream.*

Venison with Onions and Ancho Chiles

Ancho chiles are dried poblanos. They have a little heat, but they are best known for a deep, earthy flavor.

1 pound (450 g) Spanish onions
¼ pound (225 g) ancho chiles
1 venison roast, loin, rib, or top round, about 3 pounds (1¼ kg)
2 tablespoons (28 g) butter, melted

Preheat the oven to 325°F (170°C, gas mark 3).

Peel and slice onions and place in a roasting pan. Break off the stems of the anchos and remove the seeds. Add the chilies to the onion. Put the venison on top of this bed of onions and anchos. Season with salt and pepper and drizzle with 2 to 3 tablespoons (30 to 45 ml) olive oil.

Roast the venison to the desired degree of doneness, about 20 minutes per pound for medium rare. Your meat thermometer should read about 130°F (50°C). When the meat is done, remove it from the pan and allow it to rest, covered, in a warm place. Put the roasting pan over medium heat on the stovetop and deglaze with 1 cup (235 ml) water. Scrap up the browned bits from the pan and reduce the water by one-half. Scrape all of this into a food processor and process until smooth, then strain through a medium-mesh strainer. Whisk in the butter and adjust the seasoning.

Slice the roast and spoon some of the sauce over, passing the rest on the side.

YIELD: 6 servings

14

Fish and Shellfish

We love seafood. We're not picky: finned fish, mollusks and crustaceans, freshwater or salt water, they're all good. We also love fish and shellfish when thinking in terms of three ingredients, because fish fits into this credo so very well. The clean, pure flavor of seafood, the breadth of the palette of tastes and textures, the wealth of cherished ethnic preparations, and our wish to simply enhance, not embellish, a beautiful piece of seafood all play to this idea.

The first rule of cooking with any kind of fish or shellfish is an insistence on quality. Ask the fish-counter attendant to let you smell the fish before you buy. Find a fishmonger you trust and nurture that relationship. You can never make a good fish dish with a poor-quality piece of fish.

STUFFED HADDOCK

A simple Down East favorite. Serve with parsley potatoes and steamed green vegetables.

1 pound (450 g) skinless haddock fillet
About 20 Ritz crackers
½ pound (225 g) lump crabmeat
8 tablespoons (115 g) butter

Preheat the oven to 350°F (180°C, gas mark 4).

Place the crackers in a resealable plastic bag and crush them into crumbs. Melt half the butter and mix the cracker crumbs, the crab, and melted butter in a small mixing bowl. Put this stuffing mix in a shallow baking dish. Cut the fish into 4 serving pieces and arrange them over the stuffing. Dot the fish with the remaining butter and season with salt and pepper.

Bake for about 20 minutes.

YIELD: 4 servings

ADD IT!
Lemon juice in the stuffing is good, as is a bit of white wine or sherry.

Roast Striped Bass with Raspberry-Mustard Cream Sauce

We believe that striped bass is the king of East Coast fishes. It's meaty, flavorful, mild, and lots of fun to catch. Known to those in the Tidewater as rockfish, this once severely depleted fish has made a huge comeback.

2 pounds (900 g) striped bass fillet, bones removed, skin on
¼ cup raspberry Dijon mustard
1 cup (235 ml) heavy cream
4 tablespoons (55 g) butter

Preheat the oven to 450°F (230°C, gas mark 8). Oil a baking sheet.

With a sharp knife, slash through the skin of the fillet in a cross-hatch pattern to prevent the fish from curling when cooked. Place on the baking sheet and season with salt and pepper. Drizzle with 2 tablespoons (30 ml) olive oil and roast for about 15 minutes, until the fish feels firm and is opaque throughout.

While the fish is roasting, heat the cream and mustard in a saucepan until reduced by half. Whisk in the butter and adjust the seasoning. Place a piece of fish on each of 4 plates and spoon the sauce over it.

YIELD: 4 servings

NOTE: *A good side dish to this recipe would be Oven Fries (Page 438).*

ROAST STRIPED BASS
WITH DILLED CORN PUREE

Striped bass and corn—two flavors that work together like riding in a convertible on a sunny summer day.

2 pounds (900) striped bass fillet, bones removed, skin on
¼ cup (8 g) chopped fresh dill
2 cups (475 ml) sweet corn soup (see note)
4 tablespoons (55 g) butter

Preheat the oven to 450°F (230°C, gas mark 8). Oil a baking sheet.

With a sharp knife, slash through the skin of the fillet in a cross-hatch pattern to prevent the fish from curling when cooked. Place on the baking sheet and season with salt and pepper. Drizzle with 2 tablespoons (30 ml) olive oil and roast for about 15 minutes, until the fish feels firm and is opaque throughout.

While the fish is roasting, heat the soup in a small saucepan and add half of the dill, reserving the rest. Whisk in the butter, 1 tablespoon (15 g) at a time, to form a smooth sauce. Be sure to monitor the heat and remove as soon as the last of the butter is melted, to make sure the sauce doesn't break. Divide the sauce among 4 large shallow bowls and place a piece of fish in each bowl. Sprinkle the reserved dill over the fish and serve.

YIELD: 4 servings

🧂 ADD IT!
Spike the sauce with chopped mild green chiles and a spritz of lime juice.

NOTE: *We find the sweet corn soup in cardboard containers, like juice boxes, at our market and at natural food stores. If you can't find a close approximation, steam 2 ears of corn, remove the kernels, and puree them along with 1 cup (235 ml) cooking water and a half cup (120 ml) cream.*

MILK-BAKED COD

A real Yankee favorite. Our Ma's Ma cooked cod this way, though we've updated the recipe by adding leeks.

2 leeks
1½ pounds (675 g) cod fillet
1½ cups (350 ml) milk

Trim the roots and dark green part from the leeks and split lengthwise, then in thin half-moons. Cut the leeks in half lengthwise, then cut into thin half moons. Place the leeks in a bowl of cold water and swish them around to clean. Remove them from the water by lifting them out with a slotted spoon, leaving any dirt in the water. Leeks are notorious dirt carriers, so you might have to wash them a couple of times. Put the leeks in a 1-quart (1-L) saucepan, along with 2 tablespoons (30 ml) oil. Cover and cook over low heat until the leeks are wilted and translucent—about 15 minutes. Season with salt and pepper.

Preheat the oven to 350°F (180°C, gas mark 4).

In a shallow 1-quart (1-L) baking dish, spread the leeks and top with the cod fillet. Season the fish with salt and pepper and pour the milk over the fish and leeks. Bake for about 20 minutes, until the cod is cooked through and flakes apart with a fork.

YIELD: 4 servings

SPINACH-STUFFED FLOUNDER

Pretty much any flat fish fillet will do for this recipe. White fish and spinach is a great classic combination.

    10 ounces (280 g) fresh spinach
    1 tablespoon (10 g) minced garlic
    1½ pounds (675 g) flounder fillets, 4 to 6 ounces (115 to 170 g) each
    4 tablespoons (55 g) butter

Pick the spinach over to remove any large stems or bruised leaves. Rinse it well. Put the spinach in a 4-quart (4-L) pot and add 2 cups (475 ml) water; season with salt. Bring to a boil over high heat and cook until the spinach is just wilted—1 to 2 minutes after water boils. Drain and cool the spinach, then squeeze as much water out as possible and chop it coarsely. Set aside.

Heat a medium-size sauté pan or skillet over medium heat; add 2 tablespoons (28 g) of the butter and when melted, add the garlic. Let the garlic cook in the butter for a minutes, then stir in the spinach. Season with salt and pepper and set aside.

Preheat the oven to 350°F (180°C, gas mark 4).

Divide the spinach mixture among the fillets. Lay a fillet out on a cutting board and put a portion of the spinach mixture in the middle. Roll up the fillet and place, seam side down, in a shallow baking dish that will just accommodate all of the flounder rolls. Secure each fillet with a toothpick if you'd like. Repeat with the remaining fish and spinach. Season the fish with salt and pepper, melt the remaining butter, and brush it over the top of the fish rolls. Bake for 15 minutes and serve.

YIELD: 4 servings

🥫 ADD IT!
Pour ½ cup (120 ml) dry white wine in the baking dish with the flounder rolls.

GRILLED HALIBUT WITH SCALLIONS

A simple grilled fish dish. Despite its white flesh, halibut handles strong flavors well.

> 4 halibut steaks, ½ inch (1 cm) thick, about 2 pounds (900 g)
> ½ cup (120 ml) steak sauce
> 1 bunch scallions

Prepare a grill.

When it is ready, brush the halibut with the steak sauce. Grill for 5 minutes per side, until just done through—the fish will feel firm when pressed with your finger. While the fish is grilling, trim the scallions and grill them too.

Place a fish steak on a plate and top with a grilled scallion or two.

YIELD: 4 servings

Phyllo-Wrapped Halibut

Phyllo is surprisingly easy to work with, as long as you respect its need to stay damp. (See page 20 in Chapter 2, "Techniques and Terms," for more help on working with phyllo dough.) This recipe will also work well with salmon, sea bass, or mahimahi. It is great served with tzatziki (yogurt with chopped mint and garlic) as a sauce.

> 2 leeks
> 2 pounds (900 g) skinned halibut fillet
> 6 sheets phyllo dough, thawed, each 14 x 18 inches (about 35 x 46 cm)
> 8 tablespoons (115 g) butter, melted

Trim the root ends and remove the dark green portions of the leeks. Cut the leeks in half lengthwise, then cut into thin half moons. Place the leeks in a bowl of cold water and swish them around to clean. Remove them from the water by lifting them out with a slotted spoon, leaving any dirt in the water. Leeks are notorious dirt carriers, so you might have to wash them a couple of times. Put the leeks in a 1-quart (1-L) pot. Add 2 tablespoons (30 ml) oil, cover, and cook over low heat until the leeks are wilted and translucent—about 15 minutes. Season the leeks with salt and pepper and set aside to cool.

Preheat the oven to 350°F (180°C, gas mark 4).

Cut the halibut into 4 serving portions, season each with salt and pepper, and top each with one-fourth of the cooked leeks. Place a layer of phyllo dough on a cutting board and brush with melted butter. Top with another phyllo leaf, butter again, and top with a third phyllo sheet, buttering the top of this one as well. Cut the phyllo in half crosswise and place a piece of halibut on each half. Wrap the dough around the fish, tucking in to form a neat package and leaving the leek-covered side on top. Brush each package with butter. Place on a baking sheet. Repeat with the rest of the phyllo and fish.

Bake for 25 minutes, until the phyllo is golden brown.

YIELD: 4 servings

GRILLED MAHIMAHI WITH GINGER AND GRAPEFRUIT

Mahimahi is a versatile fish, pairing well with fresh fruit.

1½ pounds (675 g) mahimahi fillet, cut into 4 serving pieces
2 grapefruits
1 tablespoon (10 g) minced fresh ginger

Prepare the grill.

Season the fish with salt and pepper and grill for about 5 minutes per side per inch of thickness, until just done through. While the fish is cooking, cut away the peel and inner membrane of the grapefruit. Over a bowl to catch the juice, cut the individual sections out from the membranes. Mix the ginger with the grapefruit. Add 2 tablespoons (30 ml) extra-virgin olive oil and salt and pepper to taste.

To serve, place a piece of fish on a plate and spoon the grapefruit mixture over it, with some of the juice.

YIELD: 4 servings

🫙 ADD IT!
For a great herbal touch, sprinkle chopped fresh cilantro over the fish just before serving.

MONKFISH WITH TOMATO SAUCE

A nickname for monkfish is "poor man's lobster." We don't think this has to do with the taste, which is typically white-fish neutral, but with the texture. Monkfish gets firm when cooked—almost like the texture of lobster tail.

    1 pound (450 g) monkfish fillet
    1 cup (125 g) all-purpose flour
    2 cups (500 g) mushroom tomato sauce, or other favorite pasta sauce

If the monkfish has the outside membrane still on it—it is transparent and light blue—you will need to remove it. Better to have your fishmonger do it for you.

Line a plate with paper towels. Heat ¼ cup (60 ml) olive oil in a medium-size sauté pan or skillet over medium-high heat. In a bowl or pie plate, combine the flour with salt and pepper to taste and dredge the monkfish in the flour. When the oil shimmers and begins to smoke, add the fish and sauté until it is golden brown on all sides and done through, about 10 minutes. Drain the fish on the paper-towel-lined plate.

Heat the pasta sauce in a small saucepan over low heat. Arrange the fish on 4 plates and top with the sauce.

YIELD: 4 servings

Whole Salmon Grilled with Dill and Lemon

We are going to steam and grill salmon at the same time. This dish makes a great center attraction at a Fourth of July cookout, but try it anytime of the year.

1 whole salmon, gutted and scaled, 8 to 10 pounds (3½ to 4½ kg)
2 large bunches dill
6 lemons
1 cup (235 ml) extra-virgin olive oil

Prepare a grill.

Rinse the salmon inside and out, making sure the scales are all removed. Pat dry. Slice 4 of the lemons into thin round slices. Lay a large piece of heavy foil on a flat surface.

Reserve a few stems of the dill for garnish. Cut 2 lemons into wedges and set aside.

Spread 1 bunch dill so that it covers an area as long and wide as the salmon. Scatter one-third of the lemon slices over the dill. Sprinkle with kosher salt and plenty of fresh-cracked black pepper and place the salmon on top. Season the cavity of the salmon with salt and pepper and spread one-third of the lemon slices in the cavity. Top the salmon with the remaining lemon slices and dill, and season with salt and pepper. Drizzle the olive oil over all.

Wrap the salmon in the foil, making a neat package, but not too tight. You might want to use two thicknesses of foil—it is important to use a really heavy-duty foil.

Place the salmon on the grill and cook for 15 to 20 minutes, then turn over carefully and cook for another 15 to 20 minutes. You don't want an extremely hot grill for this operation. If flames flare up, douse them with water.

Open the foil and carefully lift the salmon with spatulas onto a serving platter. Garnish with the reserved dill and lemon wedges.

YIELD: 15 to 20 servings as part of a buffet

EASY GRAVLAX

Delicious cured salmon is only 72 hours away! You will need two roasting pans that nest within each other.

> 1 side salmon, pin bones removed but skin on, about 3 pounds (1¼ kg)
> 1 large bunch fresh dill
> ½ pound (225 g) brown sugar
> ½ pound (225 g) kosher salt

Place the salmon, skin side up, on a cutting board. With a sharp knife, slash through the skin at three or four intervals along the length of the fish, not quite all the way from top to bottom.

Chop the dill and combine in a bowl with the sugar and salt. Lay a piece of plastic wrap on a flat surface and spread one-half of the sugar-salt mixture on it. Brush the salmon with olive oil on both sides, then place the salmon, skin side down, on the sugar-salt curing mixture and top with the remaining mixture. You will want to have more mixture at the thick end of the fish than at the thin end. Wrap the salmon well in plastic and place in one of the pans. Place the other pan on top and weight it with a couple of bricks or heavy cans of food. You want 4 to 5 pounds (1¾ to 2¼ kg) of weight. Refrigerate for 72 hours, turning once each day.

After 72 hours, unwrap the salmon and rinse off the curing mixture with a bit of cold water. Dry the gravlax. Slice thin and enjoy with mustard and pumpernickel bread, plus capers, hard-boiled egg, and red onion.

YIELD: One side serves 10–15 as an appetizer

GRILLED SALMON WITH LEMON CREAM SAUCE

Break this one out for that "first day of spring, kick off the grilling season" dinner. Or any other time of the year.

4 pieces skinless salmon fillet—about 2 pounds (900 g)
1 lemon
1 cup (235 ml) heavy cream
3 tablespoons (43 g) butter

Prepare a grill.

When it is ready, oil the grill with a cloth soaked in vegetable oil. Season the salmon with salt and pepper and grill for about 5 minutes per side. Don't try to force the spatula under the fish to turn it. It will release from the grill eventually—give it time.

While the salmon is cooking, grate the zest from the lemon and add it to the cream in a small saucepan. Cook over medium-high heat until the cream is reduced by half. Squeeze the lemon and add the juice to the cream. Whisk in the butter, 1 tablespoon (15 g) at a time, to form a smooth sauce. Be sure to monitor the heat and remove as soon as the last of the butter is melted, to make sure the sauce doesn't break. Season the sauce with salt and pepper.

To serve, place a piece of salmon on a plate and spoon the sauce over it.

YIELD: 4 servings

ADD IT!
Mix a spoonful of chopped fresh dill in the sauce at the last moment.

GRILLED SALMON WITH WATERCRESS SAUCE

Pink salmon + bright green sauce = a beautiful plate.

   4 pieces of skinless salmon fillet, about 2 pounds (900 g)
   1 bunch watercress
   1 cup (235 ml) heavy cream
   3 tablespoons (43 g) butter

Prepare a grill.

When it is ready, oil the grill with a cloth soaked in vegetable oil. Season the salmon with salt and pepper and grill for about 5 minutes per side. Don't try to force the spatula under the fish to turn it. It will release from the grill eventually—give it time.

While the salmon is cooking, remove the stems from the watercress and place the leaves in a blender. Put the cream in a small saucepan and simmer over medium-high heat until the cream is reduced by half. Pour the hot cream into the blender and blend until you have a smooth, bright green sauce. Return this to the saucepan and whisk in the butter, 1 tablespoon (15 g) at a time, to form a smooth sauce. Be sure to monitor the heat and remove as soon as the last of the butter is melted, to make sure the sauce doesn't break. Season the sauce with salt and pepper.

To serve, place a piece of salmon on a plate and spoon the sauce over it.

YIELD: 4 servings

ADD IT!
Mix 2 tablespoons (20 g) sautéed minced shallots with the cream.

SALMON WITH HORSERADISH CRUST

The key to this dish is letting the crust firm up in the refrigerator, on the fish, prior to cooking.

4 slices home-style white bread
2 tablespoons (30 g) prepared horseradish
4 tablespoons (55 g) butter, melted
2 pounds (900 g) skinless salmon fillet, cut into 4 serving pieces

Cut the crusts from the bread and discard. Put the bread in a food processor fitted with the metal blade. Pulse until you have coarse crumbs. Mix the crumbs, horseradish, melted butter, and salt and pepper to taste. Place the salmon on a plate with the former skin side down; season the fish with salt and pepper and put one-fourth of the crumb mixture on each, pressing the crumbs firmly onto the fish. Cover with plastic wrap and refrigerate for at least 1 hour and up to overnight to set the crust.

Preheat the oven to 400°F (200°C, gas mark 6).

Heat ¼ cup (60 ml) oil in a wide sauté pan or skillet over medium-high heat. When the oil starts to shimmer, carefully place the salmon in the pan, crust side down, and cook for about 5 minutes, until the crust becomes golden brown. (We find it easiest to put the fish in the pan by putting it crust side down on a spatula and gently sliding it into the pan.) Be careful not to let the crust burn. Carefully remove the fish from the pan by sliding a spatula under the crust. Place the fish on a baking sheet with the crust side up. Finish cooking in the oven for 7 to 8 minutes, until still just underdone in the center, or to your desired degree of doneness.

YIELD: 4 servings

 ADD IT!
Mix the juice of 1 lemon in the crust mixture.

SEARED SALMON WITH CARROT-ORANGE-GINGER BROTH

We aren't sure which culinary tradition this combination came out of, but the flavors go together really well. If you can't find carrot-orange juice, then buy carrot juice and add some orange juice.

> 4 pieces skinless salmon fillet, 7 to 8 ounces (200 to 225 g) each
> 2 cups fresh carrot-orange juice
> 1 tablespoon (6 g) finely minced fresh ginger

Preheat the oven to 450°F (230°C, gas mark 8).

Heat 3 tablespoons (45 ml) oil in a wide sauté pan or skillet over high heat. Season the salmon with salt and pepper and sear, with the former skin side up, for 3 to 4 minutes, until the side being seared is nice and browned. Do not sear the other side. Using a spatula, transfer the salmon to a baking sheet, browned side up, and finish cooking in the oven for 6 to 8 minutes, until just undercooked in the middle (cook longer if you want it to be cooked through.)

While the salmon is in the oven, combine the juice and ginger in a small saucepan and bring to a simmer. Season to taste with salt and pepper and pour ½ cup (120 ml) of the broth into each of 4 large, shallow bowls. Place a piece of fish in each bowl and serve.

YIELD: 4 servings

ADD IT!
Sprinkle shredded mint leaves over the fish as a final garnish.

SEARED SALMON WITH TERIYAKI GLAZE AND SEAWEED SALAD

We love seaweed salad. This recipe may be an excuse to eat some. (Well, it does go well with the fish too.) At the Three Stallion Inn, Bob does variations on this recipe all the time. Customers love it.

4 pieces skinless salmon fillet, 7 to 8 ounces (200 to 225 g) each
1 cup (235 ml) teriyaki sauce
1 pound (45 g) wakame or other seaweed salad

Preheat the oven to 400°F (200°C, gas mark 6).

Heat 3 tablespoons (45 ml) olive oil in a sauté pan or skillet over medium-high heat. Season the salmon with salt and pepper. When the oil shimmers and begins to smoke, sear the fillets on one side—for 4 to 5 minutes. Carefully remove the fish from the pan using a spatula and place on a baking sheet with the seared side up. Finish cooking in the oven for 8 to 10 minutes, until just underdone (but not raw) in the center.

While the salmon is cooking, heat the teriyaki sauce in a small saucepan over low heat. Divide the seaweed salad among 4 plates, top with a piece of salmon, and spoon the teriyaki sauce over it.

YIELD: 4 servings

Pesto Poached Sea Bass

You can try this recipe with salmon, striped bass, or halibut too. Zesty Pearl Couscous (page 351) and Asparagus with Garlic and Parsley (page 371) would be nice accompaniments.

½ cup (120 ml) basil pesto
1 cup (235 ml) white wine
4 pieces sea bass fillet, about 1½ pounds

In a pan just large enough to comfortably hold the fish in one layer, mix the wine and the pesto with a cup of water. Bring to a simmer. Season the fish with salt and pepper and carefully place in the poaching liquid—it should just cover the fish. If it doesn't, add more water until it does.

Simmer the fish until it is cooked through, 12 to 15 minutes. Remove carefully with a slotted spoon, blot dry with a paper towel, and serve. Some of the pesto should cling to the fish.

YIELD: 4 servings

Snapper Braised with Thai Red Curry

While we specify snapper, you have considerable latitude on the fish used in this recipe. Buy what looks the best. Mahimahi, striped bass, wahoo, and grouper would all be good. Steamed jasmine rice is a good accompaniment.

1½ pounds (675 g) red snapper
2 tablespoons (30 g) Thai red curry paste
1 can (14 ounces, or 415 ml) coconut milk

Place the snapper in a 2-quart (2-L) saucepan and season with salt and pepper. Combine the curry paste and the coconut milk in a bowl, mix well, and pour over the fish. Cover the saucepan and put over medium heat. Simmer gently (you may need to lower the heat) for 20 minutes.

YIELD: 4 servings

🧂 ADD IT!
A squeeze of lime and fresh cilantro sprinkled over the fish will enliven it.

BAKED SOLE WITH SORREL SAUCE

There are lots of fish marketed as sole in the United States. If you can find true sole, great, but grey sole, petrale sole, and even flounder will work well.

1½ pounds (675 g) sole fillet
1 bunch sorrel
1 cup (235 ml) heavy cream
2 tablespoons (28 g) butter

Preheat the oven to 400°F (200°C, gas mark 6).

Season the fish with salt and pepper and lay in a shallow baking pan that just accommodates the fish comfortably. Bake for 10 to 12 minutes, or until just cooked through.

While the fish is cooking, simmer the cream in a 1-quart (1-L) saucepan on the stovetop to reduce by half. Pick over the sorrel, removing the stems, rinse it well, and chop the leaves roughly. Put the sorrel in a blender and add the hot cream. Puree until the sauce is smooth and bright green. Add the butter and continue to puree. Season to taste with salt and pepper.

Remove the fish from the oven, divide the fillets among 4 plates, and top with the sauce.

YIELD: 4 servings

MUSHROOM-STUFFED SOLE

Dover sole, petrale sole, grey sole, or flounder all work well. This is a classic combination in French cooking.

> 10 ounces (280 g) fresh white or brown mushrooms
> 1½ pounds (675 g) sole fillet
> 1 cup (235 ml) heavy cream

Clean the mushrooms, place them in a food processor, and process until finely chopped. Heat 2 tablespoons (30 ml) olive oil in a medium-size sauté pan or skillet over medium-high heat. Sauté the mushrooms until their water has been released and evaporates. Season with salt and pepper and set aside.

Preheat the oven to 350°F (180°C, gas mark 4).

Lay a fillet on a cutting board and place a quarter or so of the mushroom mixture on top. Roll it up, leaving the seam side down, and place in a shallow baking dish. Repeat with the rest of the fish and mushrooms. Season the fish with salt and pepper, pour the cream over it, and bake for 20 minutes.

YIELD: 4 servings

ADD IT!
Sauté a handful of chopped fresh tarragon with the mushrooms.

BRAISED SWORDFISH WITH ARTICHOKES

You can substitute canned artichoke hearts or—even better— frozen artichoke hearts for the fresh ones. Couscous and a simple salad would complement the fish well.

2 pounds (900 g) baby artichokes
4 swordfish steaks—about 2 pounds (900 g)
1 can (14 ounces, or 400 g) diced tomatoes with garlic

Clean the artichokes. Remove the tough outer leaves and the top ½ inch (1 cm) or so of each artichoke. Split each in half lengthwise, and remove the choke with a melon baller.

Heat 2 quarts of water to a boil, salt it, and blanch the artichokes for 3 to 4 minutes. Drain and set aside.

Heat 2 to 3 tablespoons (30 to 45 ml) olive oil in a wide sauté pan or skillet that has a tight-fitting cover over high heat. Season the swordfish with salt and pepper. When the oil starts to smoke, sear the swordfish for 1 to 2 minutes per side, until browned. Add the artichokes and tomatoes, turn the heat to low, and cover. Simmer for 20 minutes, until the artichokes are tender.

YIELD: 4 servings

 ADD IT!
After you trim the artichokes, you can soak them in acidulated water to prevent browning. Squeeze the juice of one lemon into 2 quarts (2 L) water.

GRILLED MARINATED SWORDFISH WITH TARRAGON

Tarragon and swordfish may be one of our favorite flavor combos.

4 swordfish steaks, ¾-inch (1½-cm) thick, about 2 pounds (900 g)
4 to 5 sprigs tarragon
2 lemons
¼ cup (60 ml) extra-virgin olive oil

Lay the swordfish out on a shallow dish and season with salt and pepper. Remove the stems from the tarragon and chop the leaves. Scatter over the fish. Squeeze 1 of the lemons and combine the juice with the olive oil. Spoon over the fish. Allow to marinate, refrigerated, for at least 1 hour and up to 4 hours.

Prepare a grill.

When it is ready, remove the swordfish from the marinade, making sure that some of the tarragon clings to the fish. Grill the swordfish for 5 to 6 minutes per side, until cooked through but still juicy. Cut the remaining lemon into wedges and serve with the fish.

YIELD: 4 servings

GRILLED SWORDFISH PUTTANESCA

The meaty texture and assertive flavor of the swordfish embraces the lusty puttanesca sauce, a zesty mix of tomatoes, onions, capers, black olives, anchovies, oregano, and garlic. Wow.

4 swordfish steaks, ¾-inch (1½-cm) thick, about 2 pounds (900 g)
2 medium-size red onions
2 cups (500 g) puttanesca pasta sauce

Prepare a grill.

Season the swordfish with salt and pepper and drizzle with olive oil. Peel each onion and cut it into quarters, leaving the root core intact so the onion quarters hold together. Season the onions with salt and pepper and drizzle with olive oil.

Grill the swordfish and onion for 5 to 6 minutes per side until just cooked through. The swordfish should be fully cooked, but one must be careful not to overcook, or it will be dry.

While the fish is cooking on the grill, heat the puttanesca sauce in a small saucepan over low heat, or on the edge of the grill. Divide the swordfish and grilled onion among the plates, and top with the sauce.

YIELD: 4 servings

GRILLED SWORDFISH
WITH SAUTEÉD CUCUMBERS

Here's a recipe that makes use of your grill's side burner. Isn't it nice to use it?

> 4 swordfish steaks, ¾-inch (1½-cm) thick, about 2 pounds (900 g)
> 1 cucumber
> 2 tablespoons (30 ml) sherry vinegar
> 2 tablespoons (28 g) butter

Prepare a grill.

While the grill is getting ready, season the swordfish with salt and pepper. Grill for 6 to 7 minutes per side, until just done throughout.

While the fish is grilling, peel the cucumber, halve it lengthwise, and remove the seeds. We find it easiest to remove seeds using a melon baller. Cut it on the bias into half rounds. Heat 2 tablespoons (30 ml) oil in a medium-size sauté pan or skillet over high heat. When the oil begins to smoke, sauté the cucumbers for 4 to 5 minutes. Allow the cucumbers to brown a bit. Season with salt and pepper and add the vinegar. Allow the vinegar to reduce just a bit and stir in the butter.

To serve, place a piece of fish on a plate and spoon the cucumber sauce over it.

YIELD: 4 servings

🥫 ADD IT!
Stir in 1 tablespoon (10 g) minced garlic with the cucumbers.

GRILLED SWORDFISH WITH TEQUILA-TOMATILLO SAUCE

Tomatillos, also known as ground tomatoes or husk tomatoes, are a pleasantly tart green vegetable that comes wrapped in a papery husk. They're popular in salsa, and we regularly find them at our local supermarket. If you have less luck, you can substitute green tomatoes with a dash of fresh lemon juice, or use canned tomatillos, which are available in many supermarkets, often already ground up.

> ½ pound (225 g) tomatillos
> 2 ounces (60 ml) tequila
> 2 tablespoons (30 ml) olive oil
> 4 swordfish steaks, ¾-inch (1½-cm) thick, about 2 pounds (900 g)
> 4 tablespoons (55 g) butter

Peel the outer husk from the tomatillos. Bring 1 quart (1 L) of water to a boil, salt the water, and blanch the tomatillos for 3 to 4 minutes. Drain and place whole in a food processor. Process the tomatillos until they are pureed. Set aside.

Prepare a grill.

While the grill is heating, season the swordfish with salt and pepper and drizzle with 2 tablespoons (30 ml) olive oil. When the grill is ready, grill the swordfish for 6 to 7 minutes per side, until just done through but moist inside.

While the swordfish is grilling, heat the tomatillo puree in a 1-quart (1-L) saucepan over medium-high heat. Add the tequila and cook for 5 minutes. Season with salt and pepper and whisk in the butter, 1 tablespoon (15 g) at a time, to form a smooth sauce. Be sure to monitor the heat and remove as soon as the last of the butter is melted, to make sure the sauce doesn't break.

To serve, place a swordfish steak on a plate and spoon the sauce around and over it.

YIELD: 4 servings

CORNMEAL PANFRIED TROUT

A classic, and with good reason. This recipe works well with catfish, too. Serve with lemon wedges.

- 4 rainbow trout, boneless, 8 ounces (225 g) each
- 2 eggs, slightly beaten
- 2 cups (275 g) cornmeal

Fillet the trout by removing the head, tail, and all the fins. Split into two sides along the backbone. (Strangely, boneless trout contain a backbone.) Season each fillet with salt and pepper, dip into the egg, and dredge in the cornmeal.

Heat ¼ cup (60 ml) oil in a wide sauté pan or skillet over medium-high heat. Add the trout to the hot oil, not crowding the pan. Panfry on each side for about 5 minutes. Remove the fillets from the pan as they are done and keep warm, covered. Repeat until all the fish is cooked, adding oil to the pan as needed.

YIELD: 4 servings

ADD IT!
Mix 1 teaspoon rubbed sage with the cornmeal.

GRILLED TROUT WITH PECANS

One of the nicest additions to the American food supply over the past few years is farm-raised rainbow trout. A really fresh trout has slimy skin. (Not nice to talk about, but there it is.) It should also have clear, bright eyes and the cavity should have a slight smell of cucumbers.

4 rainbow trout, boneless, 8 ounces (225 g) each
4 tablespoons (55 g) butter
1 tablespoon (15 ml) sherry vinegar
½ cup (60 g) chopped pecans

Fillet each trout by removing the head, tail, and all the fins. Split into two fillets along the backbone. (Strangely, boneless trout contain backbones.) Season each fillet with salt and pepper.

Prepare a grill.

When ready, oil the grate using a cloth soaked with vegetable oil and grill the trout fillets for about 4 minutes per side. Don't force the fish off the grill with your spatula—when it is ready, it will release itself.

While the fish is grilling, heat a medium-size sauté pan or skillet over medium-high heat and add 2 tablespoons (28 g) of the butter. When the butter has melted, add the pecans and cook, stirring, for 5 minutes. Add the vinegar and cook for 1 minute. Whisk in the remaining butter, 1 tablespoon (15 g) at a time, to form an emulsified sauce. Season the sauce with salt and pepper.

To serve, place 2 trout fillets on each plate and spoon the nut sauce over it.

YIELD: 4 servings

🧂 ADD IT!
Sauté a little chopped fresh tarragon along with the pecans.

TROUT STUFFED WITH BACON AND WATERCRESS

Watercress grows wild on the banks of many prime trout streams; thus we feel they are a natural pairing.

- 8 strips bacon
- 2 bunches watercress
- 4 boneless rainbow trout, 8 ounces (225 g) each
- 2 tablespoons (28 g) butter

In a sauté pan or skillet over medium heat, cook the bacon until crisp.

While the bacon cooks, clean the watercress by removing the large stems, rinsing, and spinning it dry in a salad spinner. Remove the bacon from the pan when done and place on a paper towel to drain. Return the pan to the burner, turn up the heat to high, add the watercress, and stir-fry in the bacon grease until wilted, about 3 to 4 minutes. Season with salt and pepper. Remove from heat and allow to cool.

Preheat the oven to 400°F (200°C, gas mark 6).

Grease a baking sheet with pan spray and place the trout on it. Season the fish inside and out with salt and pepper. Chop the bacon and the cooked watercress, then mix the two together. Stuff each trout with one-fourth of the mixture.

Melt the butter and brush over the trout. Bake the trout for about 20 minutes. The trout is done when the flesh inside at the backbone is no longer pinkish. You can gently lift up one side of the fish to check.

YIELD: 4 servings

ADD IT!
Stir in 1 teaspoon of minced garlic with the watercress as it cooks.

Rainbow Trout Stuffed with Fennel and Lemon

Farm-raised rainbow trout is now a staple at most markets. We find that the quality is consistent and the price is reasonable. As with all members of the salmon family, slimy skin is a good indicator of freshness. The eyes should also be full, clear, and bright, and the cavity should have a slight smell of cucumbers. Try serving this dish with Tomato-Braised Brown Rice (page 357).

> 4 boneless rainbow trout, 8 ounces (225 g) each
> 2 bulbs fennel
> 3 lemons

Remove the tops from the fennel and reserve some fronds as garnish. Halve the bulbs lengthwise, remove the core, and cut into long, thin pieces. Put the fennel in a saucepan with about 2 tablespoons (30 ml) olive oil and place over medium-low heat. Cover and cook for 45 minutes, stirring often, until the fennel is caramelized and soft. Set aside.

Preheat the oven to 400°F (200°C, gas mark 6) and oil a baking sheet.

Slice 2 lemons very thin. Salt and pepper the fish inside and out. Place a row of lemon slices inside each fish and then top those slices with cooked fennel to form a stuffing. Place fish the baking sheet, brush the fish with olive oil, and bake for about 20 minutes. The trout is done when the flesh inside at the backbone is no longer pinkish. You can gently lift up one side of the fish to check.

Cut the remaining lemon into wedges. Arrange the trout with the reserved fennel fronds and the lemon wedges as garnish.

YIELD: 4 servings

🪣 ADD IT!
As the fennel cooks, add 2 tablespoons (10 g) minced garlic.

Rainbow Trout with
Lemon Brown-Butter Sauce

This is a classic, also known as a la meunière, French for "in the manner of the miller's wife." It is also really good, as well as quick and easy to prepare. The quality of your fish will shine through here. You can also try this preparation with catfish, snapper, or bluefish.

    4 rainbow trout, boneless, 8 ounces (225 g) each
    1 cup (125 g) all-purpose flour
    6 tablespoons (85 g) butter
    2 lemons

Preheat the oven to 400°F (200°C, gas mark 6) and oil a baking sheet.

Season the trout inside and out with salt and pepper. Put the flour in a pie plate or similar pan and dredge the outside of the trout on both sides. Heat a wide sauté pan or skillet over medium-high heat. Add 2 tablespoons (30 ml) oil and 2 tablespoons (28 g) of the butter to the pan; when it starts to shimmer and just begins to smoke, add two of the trout. Brown on one side, about 3 to 4 minutes; turn carefully and brown for 3 to 4 minutes on the other side.

Remove the fish to the baking tray and repeat with the other two fish, adding oil if needed. Finish cooking all of the trout in the oven for about 10 minutes. The trout is done when the flesh inside at the backbone is no longer pinkish. You can gently lift up one side of the fish to check. While the trout is in the oven, squeeze the juice from 1 lemon. Add the remaining 2 tablespoons (28 g) butter to the pan and return to medium heat. Add the lemon juice and season with salt and pepper. Stir the butter occasionally; when it turns a golden brown, remove from heat.

Cut the remaining lemon into wedges. To serve, place a trout on a plate and pour some of the brown butter sauce over it, garnishing with lemon wedges.

YIELD: 4 servings

🧂 ADD IT!
Stir 2 tablespoons (8 g) chopped fresh parsley into the butter sauce just when the butter browns.

CRUMB-CRUSTED TUNA WITH LIME BUTTER

To make fresh bread crumbs, simply remove the crust from any home-style bread and put it into the food processor, fitted with the metal blade. Pulse until it is turned into crumbs.

> 2 cups fresh bread crumbs made from white home-style bread
> 8 tablespoons (115 g) butter
> 4 tuna steaks, about 1-inch (2½-cm) thick—2 pounds (900 g) total
> 2 limes

Melt half the butter and mix with the bread crumbs. Season the tuna with salt and pepper and press the crumbs onto the top and bottom of the tuna steaks. Place on waxed paper on a plate and refrigerate for at least ½ hour.

Peel the zest from 1 lime and mince the zest finely. Squeeze the lime into a small mixing bowl or food processor. Mash the juice, zest, and remaining butter together, with some salt and pepper. Roll the butter up like a log in plastic wrap and refrigerate for at least ½ hour.

Heat ¼ cup oil in a wide sauté pan or skillet over medium-high heat. When the oil begins to smoke, add the tuna steaks. Cook for 4 to 5 minutes per side, turning carefully so as to leave the crust intact, for medium-rare tuna. Cook for less or more time according to how you like your tuna done. Figure about 7 minutes per side for medium to medium well, and 10 minutes per side for well.

To serve, place a tuna steak on a plate. Remove the plastic from the butter, cut into disks, and place on the tuna.

YIELD: 4 servings

GRILLED LEMON-PEPPER TUNA WITH GUACAMOLE

What is better than a beautiful piece of fish simply grilled? Here we embellish just a little. This is a great recipe for that summer day when you don't want to linger inside the supermarket. You can make the guacamole yourself (page 56) if you'd prefer.

> 4 tuna steaks, 1-inch (2½-cm) thick, about 2 pounds (900 g) total
> 1 cup (235 ml) lemon-pepper marinade (purchased or homemade, see note)
> 1 cup (225 g) guacamole

Marinate tuna in the lemon-pepper marinade for at least 1 hour and up to 6 hours. Prepare a grill. When it is ready, remove the tuna from the marinade and grill for 5 minutes per side for medium rare. You can cook to the temperature you like best: figure about 7 minutes per side for medium to medium well, and 10 minutes per side for well.

Place a tuna steak on a plate and top with some of the guacamole.

YIELD: 4 servings

 ADD IT!
A shot of tequila in the marinade would be good—hey, you're making margaritas anyhow, right?

NOTE: *To make 1½ cups of your own marinade, whisk together the following ingredients until the sugar is dissolved:*

½ cup (120 ml) water
2 tablespoons (30 ml) cider or rice vinegar
¼ cup (50 g) sugar
¼ cup (60 ml) lemon juice
¼ cup (60 ml) oil
½ teaspoon garlic powder
½ teaspoon onion powder
1 teaspoon salt
2 teaspoons black pepper

GRILLED TUNA WITH WASABI CREAM SAUCE

This is a westernized interpretation of a classic flavor combination.

> 4 tuna steaks, 1-inch (2½-cm) thick, about 2 pounds (900 g)
> 1 tablespoon (10 g) wasabi (Japanese horseradish) powder
> 1 cup (235 ml) heavy cream
> 3 tablespoons (43 g) butter

Prepare a grill.

When the grill is ready, season the tuna with salt and pepper and grill for 5 minutes per side for medium rare. You can cook to the temperature you like best, figure about 7 minutes per side for medium to medium well, and 10 minutes per side for well. If you are cooking to medium well or well, finish the cooking on the cooler part of the grill.

While the tuna is cooking, heat a medium-size sauté pan or skillet over high heat. Add the cream and wasabi, whisking to mix well. Reduce the cream by half, season with salt and pepper, and whisk in the butter, 1 tablespoon (15 g) at a time, to create a smooth sauce. Be sure to monitor the heat and remove as soon as the last of the butter is melted, to make sure the sauce doesn't break.

To serve, place a tuna steak on each of 4 plates and spoon the sauce over it.

YIELD: 4 servings

ADD IT!
Serve with some pickled ginger on the side.

Sesame Seed-Crusted Tuna with Ponzu Sauce

To us, Asian flavors work with tuna like no other—especially Japanese flavors. Ponzu is a traditional Japanese dipping sauce based on soy and citrus.

½ cup (60 g) sesame seeds—half white and half black if possible
4 tuna steaks, each 6 to 8 ounces (170 to 225 g)
1 cup (235 ml) ponzu sauce

Put the sesame seeds in a pie plate or similar dish. If using two colors of sesame seeds, keep the two colors separate, but allow them to butt up against each other. Season the tuna with salt and pepper and press into the sesame seeds on both sides of the steak, so that half of each side is white and half is black.

Preheat the oven to 450°F (230°C, gas mark 8).

Heat ¼ cup (60 ml) oil in a wide sauté pan or skillet over high heat. When the oil starts to smoke, add the tuna and sear 3 to 4 minutes, until the sesame seeds are browning. Using tongs and gripping the sides of the tuna steaks, carefully turn the tuna and sear the other side, also for 3 to 4 minutes. Put the tuna on a baking sheet and finish in the oven to the desired degree of doneness.

The best way to tell if the tuna is done is by the pressing method. In this case squeeze from the sides, as otherwise the seeds will burn your fingers. You can also make a discreet cut to see how done it is. Many people like their tuna, especially a really fresh piece, no more than medium rare. Others prefer theirs more well done.

While the tuna is in the oven, heat the ponzu in a small saucepan over low heat.

To serve, place a piece of tuna on each of 4 plates and spoon the ponzu sauce over it.

YIELD: 4 servings

ADD IT!
Chopped fresh cilantro as a garnish is nice.

FRIED CALAMARI

Calamari can be cooked only two ways—on high heat for a very short time, or on low heat for a much longer time. Any other way, you end up with hot rubber bands. We choose the hot and fast method here. These are easier to do in a deep fat fryer, but you can use a heavy pot on the stove, too.

> 1 pound (450 g) cleaned calamari, tubes and tentacles
> 2 lemons
> 2 cups (250 g) all-purpose flour

Cut the calamari tubes into ½-inch (1-cm) rings. Place the tentacles and rings in a bowl and squeeze the juice of 1 lemon over them, then season with salt and pepper.

Heat 2 inches of oil in a deep fryer. You can also use a wide sauté pan or skillet or 4-quart (4-L) pot. Heat the oil until a candy thermometer measures 375°F (190°C) or until the oil shimmers on top. While the oil is heating, dredge the squid in the flour. Fry in the hot oil for 1 to 2 minutes, in batches if necessary. Do not crowd the fryer. It is important that the oil maintains its temperature, or the calamari will be greasy. Drain on paper towels for a bit and season with salt and pepper.

Cut the remaining lemon into wedges and serve with the calamari.

YIELD: 4 servings

🍶 ADD IT!
Mix 2 tablespoons (15 g) paprika with the dredging flour; serve with aioli for dipping.

Garlic and Basil Baked Clams

To open clams, use a clam knife (available at any kitchen store for a couple of dollars). Press the edge of the knife into the seam between the two shells at the front of the clam. Cold clams are easier to open—they seem to relax and to grip the shells together less tightly.

20 littleneck clams
6 slices home-style white bread
½ cup (130 g) basil pesto
4 tablespoons (55 g) butter

Preheat the oven to 400°F (200°C, gas mark 6).

Scrub the clams under cold water, then open them, leaving each clam on the half shell. Cut off and discard the crusts of the bread. Process the bread slices in a food processor fitted with the metal blade until you have coarse crumbs. Mix the crumbs and pesto in a bowl.

Melt the butter in a small saucepan over low heat; add the melted butter to the crumb mixture. Season with salt and pepper to taste. Put 1 to 2 tablespoons of the crumb mixture on each clam, pressing the crumbs in lightly. Place the clams on a baking sheet and bake the clams for 8 to 10 minutes, until the crumbs are golden brown on top.

YIELD: 4 servings

🧂 ADD IT!
Stir 1 clove minced garlic into the pesto-crumb mixture to kick it up a notch.

PAN ROAST OF CLAMS WITH TOMATO

Another way to eat clams—ain't life grand? This one is a real snap to prepare, too.

20 littleneck clams
½ pound (225 g) fresh tomatoes
2 tablespoons (30 ml) tarragon vinegar
8 tablespoons (115 g) butter

Rinse the clams under cold water to remove any grit. Discard any clams that are not tightly shut.

Prepare a large bowl of ice water. Bring a large pot of water to a boil. Core the tomatoes and mark an X at the base with a paring knife. Drop the tomatoes in the boiling water for 15 to 30 seconds, or until the skin starts peeling. When you see that first sign of peeling, remove the tomatoes and plunge them immediately into the ice water. Drain the tomatoes and peel them—the skin should pop right off. Cut the tomatoes in half; scoop out the seeds and roughly chop the remaining tomato flesh.

Put the clams, the tomatoes, the vinegar, and salt and pepper to taste into a 2-quart (2-L) heavy-bottomed pot with a tight-fitting lid. Cover and cook over high heat for 10 to 12 minutes, until the clams have opened.

Cut the butter into small pieces and stir into the pan sauce. Serve the clams and the sauce in bowls.

YIELD: 4 servings

CLAMS WITH CHINESE BLACK BEAN SAUCE

When we first tried this dish in a Chinatown restaurant it was a shock—the first 20-something years of our lives had suddenly become meaningless, and we had a new yardstick by which to measure what tastes good. Steamed white rice and a vegetable stir-fry would add the finishing touches to a fine meal.

    20 littleneck clams
    1 jar (10 ounces, or 280 g) Chinese black bean sauce
    4 scallions

Scrub the clams under cold water, discarding any that are not tightly closed. Put the clams and black bean sauce into a heavy-bottomed 2-quart (2-L) pot, cover, and cook over medium-high heat until the clams open—about 8 to 10 minutes. Chop the scallions, both green and white parts, and sprinkle over the clams.

YIELD: 4 servings

STEAMED CRABS

This is the recipe that will make you think of crab houses on the Chesapeake, with humidity hanging in the air like a fog, brown paper on the tables, and wooden mallets for pounding the crabs.

    1 dozen live blue crabs—or 4 Dungeness crabs, 1 pound (450 g) each
    ½ cup (50 g) crab-boil spice (the traditional one is Old Bay seasoning)
    2 cups (475 ml) beer

Rinse the crabs under cold water and put them in an 8-quart (8-L) pot that has a tight-fitting lid. Sprinkle the crab-boil spice in the pot and add the beer and 2 cups (475 ml) water. Bring to a boil over high heat and cook for 12 to 15 minutes for blue crab, or about 15 to 20 minutes for Dungeness.

Serve with melted butter, mallets, and nut crackers, preferably outdoors. If you can find a creaky old dock and throw the shell over your shoulders into the water, even better.

YIELD: 4 servings

BAKED STUFFED LOBSTER

This is how we had baked stuffed lobster growing up in Marblehead, Massachusetts. You could use other crackers than Ritz, but that would be Just Wrong.

4 lobsters, 1¼ to 1½ pounds (575 to 675 g) each
4 cups (400 g) crushed Ritz crackers
3 lemons
16 tablespoons (½ pound, or 225 g) butter

Bring 4 quarts (4 L) salted water to a boil in an 8-quart (8-L) pot with a tight-fitting lid. Parboil the lobsters for 4 to 5 minutes, then drain and cool. When the lobsters are cool enough to handle, lay them on their backs on a cutting board and split them open from just under the mouth to halfway down the tail. Be careful to not cut all the way through—leave the top part of the shell intact. Break the lobsters apart a bit by carefully prying the split part open.

Heat the oven to 350°F (180°C, gas mark 4).

Put the Ritz crumbs in a mixing bowl. Squeeze the juice from 2 of the lemons. Melt the butter in a small saucepan and add the lemon juice. Mix this with the crackers and season with salt and pepper. Spoon one-fourth of this mixture into the cavity of each lobster.

Put the lobsters on a baking sheet and bake them for about 15 minutes, until the crumbs are golden brown and the lobster meat is cooked through (check the tail meat).

Serve with additional drawn butter and lemon wedges.

YIELD: 4 servings

GRILLED LOBSTER WITH CHERVIL BUTTER SAUCE

This is a loose adaptation of a recipe made famous by chef Jasper White at his landmark Boston restaurants. Chervil—a fragrant herb with a faint licorice flavor—is underutilized, in our opinion. Oven Fried Potatoes (page 438) and steamed asparagus would round this meal out nicely.

4 lobsters, 1¼ to 1½ pounds (575 to 675 g) each
¼ cup (5 g) minced chervil
1 cup (235 ml) white wine
16 tablespoons (½ pound, or 225 g) butter, cut into tablespoon-size pieces

In an 8-quart (8-L) pot with a tight-fitting lid, bring to a boil 4 quarts (4 L) salted water. Parboil the lobsters for 8 to 9 minutes, then drain and cool. When the lobsters are cool enough to handle, lay them on their backs on a cutting board and split them in half.

Prepare a grill.

While the grill is heating, put the wine in a 1-quart (1-L) saucepan over high heat and reduce by two-thirds. Reduce the heat to medium and whisk the butter into the wine, a couple of cubes at a time, to create an emulsified sauce. Be sure to monitor the heat and remove as soon as the last of the butter is melted, to make sure the sauce doesn't break. Stir in the chervil and season with salt and pepper. Set aside in a warm (not hot) place.

Season the cut side of each lobster half and brush the meat with a little oil. Grill the lobster for 5 to 6 minutes, meat side down, until the lobster is heated through and the meat is grill marked. Crack the claws with a nut cracker, arrange 2 halves of lobster on each of 4 plates, meat side up, and spoon the sauce over them.

YIELD: 4 servings

🏺 ADD IT!
To deepen the flavor, add 1 tablespoon (15 ml) champagne vinegar and 2 tablespoons (20 g) minced shallot to the wine reduction.

SIMPLE STEAMED MUSSELS

This is a basic way to make mussels, and it lets the sweet flavor of the shellfish shine through.

2 pounds (900 g) mussels
4 tablespoons (35 g) minced garlic
1 cup (235 ml) white wine

Clean the mussels by removing any beards, rinsing off grit under cold water, and discarding any mussels that have their shells open and do not close up when gently tapped. Heat a 4-quart (4-L) pot with a tight-fitting lid over medium-high heat and put in the mussels, garlic, and wine. Season with salt and pepper and cover, cooking until the mussels are opened—about 5 to 6 minutes.

YIELD: 4 servings as an appetizer, 2 as a main course

MUSSELS WITH PESTO

In Belgium, there are restaurants that specialize in mussels and serve them in many ways. Here's another way to make a quick and easy mussel dish. While we are at it, let's emulate the Belgians and serve the mussels with a side of good, homemade French fries.

2 pounds (900 g) mussels
½ cup (130 g) pesto
1 cup (235 ml) white wine

Clean the mussels by removing any beards, rinsing off grit under cold water, and discarding any mussels that have their shells open and do not close up when gently tapped. Combine all ingredients in a 4-quart (4-L) pot with a tight-fitting cover. Season to taste with salt and pepper. Cook over high heat for 8 to 10 minutes, until the mussels have opened. Serve in bowls with the cooking liquid.

YIELD: 4 servings as an appetizer, 2 as a main course

ORANGE-GLAZED MUSSELS

At the Three Stallion Inn, Bob always has a mussels preparation on the appetizers list. This one has been popular, with the marmalade forming a clinging glaze.

    2 pounds (900 g) mussels
    1 cup (320 g) orange marmalade
    3 cloves minced garlic

Clean the mussels by removing any beards, rinsing off grit under cold water, and discarding any mussels that have their shells open and do not close up when gently tapped.

Melt the marmalade over medium heat in a 4-quart (4-L) pot with a tight-fitting cover. Add the garlic and mussels and season to taste with salt and pepper. Cover and cook over high heat for 8 to 10 minutes, until the mussels have opened.

YIELD: 4 servings as an appetizer, 2 as a main course

THAI GREEN CURRY MUSSELS

Spicy, yet with an intriguing mix of flavors all hitting your taste buds at once.

    2 pounds (900 g) mussels
    2 tablespoons (30 g) Thai green curry paste
    1 can (14 ounces, or 415 g) coconut milk

Clean the mussels by removing any beards, rinsing off grit under cold water, and discarding any mussels that have their shells open and do not close up when gently tapped.

Put the mussels in a 4-quart (4-L) pot with a tight-fitting cover. In a small mixing bowl, whisk together the curry paste and the coconut milk until just combined. Add this mixture to the pot. Season to taste with salt and pepper. Cook over high heat for 8 to 10 minutes, until the mussels have opened. Serve in bowls with the cooking liquid.

YIELD: 4 servings as an appetizer, 2 as a main course

MEXICAN MUSSELS

Steamed mussels are quick and easy. With the advent of farm-raised mussels, the main ingredient is now available at almost any decent supermarket or fishmonger.

  2 pounds (900 g) mussels
  1 cup (225 g) salsa
  ½ cup chopped fresh cilantro

Clean the mussels by removing any beards, rinsing off grit under cold water, and discarding any mussels that have their shells open and do not close up when gently tapped.

Combine the mussels and the salsa, along with ½ cup (120 ml) water, in a 4-quart (4-L) pot with a tight-fitting cover. Season to taste with salt and pepper. Cook over high heat for 8 to 10 minutes, until mussels have opened. Tip the whole pot into a nice serving bowl and sprinkle the cilantro over it.

YIELD: 4 servings as an appetizer, or 2 as a main course

ADD IT!
Substitute white wine for the water.

CORNMEAL-CRUSTED OYSTERS WITH SALSA

As always, when cooking oysters, do not overcook.

> **20 oysters in the shell**
> **1 cup (140 g) cornmeal**
> 2 cups (475 ml) oil (more or less)
> **1 cup (225 g) fresh salsa**

Shuck the oysters, putting the meats into a bowl and keeping the bottom shell (the one with the deeper indent) from each. Wash the shells thoroughly and set aside.

Season the oysters with salt and pepper and dredge them in the cornmeal, laying them out on waxed paper. Heat a wide sauté pan or skillet over medium-high heat and add ¼ inch (½ cm) oil. When the oil starts to smoke, fry the oysters in batches for 1 minute per side, draining on paper towels and keeping them warm. Place each fried oyster on a shell and spoon salsa over it.

YIELD: 4 servings

TEMPURA SCALLOPS WITH SWEET-HOT GLAZE

This one flies out the door when we run it as a special at the Three Stallion Inn served with steamed jasmine rice. Thai sweet chile sauce is available at any Asian market and often at supermarkets. Once you have some of this in the house, you won't want to be without it.

> 1½ pounds (675 g) scallops (wet-pack scallops are OK)
> 2 cups (225 g) tempura batter mix
> 2 cups (450 g) Thai sweet chile sauce

Special equipment needed: a deep-fat fryer or a deep heavy sauté pan or skillet and a candy thermometer.

Clean the scallops by removing the side muscle. Make the tempura batter according to the package directions. Heat oil to 350°F (180°C).

Dip the scallops in the batter and fry them, not crowding, until golden brown—about 4 minutes. Drain the scallops on paper towels and keep them warm. It is a good idea when frying tempura to test one first, to make sure the batter consistency is correct.

Heat the sweet chile sauce in a 16-inch sauté pan or skillet. Add the fried scallops and toss to coat well. If your pan is not large enough (we don't want to knock off the tempura crust while tossing the scallops), you can heat the sauce in a saucepan, combine the sauce and scallops in a large bowl, and toss to coat.

YIELD: 4 servings

🧂 ADD IT!
Sprinkle chopped fresh cilantro over the scallops.

SCALLOPS WITH ENDIVE AND CRÈME FRAÎCHE

Crème fraîche is a lovelier, tastier, more useful version of sour cream. It tastes better and does not break when cooked. You must use dry-pack, also called natural or "no water added," scallops. Wet-pack scallops will simply leak out all the added water when you try to sear them, and you get no caramelization.

> 2 pounds (900 g) large dry-pack sea scallops, 20 to 40 total
> 2 heads Belgian endive
> ½ cup (115 g) crème fraîche

If necessary, clean the scallops by removing the side muscle. Season with salt and pepper. Heat a wide sauté pan or skillet over high heat. When the pan is very hot, add 3 tablespoons (45 ml) oil and carefully place scallops in the pan. Do not crowd the pan—cook the scallops in batches if needed. Cook for 3 to 4 minutes per side until well browned. When turning them over, do not try to force the scallops off the pan. They will release themselves when they are ready to be turned. When the scallops are cooked, set them aside in a warm place.

While the scallops are cooking, cut the endive crosswise in ½-inch (1-cm) slices. Using the same pan as you used to cook the scallops, still over high heat, sauté the endive until it begins to caramelize—about 5 minutes. Add the crème fraîche and bring to a boil, scraping the pan to get the brown bits from the scallops into your sauce.

Divide the endive-crème fraîche mixture among 4 plates and arrange the scallops on top.

YIELD: 4 servings

MISO-SEARED SCALLOPS

There are all sorts of miso pastes; some have wheat, some soy, some both. Any Asian market will have a selection, as will upscale grocers and increasingly, your local supermarket. You don't need to use red miso; any will do. The powdered stuff, however, is not recommended. You must use dry-pack, also called natural or "no water added," scallops. Wet-pack scallops will simply leak out all the added water when you try to sear them, and you get no caramelization.

2 pounds (900 g) large dry-pack sea scallops, 20 to 40 total
½ cup (125 g) red miso paste
1 bunch scallions

If necessary, clean the scallops by removing the side muscle. Season the scallops with pepper and brush liberally with the miso paste. Heat a wide sauté pan or skillet over high heat. When the pan is very hot, add 2 tablespoons (30 ml) oil and carefully place scallops in the pan. Do not crowd the pan—cook the scallops in batches if needed. Cook for 3 to 4 minutes per side until well browned. When turning them over, do not try to force the scallops off the pan. They will release themselves when they are ready to be turned.

While the scallops are cooking, slice the scallion, both green and white parts, crosswise into thin slices. To serve, arrange the scallops on plates and sprinkle the scallion over them.

YIELD: 4 servings

SEARED SCALLOPS WITH CUCUMBER

For this recipe you must use dry-pack, also called natural or "no water added," scallops. Wet-pack scallops will simply leak out all the added water when you try to sear them, and you get no caramelization.

2 pounds (900 g) large dry-pack sea scallops, 20 to 40 total
2 cucumbers
¼ cup (8 g) chopped fresh dill
4 tablespoons (55 g) butter

If necessary, clean the scallops by removing the side muscle. Season the scallops with salt and pepper. Peel and seed the cucumber and slice into ¼-inch (½-cm) slices on the bias. Heat a wide sauté pan or skillet over high heat. When the pan is very hot, add 2 tablespoons (30 ml) oil and carefully place some of the scallops in the pan. Do not crowd the pan—cook the scallops in batches if needed. Cook each batch for 3 to 4 minutes per side, until well browned. When turning them over, do not try to force the scallops off the pan—they will release themselves when they are ready to be turned.

When the scallops are cooked, set them aside in a warm place and add the cucumbers to the pan. Sauté for 4 to 5 minutes, allowing the cucumber slices to brown a bit. They should be softer than raw but still crisp. Season with salt and pepper, add the dill, and stir in the butter, 1 tablespoon (15 g) at a time until just incorporated.

To serve, arrange some of the cucumbers on a plate and top with scallops.

YIELD: 4 servings as a main course, 6 as an appetizer

BEER-STEAMED SHRIMP

If you want spicier shrimp, feel free to add hot sauce or red pepper flakes to the spice mix. This is a fun dish to serve when you plan on eating outside and don't mind a mess.

2 pounds (900 g) medium shrimp, shells on
¼ cup (25 g) pickling spice
1 bottle beer, 12 ounces (355 ml)
8 tablespoons (115 g) butter

Mix together the shrimp and the pickling spice in a bowl. Season with salt and pepper. Put the shrimp into the top of a steamer and pour the beer into the bottom of the steamer. Cover and cook over high heat for 10 to 12 minutes, until the shrimp are just cooked through. While the shrimp are cooking, melt the butter in a small saucepan over low heat. Discard the beer and serve the shrimp with melted butter for dipping.

YIELD: 4 servings

CHESAPEAKE BAKED SHRIMP

Easy. Yummy. Need we say more? Bread for sopping up the sauce is essential.

2 pounds (900 g) large shrimp, peeled and deveined
¼ cup (25 g) Old Bay or other crab-boil spice
8 tablespoons (115 g) butter
1 cup (235 ml) white wine

Preheat the oven to 400°F (200°C, gas mark 6).

In a large bowl, toss together the shrimp and the crab-boil spice. Put the shrimp into a shallow 2-quart (2-L) casserole. Melt the butter over low heat and pour it over the shrimp; add the wine. Bake for 20 to 25 minutes, until the shrimp are cooked through—they will no longer be translucent and will have turned a pink-white color.

YIELD: 4 servings

BROILED SHRIMP WITH GARLIC AND CILANTRO

Friends of ours from Costa Rica showed us this dish at a dinner party. Wow, was it good!—and easy to make, too. Steamed rice and a simple salad are all you need to complete a simple yet elegant meal.

1 bunch cilantro
6 cloves garlic, peeled
2 tablespoons (30 ml) olive oil
2 pounds (900 g) shrimp, 16 to 20 per pound, peeled and deveined
8 tablespoons (115 g) butter

Heat a broiler and place the rack 8 inches from the element. Rinse the cilantro, shake dry and cut off the coarse stems. Put the cilantro and garlic in the food processor, add the olive oil, and process to make a rough pesto.

Melt the butter in a small saucepan. Place the shrimp in a shallow baking dish that just will hold them comfortably in one layer. Season the shrimp with salt and pepper, spread the cilantro-garlic mixture over them, and pour the butter over all. Broil for 10 to 12 minutes, until the shrimp are all pink (not blue) and slightly browned.

YIELD: 4 servings

ITALIAN BROILED SHRIMP

Another quick and easy, yet elegant, shrimp dish. We use vodka pasta sauce, but any good bottled tomato-based pasta sauce will do. Toss these shrimp with your favorite pasta, round it out with a salad, and you've got a meal.

 2 pounds (900 g) large shrimp, peeled and deveined
 2 cups (500 g) vodka pasta sauce
 1 cup (80 g) shredded Parmesan cheese

Heat the broiler and place the rack 8 inches from the heating element. Toss the shrimp with the pasta sauce, then put them in a shallow 1-quart (1-L) casserole dish. Broil for 8 to 10 minutes, until the shrimp are pink-white throughout. Top with cheese and broil for another 3 to 5 minutes, until the cheese is melted and lightly browned.

YIELD: 4 servings

VERACRUZ CEVICHE

We first had this in Mexico and have made it many times since. In many ceviche recipes, the fish is "cooked" by the acid in the lime juice. In this recipe, we first poach the shrimp, then marinate it in the lime and salsa. By "fresh salsa," we mean the refrigerated kind that we find in our produce aisle.

> 4 limes
> 2 cups (250 g) fresh salsa
> 2 pounds (900 g) large shrimp (40 to 50 total) peeled and deveined

In a 4-quart (4-L) pot, bring 2 quarts (2 L) water just to a simmer over medium-low heat. Season the water with salt and pepper, squeeze in the juice of 1 lime, and drop in the rinds. Add ½ cup salsa to the water. Add the shrimp and poach the shrimp for 5 to 6 minutes, until just cooked through. You can tell when shrimp are properly poached as they get an elastic yet tender feel in the mouth. Do not let the water boil while the shrimp are poaching. Drain the shrimp; put them on a baking sheet and refrigerate immediately.

When the shrimp have cooled, remove the tails and cut the shrimp into ½-inch (1-cm) chunks. Squeeze 2 more limes and add the lime juice and the remaining salsa to the shrimp. Mix well and refrigerate for at least 2 hours and preferably overnight. Serve in cocktail glasses, such as martini glasses, with wedge of lime as garnish.

YIELD: 8 servings as an appetizer

15

Eggs

Eggs have been rudely relegated to the morning hours of the gustatory day for no particular reason other than tradition. Sure, sometimes we push the envelope by serving them at brunch, which can creep past noon. But eggs deserve more! They're high in protein, low in fat, and very high in taste and versatility. Once generally scorned as cunning little cholesterol bombs, eggs are staging a comeback, especially as low-carb diets such Atkins and South Beach make them the favored choice for breakfast. We strive to showcase eggs in dishes that work for dinner, as well as offering traditional breakfast fare.

EGG AND SAUSAGE ROLL-UPS

4 eggs
2 cups (225 g) cooked sliced sausage, about 4 sausages
2 cups (500 g) marinara sauce

Preheat the broiler. Line a baking sheet with parchment paper.

Beat the eggs together with 2 tablespoons (30 ml) water, and season with salt and pepper. Heat a teaspoon of cooking oil in a 7- or 8-inch (20-cm) nonstick sauté pan or skillet with an ovenproof handle over medium heat. Pour 3 tablespoons (45 ml) of the egg into the pan, tilt the pan so that the egg covers the bottom, and cook for 1 to 2 minutes. Put the pan under the broiler for a minute to set the top of the egg. Slide the egg sheet onto the parchment-lined baking sheet to cool. Repeat with the remaining egg mixture. You should end up with 8 to 10 egg sheets.

Preheat the oven to 350°F (180°C, gas mark 4).

Lay out an egg sheet, put some of the sausage in the middle, and roll it up into a tube. Lay the tube in a shallow baking dish and repeat with the rest of the egg sheets and sausage. Pour the marinara sauce over the roll-ups and bake for 12 to 15 minutes.

YIELD: 4 to 6 servings

ADD IT!
Sprinkle ½ cup (55 g) shredded mozzarella or Parrano cheese over the top.

Egg "Crepes" with Asparagus and Roasted Red-Pepper Coulis

An excellent way of getting vegetables into the morning meal or serving an original new dish at your next brunch.

    4 eggs
    1 bunch asparagus, about 1 pound (450 g)
    1 can (14 ounces, or 400 g) roasted red peppers, drained

Preheat the broiler. Line a baking sheet with parchment paper. Prepare a container of ice water.

Beat the eggs together with 2 tablespoons (30 ml) water, and season with salt and pepper. Heat a teaspoon of cooking oil in a 7- or 8-inch (20-cm) nonstick sauté pan with an ovenproof handle over medium heat. Pour 3 tablespoons (45 ml) of the egg into the pan, tilt the pan so that the egg covers the bottom, and cook for 1 to 2 minutes. Put the pan under the broiler for a minute to set the top of the egg. Slide the egg sheet onto the parchment-lined baking sheet to cool. Repeat with the remaining egg mixture. You should end up with 8 to 10 egg sheets.

Remove the woody bottom portion of the asparagus. In a large pot, bring 3 quarts (3 L) salted water to a boil and boil the asparagus for 2 to 3 minutes. Drain and immediately submerge the asparagus in the ice water. Drain and set aside.

Put the drained red peppers into a food processor fitted with the metal blade. Puree the peppers.

Preheat the oven to 350°F (180°C, gas mark 4).

Roll 2 stalks of asparagus in each egg sheet and lay the bundles side by side in a shallow baking dish. Pour the red-pepper coulis over the egg crepes. Bake for 10 to 12 minutes.

YIELD: 4 servings

🗴 ADD IT!
Roll up shredded Gruyère cheese along with the asparagus.

EGGS AND FETA IN PHYLLO CUPS

Wave good-bye to quiche—this elegant brunch dish is quite easy to make.

2 sheets phyllo dough, thawed, each 14 x 18 inches (about 35 x 46 cm)
4 tablespoons (55 g) butter, melted
6 eggs
3 tablespoons (30 g) crumbled feta cheese

Preheat the oven to 350°F (180°C, gas mark 4).

Lay 1 sheet of phyllo on a cutting board, brush all over with melted butter, and carefully lay the other sheet on top. Brush again with butter. Make two equidistant cuts crosswise on the phyllo, dividing it into thirds, and make one lengthwise cut to divide the pastry into 6 pieces. Lay a 1 x 6-inch (2½ x 15-cm) strip of parchment paper into each of 6 cups on a muffin pan. The ends of each strip should extend beyond the edge of the cup.

Press the phyllo rectangles gently into each muffin cup, butter side down. Crack an egg into each and sprinkle each egg with feta and black pepper. (The feta will provide plenty of salt.) Bake 12 to 14 minutes, until the phyllo is golden brown and the egg is set.

Remove the cups from the muffin pan by picking it up by the parchment strips, which can be discarded.

YIELD: 6 servings at brunch, or 3 servings as a meal

ADD IT!
Stir a teaspoon of finely minced fresh rosemary into the crumbled feta.

Eggs and Oysters

Most people pair eggs with some sort of pork product, be it bacon, sausage, or ham. But for an intriguing twist, the briny taste of oysters makes this a dish to remember.

   1 container (8 ounces, or 225 g) shucked oysters
   1 cup (125 g) all-purpose flour
   4 eggs

Drain the oysters. Season the flour with salt and pepper and put it in a mixing bowl or pie plate. Dredge the oysters in the flour. Heat about 2 tablespoons (30 ml) olive oil in a medium-size sauté pan or skillet over medium heat until the oil is hot but not smoking. Add the oysters and fry for 1 to 2 minutes on each side. Reduce the heat to medium. Spread the oysters out and crack the eggs in between. Fry the eggs until the whites are set. Serve 2 eggs along with half the oysters on a plate.

YIELD: 2 servings

ADD IT!
We love a shot of hot sauce over our eggs; a squeeze of fresh lemon might be nice, too.

Eggs in Potato Nests

2 medium potatoes (russets are good for this)
4 slices Canadian bacon or ham
4 eggs

Preheat the oven to the lowest setting.

Peel the potatoes and shred them on a box grater. Put them in a sieve to squeeze out the excess water and turn them into a bowl; season with salt and pepper. Heat 3 tablespoons (45 ml) oil in an 8-inch sauté pan or skillet over medium-high heat. When the oil is hot, spread out the potatoes in the pan. Cook for 8 to 10 minutes, flip with a spatula and cook for 5 to 6 minutes on the other side, until the potatoes are golden brown and cooked through. With the spatula, cut the potatoes into 4 wedges and put them in the oven to stay warm.

Fry the Canadian bacon for 1 to 2 minutes on each side and set aside with the potato wedges. Add 1 tablespoon (15 ml) oil to the pan and crack the eggs in. Fry the eggs as you prefer, sunny side up or over. When the eggs are nearly done, assemble the potato nests: Put 2 potato wedges on each of 2 plates and top each wedge with a slice of meat. Top each with an egg and serve.

YIELD: 2 servings

POACHED EGGS WITH BASIL MUSHROOMS

A hint for egg poaching: Put 1 to 2 tablespoons (15 to 30 ml) white vinegar in the water to keep the eggs from sticking to the bottom. Feel free to substitute other herbs for the basil.

10 ounces (280 g) white or brown mushrooms
¼ cup (10 g) chopped fresh basil
4 eggs

Rinse and slice the mushrooms; set aside. Heat 2 tablespoons (28 g) butter in a medium-size sauté pan or skillet over high heat. When the butter melts, add the mushrooms and sauté for 4 to 5 minutes. Add the basil and salt and pepper to taste, and continue to sauté until any liquid released by the mushrooms evaporates. Set the mushrooms aside. In a medium-size pan or skillet, heat 2 inches (5 cm) water to the simmer. Drop in the eggs and poach them for 4 to 5 minutes, until they are set. Do not allow the water to boil. Make a little nest of the mushrooms on each of 4 plates. Remove the eggs from the water with a slotted spoon and place one in each mushroom nest.

YIELD: 4 servings

GREEN EGGS

You don't have to be Sam I Am to like this recipe, although kids will flock to it once they've read the book. Grown-ups will appreciate the sophisticated flavor. These are always good with a side of fried ham and a toasted English muffin.

½ cup (25 g) chopped chives
½ cup (120 ml) light cream
2 tablespoons (28 g) butter
4 eggs

In a small pot, heat 2 cups (475 ml) water to a boil. Salt the water, add the chives, and cook for 5 to 10 seconds. Drain and immediately run the chives under cold water until cooled. Put the chives in a blender. Pour the cream in the blender, along with salt and pepper to taste, and puree to a smooth, bright green sauce. Put the sauce back in the small pot and warm it over low heat.

Heat the butter in a wide sauté pan or skillet over medium-high heat. When the butter is melted, crack in the eggs and fry, sunny side up or over, as you prefer. Put 2 eggs on each of 2 plates and spoon the sauce over.

YIELD: 2 servings

ITALIAN BAKED EGGS

It's a little-known fact: Marinara sauce isn't monogamous. In fact, it pairs well with all sorts of things besides pasta. Next time you need a light, quick dinner, try this recipe with a nice green salad to go with it.

2 cups (500 g) marinara sauce
4 eggs
2 tablespoons (10 g) shredded Parmesan cheese

Preheat the oven to 350°F (180°C, gas mark 4).

Put the marinara sauce in a small, shallow baking dish. With a spoon, make 4 indentations in the sauce. Break the eggs into these indentations. Sprinkle the cheese over the sauce and eggs. Bake for 10 to 12 minutes, until the eggs are set and the marinara sauce is bubbling.

YIELD: 2 servings

LOX AND CREAM CHEESE OMELET

For the carb counters, here's a way to get your lox and cream cheese without having to use a bagel to anchor the whole affair.

    3 eggs
    2 tablespoons (30 ml) half-and-half
    2 tablespoons (25 g) lox cream cheese

Preheat the oven to 400°F (200°C, gas mark 6).

In a small bowl, lightly beat the eggs with the half-and-half. Heat 1 tablespoon (15 g) butter in a nonstick 8-inch omelet pan with an ovenproof handle over medium heat. When the butter is melted, add the egg mixture to the pan. Using a heat-proof rubber spatula, shake the pan over the heat and stir the eggs with the spatula at the same time. When the eggs form a disk, dot with the cream cheese and bake in the oven for 3 to 4 minutes to set the eggs. Fold out onto a plate.

YIELD: 1 serving

 ADD IT!
Sprinkle chopped chives over the top of the omelet.

MEXICAN BAKED EGGS

1 package (8 ounces, or 225 g) Mexican rice mix (see note)
8 eggs
1 cup (115 g) shredded cheddar or Monterey Jack cheese

Preheat the oven to 350°F (180°C, gas mark 4).

Prepare the rice according to the package instructions. When it is cooked, spread it out in the bottom of a shallow 1-quart (1-L) baking pan. Make 8 little indents in the rice with a spoon and crack an egg into each indent. Spread the cheese over the rice and eggs.

Bake for 10 to 12 minutes, until the eggs are set and the cheese is melted.

YIELD: 4 servings

🥫 ADD IT!
Serve with a dollop of slightly warmed fresh salsa.

NOTE: Here's a recipe for those prefer to make their own rice.

2 teaspoons oil
¼ cup (40 g) finely chopped onion
¼ cup (40 g) finely chopped celery
1 cup (185 g) long-grain white rice
1 cup (235 ml) tomato juice

1 teaspoon dark chile powder
½ teaspoon ground cumin
1 cup (235 ml) water
Salt and pepper to taste

Combine oil, onion, and celery in a 2-quart (2-L) saucepan with a tight-fitting lid. Heat over low heat, covered, until the vegetables are softened. Stir in the rice and cook for a minute or two. Add the remaining ingredients, stir, cover, increase heat to high, and bring to a boil. Reduce heat to a simmer and cook, covered, for about 20 minutes, until the liquid is absorbed. Remove from heat and leave covered for 5 minutes. Makes about 2 cups (350 g).

Pasta Frittata

A great way to use up leftover pasta and sauce.

> 3 cups (425 g) cooked spaghetti or other long pasta
> 2 cups (500 g) marinara or other tomato pasta sauce
> 6 eggs

Heat the oven to 350°F (180°C, gas mark 4).

Choose a wide nonstick sauté pan with an ovenproof handle and spray it with pan spray. Mix the pasta and sauce together and spread out in the pan. Crack the eggs in a bowl, season with salt and pepper, and beat them with a whisk. Pour the mixture over the pasta. Bake for 10 minutes, then carefully flip the frittata. Bake for another 10 minutes, until the eggs are set. Slide onto a cutting board and allow to cool for a few minutes, then slice into wedges. You can also serve this at room temperature at a later time.

YIELD: 4 to 6 servings

ADD IT!
Sprinkle the frittata liberally with grated Parmesan cheese.

Poached Eggs and Deviled Ham on English Muffins

A quick breakfast idea. Adding a tablespoon (15 ml) white vinegar to the poaching water will keep the eggs from sticking to the pan.

> 2 English muffins
> 1 can (4½ ounces, or 128 g) deviled ham spread
> 4 eggs

Split and toast the English muffins and spread each half with the deviled ham. In a medium-size sauté pan or skillet, bring 2 inches (5 cm) water to a simmer. Crack in the eggs and poach them for 4 to 5 minutes, until the whites are set. Remove the eggs from the water, one at a time, with a slotted spoon and place them on the English muffin halves.

YIELD: 2 servings

Scotch Eggs

These taste great for brunch, breakfast on the go, or even at a picnic.

½ pound (225 g) bulk breakfast sausage
5 eggs (4 hard-boiled eggs, shelled, and 1 raw egg)
1 cup (115 g) dried bread crumbs

Preheat the oven to 350°F (180°C, gas mark 4).

Divide the sausage meat into 4 pieces and flatten each into a disk. Fully encase each hard-boiled egg in the sausage, sealing the meat with your fingertips. Beat the raw egg in a small bowl. Put the bread crumbs on a pie plate or a small mixing bowl. Dip each sausage-encased egg first in the raw egg, then into the bread crumbs. Put the eggs on a baking sheet and cook for 12 to 15 minutes. Serve hot, cold, or at room temperature.

YIELD: 4 servings

SHIRRED EGGS WITH HAM AND SCALLION

"Shirred" is a 50-cent word for "baked" and is a really easy way to make an elegant egg dish. If you don't have custard cups, a muffin pan will work too.

¼ cup (35 g) diced ham
4 teaspoons minced scallion
4 eggs

Preheat the oven to 350°F (180°C, gas mark 4).

Spray four 4-ounce (120-ml) custard cups with pan spray. Put the ham and scallion in the bottom of each cup and break an egg on top. Put the custard cups on a baking sheet and bake for 10 to 12 minutes, until the egg is just set. Serve in the cups, or flip the eggs out to show the ham and scallion on top.

YIELD: 4 servings at brunch, or 2 servings as a meal

SPANISH OMELET

Good for breakfast, brunch, or a quick supper.

> 3 medium-size potatoes, any variety
> 1 medium-size onion
> 6 eggs

Peel the potatoes and cut them in ½-inch (1-cm) cubes. Put the potatoes in a 1-quart (1-L) pot, cover with water, and gently boil over medium heat until just tender, about 15 minutes. Drain the potatoes.

Preheat the oven to 350°F (180°C, gas mark 4). Heat 2 tablespoons (30 ml) oil in a medium-size ovenproof sauté pan or skillet over medium heat. Peel and dice the onion and cook for 5 to 7 minutes, stirring, until the onions are soft and translucent. Add the potatoes. Beat the eggs, season with salt and pepper, and pour over the potatoes and onion. Put the pan in the oven and bake for 10 to 12 minutes, until the eggs are set. Cut into wedges and serve.

YIELD: 6 servings

 ADD IT!
Sprinkle grated Parmesan cheese and a teaspoon of chopped fresh thyme on the omelet before it goes into the oven.

16

Pasta, Grains,
and Beans

*The reality is that people already know how to boil spaghetti, dump
a jar of sauce in a saucepan, and open a jar of grated Parmesan cheese.
Yes, that would be three ingredients, but that recipe seems to obey the
letter of the law, not the spirit. Here is a more rigorous investigation
of the possibilities for legumes, grains, and pasta.*

PASTA

Since we have taken spaghetti with sauce off the table, we have concentrated our pasta ideas on classics that happen to have three ingredients, on interesting twists that enliven the mundane, and on making fresh pasta doughs and filled pastas.

FRESH BASIL PASTA

> 2 cups (250 g) all-purpose flour
> 2 eggs
> 2 tablespoons (30 g) basil pesto
> 1 teaspoon olive oil
> 1 teaspoon salt

Combine all the ingredients in the bowl of a stand-type mixer fitted with the dough hook. Mix together and knead until the dough is smooth, about 10 minutes. Roll out and cut using a pasta-rolling machine (see Chapter 2, "Techniques and Terms," page 19).

To cook fresh pasta, bring 4 quarts (4 L) salted water to a boil, add the pasta, and cook for 3 to 5 minutes, until the pasta is floating. Strain and serve.

YIELD: 4 servings

FRESH CHESTNUT PASTA

Chestnut flour can be found in specialty shops. This is a wonderfully nutty-tasting pasta. It matches well with Gorgonzola Cream Sauce (page 32).

1 cup (125 g) all-purpose flour
1 cup (125 g) chestnut flour
2 eggs
1 teaspoon olive oil
1 teaspoon salt

Combine all the ingredients in the bowl of a stand-type mixer fitted with the dough hook. Mix together and knead until the dough is smooth, about 10 minutes. Roll out and cut using a pasta-rolling machine (see Chapter 2, "Techniques and Terms," page 19).

To cook fresh pasta, bring 4 quarts (4 L) salted water to a boil, add the pasta, and cook for 3 to 5 minutes, until the pasta is floating. Strain and serve.

YIELD: 4 servings

CAMPANELLE WITH PORCINI CREAM SAUCE

Campanelle, or gigli, are ruffled whorls of pasta that look like the lilies they're named for (gigli is Italian for "lilies"). We like them because they look festive and because they take this sauce beautifully. You can substitute penne or rotini if your store doesn't carry these.

  1 box (1 pound, or 455 g) dried campanelle pasta
  1 tub (8 ounces, or 225 g) mascarpone cheese
  3 to 4 ounces (85 to 115 g) dried porcini mushrooms

Break the dried mushrooms into bite-size pieces and place in a small bowl. Pour about 2 cups (475 ml) boiling water over them and let sit for 20 to 30 minutes, until they rehydrate.

Set a large covered pot of salted water on to boil. When it boils, put the pasta in. Cover until it returns to a boil and then remove the cover and continue to cook the pasta, for about 10 minutes total. When pasta is cooked through but still slightly firm in the center, drain it in a colander and pour into a wide shallow bowl.

While the pasta is cooking, remove the mushrooms from their liquid with a slotted spoon and set aside in a small bowl. Fit a paper towel into a small sieve and drain the mushroom liquor through it into a small saucepan. Heat the liquid until it boils and reduces by about a half. Reduce the heat to low and add the mascarpone cheese. Stir frequently until the cheese melts into the mushroom liquid, creating a semi-thick sauce. Stir the mushrooms into the sauce and pour the sauce over the pasta. Season generously with salt and pepper and toss until the pasta is thoroughly coated with the sauce. Divide among plates and serve.

YIELD: 4 servings as a main course, or 6 as an appetizer

🥫 ADD IT!
Add a few teaspoons fresh chopped tarragon into the mushroom liquid as it reduces, and sprinkle a half cup (40 g) coarsely shaved Parmesan cheese over the sauced pasta as a finish.

Fusilli with Pancetta and Swiss Chard

Swiss chard is one of those foods that provoke a guilty "I should eat that more often it's good for me" reaction. But the truth is, eating Swiss chard is not a hardship. Try substituting it for spinach in some of your dishes, or sautéing it with garlic as a side dish. Or, as here, tossing it in pasta. Good stuff!

    1 pound (455 g) pancetta, cut into small cubes
    1 pound (455 g) ruby chard
    ¼ cup (60 ml) garlic-infused olive oil
    ⅔ pound (300 g) fusilli pasta

Set a large covered pot of salted water on to boil for the pasta.

Wash and spin-dry the Swiss chard and cut into pieces ½-inch (1-cm) wide.

Put the pancetta in a medium-size sauté pan or skillet and cook, stirring frequently, over moderately high heat, until the meat bits are crispy and most of the fat has been rendered. With a slotted spoon, remove the pancetta to drain on a paper towel. Do not clean the pan.

Add the Swiss chard and olive oil to the pan used for the pancetta and cook on moderate heat, stirring frequently. (Be sure to scrape up the brown bits from the bottom of the pan.) Cook for about 15 minutes, or until the chard is tender. Season heartily with salt and, especially, pepper.

When the pasta water boils, put the pasta into the pot. Cover until it returns to a boil, and then remove the cover and continue to cook, for about 10 minutes total. When the pasta is cooked through but still slightly firm in the center, drain it in a colander and pour into a wide shallow bowl.

Pour the Swiss chard and oil mixture onto the pasta, followed by the pancetta. Toss the whole shebang until the ingredients are thoroughly mixed, and divide among 4 plates.

YIELD: 4 servings

🥫 ADD IT!
Cut about 3 ounces (85 g) soft, mild goat cheese into small pieces and toss with the pasta. If you can't abide goat cheese, grated fresh Parmesan will also work nicely.

MAFALDE WITH ARTICHOKES

Mafalde are flat pasta ribbons with ruffles along both edges. They look like mini-lasagne. In fact, if you can't find them, a very similar noodle called lasagnette will do nicely.

> 2 cans artichoke hearts in water, 28 ounces (800 g) total
> 2 tablespoons (30 ml) garlic-infused olive oil
> ⅔ pound (300 g) mafalde pasta
> ½ cup (50 g) freshly grated Parmesan cheese

Set a large covered pot of salted water on to boil for the pasta.

Drain the artichokes and chop coarsely. Heat the olive oil in a heavy sauté pan or skillet over moderate heat. Add the artichokes and season liberally with salt and pepper. Sauté, stirring frequently, for about 5 minutes. Add ½ cup (120 ml) water. Reduce to low heat and simmer, covered, for about 10 minutes.

While the artichokes are cooking, put the pasta into the pot. Cover until it returns to a boil, and then remove the cover and continue to cook, for about 10 minutes total. When the pasta is cooked through but still slightly firm in the center, drain it in a colander and pour into a wide shallow bowl.

Pour the artichoke mixture onto the pasta, followed by the Parmesan cheese. Adjust salt and pepper, and toss until the ingredients are thoroughly mixed.

YIELD: 4 servings

PESTO CHICKEN PASTA

This recipe is amazingly elastic—you can chop a large variety of veggies and toss them into the mix along with the chicken. Some good candidates include mushrooms, cherry tomatoes, kalamata olives, and spinach.

2 whole boneless chicken breasts, about 1½ pounds (675 g)
2 tablespoons (30 ml) garlic-infused olive oil
1 package (1 pound, or 455 g) fresh linguini
One tub (7 ounces, or 200 g) pesto

Put a large pot of salted water on to boil. While the water is heating, wash the chicken in cold water and pat dry. Cut it into bite-sized pieces, removing those annoying tendon strings that tend to crop up with boneless chicken. Heat the olive oil in a midsize sauté pan or skillet over high heat. When the oil is hot but not smoking, add the chicken and cook, stirring until the chicken is golden brown and cooked through—7 to 10 minutes. Add a couple of large spoonfuls of pesto to the chicken and stir until the chicken is evenly coated. Season with salt and pepper.

When the water boils, add the linguini and cook until just tender, about 5 minutes. Drain into a colander and shake to remove the excess water. Pour into a large shallow bowl and spoon the chicken-pesto sauce on top. Toss vigorously until the sauce is evenly distributed throughout the pasta. Feel free to add more pesto if you think it needs it. Divide among 4 plates and serve.

YIELD: 4 servings

🥫 ADD IT!
The boon companion of pesto is Parmesan cheese, so sprinkle a mess of grated fresh Parmesan over each plate. You can also sauté 2 minced cloves of garlic along with the chicken.

BUTTERNUT SQUASH RAVIOLI

We love using the wonton or egg roll wrappers found in any supermarket as ravioli pasta. They are already dusted with cornstarch, so you only need a filling and water to stick them together. These ravioli are great with Sage Brown Butter Sauce (page 350).

 1 small butternut squash, about 1 pound (450 g)
 ½ teaspoon nutmeg
 2 tablespoons (28 g) butter
 36 wonton wrappers, about 3 inches (7½ cm) square

Peel the butternut, split it in half, and remove the seeds. Cut the squash into 1-inch (2½-cm) chunks and put them into a 2-quart (2-L) pot. Cover the squash with water and bring to a boil, covered. Lower the heat to a gentle boil and cook the squash until tender—about 20 minutes. Drain the squash and put it in a mixing bowl with the nutmeg, the butter, and salt and pepper to taste. Mash until smooth with a potato masher.

Lay out wonton wrappers on a cutting board. Put 1 teaspoon of the squash puree in the center of each. Wet the perimeter of each wrapper with water and top with another wonton skin. Press down on the edges to seal. You can cut the trim off the edges with a round or fluted edge cutter if you wish. Repeat with the remaining wrappers and squash.

To cook fresh pasta, bring 4 quarts (4 L) salted water to a boil, add the pasta, and cook for 3 to 5 minutes, until the pasta is floating. Strain and serve.

YIELD: 4 servings

SWISS CHARD RAVIOLI

We bless whoever discovered the fact that wonton or egg roll wrappers make great ravioli, too. These ravioli are great with a simple marinara sauce and grated Parmesan cheese.

1 bunch Swiss chard
1 cup (250 g) ricotta cheese
2 tablespoons (28 g) butter
36 wonton wrappers

Bring 2 quarts (2 L) salted water to a boil. While the water is heating, prepare the filling. Rinse the chard well. Remove the ribs from the chard and cut up the leaves into thin strips—about ½ inch (1 cm). Boil the chard for 3 to 4 minutes, drain, and immediately rinse under cold water. Squeeze the chard to remove as much water as possible. Chop the chard very fine and put it into a mixing bowl. Add the ricotta and salt and pepper to taste.

Lay out wonton wrappers on a cutting board. Put 1 teaspoon of the chard ricotta mixture in the center of each. Wet the perimeter of each wrapper with water and top with another wonton skin. Press down on the edges to seal. You can cut the trim off the edges with a round or fluted edge cutter if you wish. Repeat with the remaining wrappers and squash.

To cook fresh pasta, bring 4 quarts (4L) salted water to a boil, add the pasta, and cook for 3 to 5 minutes, until the pasta is floating. Strain and serve.

YIELD: 4 servings

RAVIOLI IN SAGE BROWN BUTTER SAUCE

If you can find butternut squash ravioli—we sometimes stumble across them in our local gourmet shop—they are perfect for this recipe. They're also relatively simple to make for yourself, what with the advent of wonton wrappers as ravioli casings. (See Butternut Squash Ravioli recipe, page 348.)

9 ounces (225 g) prepared fresh ravioli
8 tablespoons (115 g) unsalted butter
8 to 10 fresh sage leaves
½ cup (40 g) shaved fresh Parmesan cheese

Bring a large pot of salted water to a boil. Add the ravioli and cook until just tender, about 3 to 4 minutes.

As the water is boiling, heat the butter in a medium-size sauté pan or skillet over moderately high heat. After the butter has melted, add the sage leaves and fry for 3 or 4 minutes, until crisp. Remove the sage from the pan and let it drain on paper towels. Keep an eye on the butter; when it begins to turn brown, which generally takes about 4 minutes, remove from the heat. Season with salt and pepper.

Transfer the ravioli via a slotted spoon to the pan or skillet and gently toss with the sauce. Divide the ravioli among 4 plates. Crumble two sage leaves over each helping, and top with a sprinkling of shaved Parmesan cheese.

YIELD: 4 servings

ADD IT!
You can also stir a teaspoon of fresh lemon juice into the butter sauce after you remove it from the heat.

ZESTY PEARL COUSCOUS

Pearl couscous, also called Israeli couscous, is a bead-size pasta. We like to toast it in oil for just a bit as one does risotto, before adding the water.

1 cup (175 g) pearl couscous
¼ cup (60 ml) Italian dressing
1 tablespoon (4 to 5 g) chopped fresh parsley
2 tablespoons (28 g) butter

In a 1-quart (1-L) pot with a tight-fitting lid, heat 2 tablespoons (30 ml) olive oil over medium heat. Add the couscous and allow to toast, stirring every minute or so, for 4 to 5 minutes. Add the dressing and 1¼ cups (285 ml) water. Cover and cook until the water is absorbed, 12 to 15 minutes. Stir in the parsley and butter.

YIELD: 4 servings as a side dish

GRAINS AND BEANS

Grains and beans can serve as the lead actor or a supporting cast member in a meal. Again, we present basic versions of recipes that can be embellished in myriad ways. A great example of this is risotto. Once you have the basic technique of risotto down, you can easily take the dish in different directions and will eventually be able to closely approximate that dish from your favorite Italian restaurant. We have a number of side-dish ideas and also dishes that make a meal in themselves. We use familiar ingredients, as well as some that may be new to you. We also introduce tastes that may be new but are treasured and central to the cooking of other parts of the world.

BARLEY RISOTTO

It's time to give barley more screen time than an annual turn in the Beef and Barley Soup Variety Hour. Here, we substitute barley for rice in a risotto, with delicious results. It's especially wonderful with Braised Lamb Shanks with Tomatoes and Tapenade (page 263).

> 1 cup (1½ ounces, or 40 g) dried mushrooms, such as porcini
> 1 cup (200 g) pearl barley
> ½ cup (40 g) shredded Parmesan cheese

Bring 3 cups (700 ml) water to a boil and pour over the mushrooms in a bowl. Allow to sit for 15 to 20 minutes. Remove the mushrooms with a slotted spoon, reserving the water, and chop them up. Set aside. Put the reserved liquid through a paper towel set in a sieve to get rid of any grit. Put the strained liquid in a small saucepan over low heat and bring to a simmer. Just keep it hot—do not let it boil.

Heat 2 tablespoons (30 ml) olive oil in a 2-quart (2-L) pot over low-medium heat. Add the barley and sauté for 2 to 3 minutes, stirring to coat the barley thoroughly with the oil. Add one-third of the mushroom liquid and continue cooking the barley, stirring, until the liquid is absorbed. Repeat the process with half of the remaining liquid, and finally with the last of it. When all the liquid is absorbed, season with salt and pepper, stir in the cheese, and serve.

YIELD: 4 servings as a side dish

Couscous with Mint and Carrot

Couscous is, essentially, tiny grains of semolina. A staple of North African cooking, it is frequently served with large platters of meats and vegetables. We particularly enjoy it with lamb.

1 carrot
1 cup (175 g) couscous
2 tablespoons (12 g) chopped fresh mint
2 tablespoons (28 g) butter

Peel the carrot, then shred it on a box grater. Put the carrot shreds into a small pan and add 1 cup (235 ml) of water. Bring the water to a boil and cook for 2 to 3 minutes. While the carrot is cooking, combine the couscous, the mint, and salt and pepper to taste in a small mixing bowl. Pour the carrot shreds and their water over the couscous and cover immediately with plastic wrap. Wait 2 to 3 minutes and fluff the couscous with a fork. Cover it with the plastic again and wait another 5 to 6 minutes. Stir in the butter and serve.

YIELD: 4 servings as a side dish

ROSEMARY COUSCOUS

Instead of mashed potatoes with your next pork roast, try this on for size.

    1 tablespoon (2 g) minced fresh rosemary
    1 cup (175 g) couscous
    1 cup (235 ml) chicken stock or broth
    2 tablespoons (28 g) butter

Combine the rosemary and the couscous, along with salt and pepper to taste, in a small mixing bowl. Bring the chicken stock to a boil and pour it over the couscous. Immediately cover the bowl with plastic wrap. After 2 to 3 minutes, fluff the couscous with a fork, and cover it with the plastic again. After another 5 to 6 minutes, stir in the butter and serve.

YIELD: 4 servings as a side dish

SAFFRON COUSCOUS WITH GOLDEN RAISINS

The world's most expensive spice, saffron just exudes a sense of luxury, much like truffles and foie gras. Fortunately, a little goes a long way. We adore this with grilled butterflied leg of lamb.

    1 pinch saffron
    1 cup (175 g) couscous
    ½ cup (80 g) golden raisins
    2 tablespoons (28 g) butter

Put the saffron in a small saucepan with 1 cup (235 ml) water. Put the couscous into a small mixing bowl. Boil the water and pour it over the couscous. Immediately cover the bowl with plastic wrap. Wait 2 to 3 minutes, fluff the couscous with a fork, and cover it with the plastic again. Wait 5 to 6 minutes, uncover it, and fluff it again with a fork. Stir in the raisins, butter, and salt and pepper to taste.

YIELD: 4 servings as a side dish

DIRTY RICE

This Cajun specialty combines rice with ground chicken or turkey livers and gizzards, plus onions, chicken broth, bacon drippings, green pepper, and garlic. The ground giblets give the rice a "dirty" look . . . but delicious flavor.

½ pound (225 g) chicken giblets
1 cup (160 g) onion, chopped small
2 cups (390 g) medium-grain rice

Chop the giblets and set aside. Heat 2 tablespoons (30 ml) cooking oil in a medium-size sauté pan or skillet over medium-high heat. When the oil is hot, add the giblets and onion. Season with salt and pepper and sauté for 8 to 10 minutes. Set aside.

Heat 1 quart (1 L) water in a 2-quart (2-L) pot with a tight-fitting lid. When the water boils, add 1 teaspoon salt and the rice. Cover, bring to a boil, and then reduce the heat to low and simmer for 20 to 25 minutes, until the water has been absorbed. Remove the rice from the heat and let it sit, covered, for 5 minutes. Fluff the rice with a fork, then stir in the giblet mixture.

YIELD: 6 to 8 servings as a side dish

ADD IT!
Bacon drippings, chopped green peppers, and chopped garlic can all be added to the chicken liver sauté.

RISO VERDE

This is a Latin-American version of the green rice found in other Mediterranean cultures—so called because this dish is cooked with recaito, the Spanish herb base. You can find recaito in most supermarkets and any Latin grocery.

½ cup (80 g) onion, diced small
1 cup (200 g) rice
2 tablespoons (30 g) recaito
2 tablespoons (28 g) butter

Heat 2 tablespoons (30 ml) oil over low heat in a 1-quart (1-L) pot with a tight-fitting lid. Add the onion, cover, and sweat the onion for 8 to 10 minutes, until the onion is soft and translucent. Add the rice, the recaito, and 2 cups (475 ml) water. Cover, bring to a boil, then reduce the heat to low and simmer for 20 to 25 minutes, until the water is absorbed. Remove the rice from the heat and let it sit, covered, for 5 minutes, then fluff in the butter with a fork.

YIELD: 4 servings as a side dish

TOMATO-BRAISED BROWN RICE

Brown rice, which retains the bran and germ of the rice, has a mild nutty flavor and slightly chewier texture than its more highly refined cousin white rice. It's also better for you.

½ cup (60 g) diced celery
1 cup (190 g) medium-grain brown rice
1 cup (235 ml) tomato juice

Heat 1 tablespoon (15 ml) oil in a 1-quart (1-L) saucepan with a tight-fitting lid. Add the celery and cover. Cook on low for 5 to 8 minutes, until the celery has softened. Add the rice, the tomato juice, 1 cup (235 ml) water, and salt and pepper to taste. Cover and bring to a boil, then reduce heat to low and cook for 40 to 45 minutes, until the water is absorbed. Allow the rice to sit, covered, off the heat for a few minutes. If you wish, you may stir in 2 tablespoons (28 g) butter.

YIELD: 4 servings as a side dish

🗋 ADD IT!
Sauté half a small onion, minced, along with the celery.

VERY SIMPLE RISOTTO

This risotto is used as a base for many variations, but it's good on its own, too.

3 cups (700 ml) rich chicken stock
1 cup (200 g) Arborio rice
½ cup (50 g) grated Parmesan cheese

Heat the stock to a simmer. In a 1-quart (1-L) pot, heat 2 tablespoons (30 ml) olive oil over medium-high heat. Add the rice and sauté it in the oil for 4 to 5 minutes, stirring every minute or so. Season with salt and pepper (assuming your stock is not salted). Add 1 ladle of the stock and stir until the rice has absorbed the liquid. Keep adding stock as the liquid is absorbed, 1 ladle at a time, and keep stirring for about 30 minutes. When the rice is done—it should be al dente—and creamy, stir in the cheese.

YIELD: 4 servings as a side dish

ADD IT!
Risotto is yummy with many things added: Our favorites include sautéed onions and mushrooms, and cream.

WILD RICE PANCAKES

Wild rice has a lovely nutty taste, but it isn't really a rice. It's the grains of a marsh grass that grows in the Great Lakes area, and it is frequently harvested by hand, although commercial wild-rice ventures have begun to pop up. These pancakes are great with duck, venison, game hens, or pheasant. They also go well with chicken.

1 cup (160 g) wild rice, washed and cleaned (see note)
1 egg
½ cup (60 g) all-purpose flour

Put the cleaned wild rice in a 2-quart (2-L) pot and add 1 quart (1 L) water. Bring to a boil and cook at a low simmer for 45 minutes to 1 hour, until the rice "bursts" and is tender. You may need to add water to the pot, so check every now and again.

Drain the rice; allow it to cool, and pour it into a mixing bowl. In a small bowl, beat the egg slightly and add it to the rice. Add the flour and salt and pepper to taste and stir everything together. It should form a slightly runny batter, but you may need to add just a bit of water.

Heat ½ cup (120 ml) oil in a sauté pan or skillet over medium heat. Drop spoonfuls of batter into the oil and flatten them with the back of the spoon. Cook for 3 to 4 minutes per side. Drain on paper towels.

YIELD: 4 servings as a side dish

NOTE: *It's important to clean wild rice thoroughly before cooking. Soak the rice in a bowl of cold water for 10 minutes or so, and drain off any debris that rises to the top.*

WILD RICE PILAF

½ cup (80 g) wild rice, washed and cleaned (see note)
1 cup (200 g) white rice
1 pinch saffron
2 tablespoons (28 g) butter

Put the wild rice in a 1-quart (1-L) pot. Add 3 cups (700 ml) water and bring to a boil. Cook at a low simmer for 40 to 45 minutes, adding water if needed, until the rice until the rice "bursts" and is tender. Drain and set aside.

When the wild rice is done, or while it is cooking, heat 2 cups (475 ml) water in a 2-quart (2-L) pot with a tight-fitting lid. Add salt and pepper, the saffron, and the butter. Bring to a boil and add the regular rice. Cover, then reduce the heat to low and simmer for 20 to 25 minutes, until the water is absorbed. Remove the rice from the heat and let it sit, covered, for 5 minutes. Stir in the wild rice.

YIELD: 4 to 6 servings as a side dish

NOTE: *It's important to clean wild rice thoroughly before cooking. Soak the rice in a bowl of cold water for 10 minutes or so, and drain off any debris that rises to the top.*

Fava Beans Stewed in Marinara Sauce

Poor fava beans—ruined for a generation by one line from Hannibal Lecter. And that's too bad, because fava beans are good stuff, as this recipe shows.

> 1 pound (450 g) dried fava beans (large dried lima beans work also)
> 1 medium-size onion
> 2 cups (500 g) marinara sauce

Pick over the beans and put them in a 2-quart (2-L) pot. Cover with water twice the depth of the beans. Bring to a boil, then turn off the heat, cover the beans, and leave them for 1 hour.

Drain the beans, return them to the pot, and re-cover with water by 2 inches. Bring to a boil, reduce the heat, and simmer for 30 to 45 minutes, until al dente. Drain the beans and set them aside.

Put the pot back on low heat and add 2 tablespoons (30 ml) oil. Chop the onion into small pieces and add to the pot. Cook, covered, for 8 to 10 minutes, until the onions are soft and translucent. Add the beans and the marinara sauce. Simmer the beans for 45 minutes, until quite tender.

YIELD: 6 to 8 servings as a side dish

ADD IT!
A couple of minced garlic cloves, of course—and you could add all kinds of herbs: chopped basil, thyme, or rosemary would all be lovely.

STEWED CURRIED LENTILS WITH SAUSAGE

Serve this with a salad and some chewy bread, and you've got a great meal.

- 1 pound (450 g) lentils
- 1 teaspoon Madras curry powder
- 1 pound (450 g) kielbasa or other sausage

Put the lentils in a 2-quart (2-L) pot and add water to cover. Bring to a boil, reduce the heat, and simmer until the lentils are tender, about 30 minutes. Add the curry powder. Slice the sausage into ½-inch (1-cm) slices and add to the pot. Season with salt and pepper to taste and stew for 15 to 20 minutes, adding water if needed. You are looking to barely keep the lentils from going dry.

YIELD: 4 servings

 ADD IT!
You can stew the lentils in chicken stock or tomato juice for a deeper flavor.

Side Dishes

17

Vegetables

For many of us, a three-ingredient recipe actually increases the complexity of how we cook veggies, which are often just steamed or boiled. These recipes can show you how to cook vegetables you may not have tried before, and how to add fresh flair to perennial favorites. Above all, we hope that our recipes will help you regard vegetables as something to be anticipated with gusto, rather than eaten because they're good for you. We tell our kids that it's important to be curious eaters, and this is the place to start.

TURNIPS FRIED WITH APPLES

Try this with Pan Fried Turkey Cutlets (page 170) and Wild Rice Pancakes (page 359).

- 1 pound (450 g) purple-top turnips
- 2 medium-size tart apples, such as Granny Smith
- 1 teaspoon nutmeg

Thoroughly scrub the turnips in cold water. Cut off the stem and root of each turnip, then peel and cut the turnips into ½-inch (1-cm) cubes. Put the turnips in a 1-quart (1-L) pot with enough salted water to cover. Bring the turnips to a boil, then lower the heat and simmer them for 10 minutes, until they are soft, but not quite fully done. Drain.

Peel and core the apples, then cut into ½-inch (1-cm) cubes. Heat ¼ cup (60 ml) vegetable oil in a wide sauté pan or skillet over high heat. When the oil begins to smoke, add the turnips and apples. Season with salt and pepper, add the nutmeg, and sauté for 8 to 10 minutes, until the turnips and apples have browned.

YIELD: 4 servings

🫙 ADD IT!
Peel and slice an onion into ½-inch (1-cm) rings and add it to the pan.

Roasted Acorn Squash

Probably one of the best things we did as kids was to tap our neighbor's grove of sugar maples each winter. We generally collected enough sap to supply us with maple syrup for the entire year. Maple syrup is wonderful stuff, and it pairs beautifully with autumn vegetables such as squashes and turnips.

2 acorn squashes
¼ cup (60 ml) maple syrup
2 teaspoons rubbed (ground) sage
4 tablespoons (55 g) butter

Preheat the oven to 325°F (170°C, gas mark 3).

Split the squashes in half and scoop out the seeds. Place them on a baking sheet, cupped side up.

Divide the remaining ingredients evenly among the four pieces and put them in the middle of the hollowed-out cups. Season each piece with salt and pepper to taste.

Roast for 45 to 50 minutes, until the squash is easily pieced by a paring knife.

YIELD: 4 servings

STUFFED ACORN SQUASH

Like mushrooms, a halved squash's spot-on impersonation of a bowl just begs for it to be stuffed. Who are we to argue?

> 2 acorn squash
> 14 ounces (400 g) stuffing mix
> 2 cups (475 ml) chicken broth
> 4 tablespoons (55 g) butter

Split the squash in half and scoop out the seeds. Set the squash in the top of a large steamer over boiling water and cook, covered, for 12 to 15 minutes, until just getting tender. Remove the squash from the steamer and set aside. Prepare the stuffing mix using the chicken stock and butter.

Preheat the oven to 350°F (180°C, gas mark 4).

Put the squash on a baking sheet and pile the stuffing into the hollows. Bake for 20 to 25 minutes.

YIELD: 4 servings

ADD IT!
Another popular stuffing is a cup (165 g) cooked wild rice per squash half.

FRIED BABY ARTICHOKES

We could eat these until the cows came home. Frankly, we wouldn't care if the cows ever did come home as long as the artichokes didn't run out.

3 lemons
12 baby artichokes
½ cup (40 g) shaved Parmesan cheese

Prepare a bowl of acidulated water by squeezing 1 of the lemons into 2 quarts (2 L) water. Trim the tops and stems of the artichokes; remove the tough outer leaves and split the artichokes in half lengthwise. Remove the choke from each artichoke with a melon baller and drop it into the acidulated water.

Heat ½ inch (1 cm) olive oil in a wide sauté pan or skillet to 375°F (190°C), using a thermometer to test.

Remove the artichokes from the water and pat them dry on a kitchen towel. Fry the artichokes for 5 to 7 minutes, until golden brown and soft. Drain on paper towels, sprinkle with salt and pepper, squeeze lemon juice over them, and scatter the Parmesan shavings on top. Cut the remaining lemon into wedges and serve as a garnish with the artichokes.

YIELD: 4 servings

ARTICHOKE HEART CASSEROLE

We'll take artichokes any way we can get them, but this is one of our favorites.

- 20 ounces (560 g) frozen artichoke hearts, thawed
- 2 cups (230 g) seasoned dried bread crumbs
- 2 lemons
- 8 tablespoons (115 g) butter

Preheat the oven to 350°F (180°C, gas mark 4).

Toss together the artichoke hearts, half of the crumbs, and the juice of the lemons in a bowl. Put the mixture into a 1- to 2-quart (1- to 2-L) shallow baking dish and season with salt and pepper. Top with the remaining crumbs. Dot with the butter and bake for 25 to 30 minutes, until golden brown.

YIELD: 6 to 8 servings

 ADD IT!
Sprinkle shaved fresh Parmesan cheese on the casserole. You can also put a little chicken stock in the bottom of the casserole dish if you'd like to add moisture.

ASPARAGUS WITH GARLIC AND PARSLEY

In the words of Ogden Nash, many people think that "parsley is gharsley." Perhaps that's because they've only made its acquaintance dressing up a dinner plate at a restaurant. Parsley deserves a better rap.

- **1 tablespoon (10 g) minced garlic**
- **2 tablespoons (8 g) minced parsley**
- 4 tablespoons (55 g) butter
- **1 pound (450 g) asparagus**

Mix the garlic, parsley, and butter in a small pan and melt over low heat. Set aside.

Trim the asparagus, either by peeling the stalk at the woody end, or by snapping the stalks off at the point where they seem to want to snap. Heat 1 to 2 inches (2½ to 5 cm) water in a pan or skillet large enough to accommodate the asparagus in one layer. Salt the water, and when it comes to a boil, put the asparagus in the pan. Cook for 2 to 3 minutes, until the asparagus is tender but still crisp. Drain the asparagus and toss lightly with the butter mixture, until it has coated the asparagus.

YIELD: 4 servings

LEMON ANCHOVY ASPARAGUS

Anchovies are one of those misunderstood denizens of our kitchens. On their own, they can be a bit strong—although there are plenty of folks who like them straight up. When melded with other ingredients and used with a subtle touch, however, anchovies add a depth of flavor vital to many dishes.

2 anchovy fillets
4 tablespoons (55 g) butter, softened
1 lemon
1 pound (450 g) asparagus

Mince the anchovies, then mash them with the side of a chef's knife. Combine the butter, juice of the lemon and anchovy paste in a bowl and mix thoroughly.

Trim the asparagus, either by peeling the stalk at the woody end, or by snapping the stalks off at the point where they seem to want to snap. Heat 1 to 2 inches (2½ to 5 cm) water in a pan large enough to accommodate the asparagus in one layer. Salt the water, and when it comes to a boil, put the asparagus in the pan. Cook for 2 to 3 minutes, until the asparagus is tender but still crisp.

Drain the asparagus and toss lightly with the butter mixture, until the butter has melted and coated the asparagus.

YIELD: 4 servings

ASPARAGUS WITH ONIONS AND ORANGE BUTTER

The traditional citrus for asparagus is lemon, but this sauce provides a delicious twist. This is great with grilled steaks or lamb.

1 pound (450 g) asparagus
1 large onion
¼ cup (60 ml) orange juice
3 tablespoons (43 g) butter

Remove the woody ends of the asparagus stems. Peel the onion and slice it thin. Heat 2 tablespoons (30 ml) olive oil in a medium-size sauté pan or skillet over medium-high heat. Add the onion and sauté for 5 to 6 minutes, stirring, until softened and browned a bit. Season with salt and pepper and set aside.

In a small saucepan, combine the orange juice and butter and cook over low heat until just melted together. Set aside. Bring a large pot of water to a boil. Salt the water and add the asparagus. Cook for 3 to 4 minutes, then drain. Put the asparagus on a platter, top with the onions, and pour the butter sauce over all.

YIELD: 4 servings

BEETS WITH ORANGE HORSERADISH GLAZE

Beets are another orphaned vegetable that we love. They're sweet, they adapt well to many cooking styles, and best of all, they have a really delightful color. They do stain clothing if you're not careful.

2 pounds (900 g) beets
3 tablespoons (45 ml) orange juice concentrate, thawed
2 tablespoons (30 g) prepared horseradish
3 tablespoons (43 g) butter

Wash the beets in cold water and scrub clean. Nip the root ends off and cut off the tops if there are any (save them to boil as a separate vegetable if you like). Put the beets in a 2-quart (2-L) pot, cover with water, and bring to a boil over high heat. Reduce the heat to medium and cook at a gentle boil for about 45 minutes, until the beets are tender when pierced by a paring knife. Drain the beets and cool.

When the beets are cool enough to handle, trim the stem area and, using your fingers, slip and rub off the skin. Rinse the beets and slice or cube them as you like. In a wide sauté pan or skillet combine the remaining ingredients over medium heat.

When the butter melts, add the beets and salt and pepper to taste. Toss to coat the beets and heat them through.

YIELD: 4 to 6 servings

BEETS WITH TARRAGON

2 pounds (900 g) beets
2 tablespoons (2 g) chopped fresh tarragon
¼ cup (60 ml) red wine vinegar
4 tablespoons (55 g) butter

Wash the beets in cold water and scrub clean. Nip the root ends off and cut off the tops if there are any (save them to boil as a separate vegetable if you like). Put the beets in a 2-quart (2-L) pot, cover with water, and bring to a boil over high heat. Reduce the heat to medium and cook at a gentle boil for about 45 minutes, until the beets are tender when pierced by a paring knife. Drain the beets and cool.

When the beets are cool enough to handle, trim the stem area and, using your fingers, slip and rub off the skin. Rinse the beets and then slice or cube them, as you like.

In a wide sauté pan or skillet, combine the remaining ingredients over medium heat. When the butter melts, add the beets and salt and pepper to taste. Toss to coat the beets and heat them through.

YIELD: 4 to 6 servings

CREAMED GOLDEN BEETS

Golden beets are a great way to sneak these veggies past the Suspicious Food Patrol. Everybody knows beets are red, right?

2 pounds (900 g) golden beets
2 tablespoons (28 g) butter
2 tablespoons (15 g) all-purpose flour
2 cups (475 ml) milk

Wash and thoroughly scrub the beets in cold water. Nip the root ends off and cut off the tops if there are any (save them to boil as a separate vegetable if you like). Put the beets in a 2-quart (2-L) pot, cover with water, and bring to a boil over high heat. Reduce the heat to medium and cook at a gentle boil for about 45 minutes, until the beets are tender when pierced by a paring knife. Drain the beets and cool. When the beets are cool enough to handle, trim the stem area and, using your fingers, slip and rub off the skin. Rinse the beets and slice them into rounds.

Preheat the oven to 350°F (180°C, gas mark 4).

While the beets are cooling, make the white sauce: Combine the butter and flour in a 1-quart (1-L) saucepan over low heat, until the butter melts and a thick paste (called a roux) is formed. Whisk in the milk, turn the heat to high, and stir until the sauce comes to a boil and thickens. Season with salt and pepper.

Combine the beet slices and the white sauce in a casserole, then bake for 25 to 30 minutes until the top is a bit browned and the sauce is bubbling.

YIELD: 6 to 8 servings

BROCCOLI WITH LEMON AND GARLIC

Here's a nice way to add zip to your midweek dinner without provoking cries of "What's THAT?" from the kids.

4 cups (280 g) broccoli florets
1 tablespoon (10 g) minced garlic
2 tablespoons (30 ml) lemon juice
4 tablespoons (55 g) butter

Put 2 quarts (2 L) salted water in a 4-quart (4-L) pot and bring to a boil. In a small saucepan heat the garlic, lemon juice, and butter over low heat, until the butter is melted. Set aside. When the water boils, drop in the broccoli florets and cook them for 4 to 5 minutes, until cooked through, but still crisp. Drain the broccoli and toss with the sauce in a large bowl.

YIELD: 4 servings

CREAMY SESAME BROCCOLI

¼ cup (30 g) sesame seeds
1 bunch broccoli
1 cup (235 ml) sour cream

Put the sesame seeds in a small sauté pan or skillet and cook them over medium heat, stirring often, until toasted, 8 to 10 minutes. Set them aside. Cut the stem off the broccoli and cut the crown into florets. Bring a large pot of salted water to a boil and add the broccoli. Cook for 4 to 5 minutes, drain, and put the broccoli into a mixing bowl. Add the sour cream, the sesame seeds, and salt and pepper to taste. Mix well to coat the broccoli.

YIELD: 4 servings

BROCCOLI WITH ORANGE HOLLANDAISE

A little different, a bit more subtle than the classic, but really good.

- **1 bunch broccoli**
- 8 tablespoons (115 g) butter
- **2 tablespoons (30 ml) frozen orange juice concentrate, thawed**
- **1 egg yolk**

Cut the stem off the broccoli and cut the crown into florets.

Melt the butter over low heat in a small pan or the microwave. Whisk the orange juice concentrate and the egg yolk in a metal mixing bowl.

Heat 2 cups (475 ml) water to a simmer in a small saucepan. Put the mixing bowl on the pan and whisk until the egg mixture has lightened and thickened and streaks of the bowl are showing as you whisk. Remove the bowl from the heat and slowly whisk in the melted butter, pouring it into the bowl in a thin stream as you whisk, until a thick yellow sauce forms. Season to taste with salt and pepper. Set aside in a warm, but not hot, place.

Fill a 4-quart (4-L) pot half full of water and bring to a boil over high heat. Salt the water and drop in the broccoli. Cook, uncovered, for 4 to 5 minutes, then drain. Top with the hollandaise.

YIELD: 4 to 6 servings

BRUSSELS SPROUTS WITH CREAM AND CHESTNUTS

We didn't discover brussels sprouts until we were adults, largely because our mother refused to serve them. She was apparently traumatized as a young child by watery, overboiled sprouts and hasn't yet recovered. We think this recipe might help.

5 to 8 chestnuts
1 pound (450 g) brussels sprouts
1 cup (235 ml) heavy cream

Preheat the oven to 400°F (200°C, gas mark 6).

In a small pan bring 2 cups (475 ml) water to a boil. Drop in the chestnuts and blanch them for 5 minutes. Drain and cut an X with the tip of a paring knife on each nut. Place them on a small baking sheet and bake for 10 to 15 minutes. The X will peel back a bit when the chestnuts are done. Allow to cool, then shell the nuts and chop them coarsely. (You can also buy chestnuts, already peeled, in a jar. We won't tell.) Trim the stems of the brussels sprouts and remove any damaged outer leaves. With a paring knife make a small X on the bottom of each stem. Heat 2 quarts (2 L) water to a boil in a 4-quart (4-L) pot. Salt the water and cook the brussels sprouts for 5 to 8 minutes, until they can be pierced with a paring knife but are still firm. As the sprouts cook, prepare a bowl of ice water. Drain and immediately plunge the sprouts into the ice water. Drain again and cut each sprout in half, lengthwise. Set them aside.

Heat the cream in a wide sauté pan or skillet and season with salt and pepper. Reduce the cream by a third, then add the sprouts and the chestnuts. Cook until the sprouts are heated through and are coated with the cream and chestnuts.

YIELD: 4 servings

ADD IT!
Sprinkle cooked, crumbled bacon over the top of the dish before serving.

Brussels Sprouts with Bacon and Vinegar

2 pounds (900 g) brussels sprouts
4 strips bacon, cooked
¼ cup (60 ml) red wine vinegar
4 tablespoons (55 g) butter

Trim the stems of the brussels sprouts and remove any damaged outer leaves. With a paring knife make a small X on the bottom of each stem. Heat 2 quarts (2 L) water to a boil in a 4-quart (4-L) pot. Salt the water and cook the brussels sprouts for 5 to 8 minutes, until they can be pierced with a paring knife but are still firm. As the sprouts cook, prepare a bowl of ice water. Drain and immediately plunge the sprouts into the ice water. Drain again and cut each sprout in half, lengthwise. Set them aside.

Bring another 2 quarts (2 L) water to a boil. While the water is heating, chop the bacon and mix it with the vinegar in a wide sauté pan or skillet. Heat over medium heat until the vinegar boils. Whisk in the butter, 1 tablespoon (15 g) at a time, to form a smooth sauce. Be sure to monitor the heat and remove as soon as the last of the butter is melted, to make sure the sauce doesn't break. Keep the sauce warm. When the water boils, drop the brussels sprouts in for 2 minutes to reheat, then drain. Put the drained sprouts in the pan with the sauce, toss to coat, and season with salt and pepper to taste.

YIELD: 6 servings

BUTTERNUT SQUASH PUREE

A classic New England autumn dish. Serve with Roast Pork with Sage and Rosemary (page 228) and round it off with baked apples.

> 1 butternut squash, about 2 pounds (900 g)
> ½ cup (110 g) brown sugar, packed
> 2 teaspoons cinnamon
> 4 tablespoons (55 g) butter

Peel the squash, split it in half, and scoop out the seeds, then cut it into 2-inch (5-cm) cubes. Put the squash in a 2-quart (2-L) pot, cover it with water and bring to a boil. Cook for 15 to 20 minutes, until the squash is easily pierced with a knife.

Drain the squash and put it into a large bowl along with the brown sugar, cinnamon, butter, and salt and pepper to taste. Mash until the squash is smooth and the ingredients are well mixed.

YIELD: 6 to 8 servings

CURRIED ROASTED BUTTERNUT SQUASH WITH SUNFLOWER SEEDS

An alternative to regular roasted squash.

> 1 butternut squash, about 2 pounds (900 g)
> 2 tablespoons (15 g) curry powder
> ¼ cup (55 g) toasted sunflower seeds

To toast the seeds: Preheat the oven to 350°F (180°C, gas mark 4). Spread the seeds in a single layer on a shallow baking sheet and bake until golden brown, 5 to 10 minutes.

While the seeds are toasting, peel the squash and scoop out the seeds, then cut it into ½-inch (5-cm) cubes. Toss the squash with ½ cup (120 ml) olive oil, the curry powder, and salt and pepper to taste in a mixing bowl. Spread out on a baking sheet and roast in the oven for 30 minutes, until the squash is soft and nicely browned. Scatter the sunflower seeds over the squash before serving.

YIELD: 6 to 8 servings

BRAISED RED CABBAGE

Cabbage is a quintessential fall-harvest vegetable, which is why you find it in so many of the simmering, long-cooking preparations typical of the cooler months. This dish is wonderful with sausages, roast pork, chicken, and duck.

1 small head red cabbage
2 Granny Smith apples
½ cup (120 ml) red wine vinegar
8 tablespoons (115 g) butter

Cut the cabbage in half lengthwise, then halve each side lengthwise again so that each quarter has part of the core at its base. Cut out the core, then thinly shred the cabbage. Put the cabbage in a pot large enough to comfortably hold it.

Peel and core the apples and cut them into small cubes. Add the apple and the vinegar, along with a cup (235 ml) or so of water, to the cabbage. Cover the pot and simmer over medium-low heat for 45 minutes, stirring every 10 minutes and adding a bit more water if needed. The cabbage should have reduced in volume considerably and be quite soft and a paler red. Season the cabbage with salt and pepper and stir in the butter until melted.

YIELD: 6 to 8 servings

🧂 ADD IT!
Add a pinch of nutmeg to the cabbage as it simmers.

CABBAGE WITH CARAWAY AND BACON

¼ pound (115 g) bacon
1 medium head green cabbage
2 tablespoons (15 g) caraway seeds

Dice the bacon into ½-inch (1-cm) pieces. Put the bacon into a 4-quart (4-L) pot and cook over medium heat until the bacon is rendered and crispy.

Core the cabbage, thinly shred it, and add it to the bacon. Add the caraway seeds, 1 cup (235 ml) water, and salt and pepper to taste. Reduce the heat to low. Cover and cook for 45 minutes, stirring every 10 minutes, until the cabbage is limp and slightly caramelized and has reduced in volume by one-half. You can add a cup (235 ml) or so of water during the cooking if needed.

YIELD: 6 to 8 servings

ADD IT!
Some folks like this cabbage with malt vinegar sprinkled over it.

MAPLE-GLAZED CARROTS

You'd think carrots would be sweet enough, but maple syrup takes them to the next level. And by "maple syrup," we mean the real stuff—it is worth the expense!

- 1 pound (450 g) carrots
- ½ cup (120 ml) maple syrup
- 1 teaspoon cinnamon
- 2 tablespoons (28 g) butter

Peel the carrots and cut them into rounds about 1 inch (2½ cm) in length. Put the carrots in a 1-quart (1-L) pot and cover with salted water. Bring to a boil and cook until the carrots are tender, 15 to 20 minutes.

While the carrots are cooking, combine the remaining ingredients in a wide sauté pan or skillet. Cook over medium heat until the butter melts, then set aside. Drain the cooked carrots and put them in the pan. Season to taste with salt and pepper. Toss the carrots to coat them with the sauce, then sauté over medium heat for 5 to 6 minutes, until the glaze really sticks to the carrots.

YIELD: 6 servings

ORANGE CARROTS

Is it the attraction of color? We don't know, but the fact remains that carrots and oranges are great flavor buddies.

> **1 pound (450 g) carrots**
> **2 oranges**
> **½ teaspoon nutmeg**
> 2 tablespoons (28 g) butter

Peel the carrots and cut them the way you prefer. We like a roll cut, where you cut about an inch (2½ cm) from the bottom on the diagonal, roll the carrot a quarter turn, and repeat, until you run out of carrot. Put the carrots in a 1-quart (1-L) pot and cover with salted water. Bring to a boil and cook at a low boil until just tender, about 15 minutes.

While the carrots are cooking, peel and finely mince the zest from one of the oranges. Squeeze the juice from both oranges and combine the zest, juice, nutmeg, and butter in a wide sauté pan or skillet over low heat until the butter is melted. Drain the carrots and put them into the pan, tossing to coat with the sauce. Season with salt and pepper to taste.

YIELD: 6 to 8 servings

MINTED BABY CARROTS

Here's a dish to serve with that Easter lamb or other "harbinger of spring"-type dish. You can use the baby carrots that come in a bag from the supermarket, but we have our suspicions about those. Are they really baby carrots, or regular carrots cut into lengths and then turned on a carrot lathe? If you can get real baby carrots—so tender they don't need peeling—from your local farm stand, farmers' market, or even your own garden, then this dish will really sing.

- **1 pound (450 g) baby carrots**
- 4 tablespoons (55 g) butter
- **2 tablespoons (10 g) minced shallot**
- **2 tablespoons (12 g) minced fresh mint**

Trim the root end of the carrots and snip off the tops, leaving about ¼ inch (½ cm) of green. Wash the carrots well, scrubbing with a vegetable brush. Put the carrots in a 1-quart (1-L) pot, cover with water, salt lightly, and bring to a boil. Cook the carrots at a low boil for 8 to 10 minutes, until they are just tender.

While the carrots are cooking, combine the butter and shallot in a wide sauté pan or skillet. Cook over medium-low heat for 5 to 6 minutes until the shallot has softened and become translucent. Drain the carrots, add them to the pan, and season with salt and pepper. Add the mint and toss to coat the carrots.

YIELD: 4 to 6 servings

Thyme-Baked Carrots

If you are mentally whimpering at the thought of dumping one more bag of frozen vegetables into one more pot of water, stop. Take a deep breath. And then make these. No water—just a lovely baking dish that you can put in the oven and forget about.

- **1 pound (450 g) carrots**
- **1 cup (235 ml) chicken stock or broth**
- **2 tablespoons (5 g) chopped fresh thyme**
- 2 tablespoons (28 g) butter

Preheat the oven to 350°F (180°C, gas mark 4).

Peel the carrots and cut them into sticks about ¼ x 3 inches (½ x 7½ cm). Lay the carrots in a shallow baking dish and pour the stock over them. Sprinkle the thyme over the carrots, season with salt and pepper, and dot with butter. Bake for 35 to 40 minutes, until the stock is absorbed and the carrots are soft.

YIELD: 4 servings

CAULIFLOWER AU GRATIN

We have found that if you disguise cauliflower with cheese and cream, many cauliflower haters won't realize what it is until they've been betrayed into saying something like, "These potatoes are very good!" After that, they're trapped.

- 1 head cauliflower
- 1 cup (235 ml) heavy cream
- 1 cup (110 g) shredded cheddar cheese

Remove the core of the cauliflower and discard. Cut into small florets. Put the florets in a 2-quart (2-L) pot, cover with water, and season with salt. Bring to a boil and cook for 6 to 8 minutes, until the cauliflower is tender. Drain the cauliflower and put it into a 1-quart (1-L) gratin dish.

Preheat the oven to 350°F (180°C, gas mark 4).

In a small saucepan, heat the cream to a simmer and add the cheese, stirring until it is melted. Season with salt and pepper. Pour the sauce over the cauliflower and bake for 15 to 20 minutes, until bubbling and golden brown on top.

YIELD: 6 servings

ADD IT!
Sprinkle buttered bread crumbs on top for a crunchy crust. A teaspoon of chopped fresh thyme in the crumbs would taste good, too.

CAULIFLOWER WITH GARLIC AND BREAD CRUMBS

This dish is about the farthest thing imaginable from the watery, overcooked vegetable of cafeteria legend.

1 head cauliflower
¼ cup (60 ml) olive oil
3 cloves garlic, peeled
½ cup (60 g) seasoned dried bread crumbs

Core the cauliflower and cut it into florets. Put the cauliflower into a 2-quart (2-L) pot, season with salt, and cover with water. Bring to a boil and cook for 4 to 5 minutes, then drain.

While the cauliflower is cooking, prepare the garlic: Slice the garlic cloves thin. Heat ¼ cup (60 ml) olive oil in a wide sauté pan or skillet over medium-high heat. When the oil starts to smoke, add the garlic.

Sauté the garlic for a minute, add the cauliflower, and toss to coat with the oil. Season with salt and pepper, then sprinkle the crumbs into the pan and toss to coat the cauliflower (the crumbs will not fully cover the cauliflower). Continue to sauté for 4 to 5 minutes, until the cauliflower is browned.

YIELD: 6 servings

ADD IT!

Cook up a pot of ribbon pasta of some sort, and toss it with this cauliflower recipe. Sprinkle with grated Parmesan cheese and freshly ground black pepper for a great quick dinner.

CELERY ROOT CHIPS

Celery root is also known as celeriac—they're knobbly and prehistoric-looking root balls found in the produce section. These are the sort of thing that you keep nibbling until you notice with guilty astonishment that the bowl is quite empty. Parsnip chips are equally addictive.

Equipment note: You will need a deep-fat fryer, or at least a sauté pan or skillet with an inch of oil. You can use a thermometer on the pan, but the fryer is much easier, because it regulates the heat. Because of the relatively high sugar content in celery root, we fry them at a slightly lower temperature than we would potatoes.

>   1 medium celery root, about 1 pound (450 g)
>   1 lemon
>   2 tablespoons (8 g) chopped fresh parsley

Heat the fryer to 325°F (170°C).

Peel and slice the celery root very thin. Fry, in batches, until crisp. Drain on paper towels and season with salt and pepper. Squeeze lemon wedges over them and sprinkle with parsley.

YIELD: 4 servings

CELERY ROOT PUREE

Celery root is such a great thing to eat because it's so unexpected—this wonderful subtle taste from a gnarled ball of roots. A puree makes a sophisticated side dish to many pork, poultry, game, and lamb recipes.

1 large celery root, about 2 pounds (900 g)
1 cup (235 ml) heavy cream
1 teaspoon nutmeg

Thoroughly wash the celery root; peel and cut it into 2-inch (5-cm) cubes. Put the cubes into a 2-quart (2-L) pot, cover with water, and bring to a boil over high heat. Reduce the heat to medium and cook at a low boil for 30 to 40 minutes, until the celery root is soft.

Drain the celery root and put it into a mixing bowl, along with the cream and nutmeg. Season with salt and pepper to taste (remember, celery root is pretty salty on its own). Mash well with a potato masher.

YIELD: 4 to 6 servings

CORN SAUTÉED WITH RED PEPPERS

Working on the local farm, we always knew which field of corn was being picked, presenting a philosophical question: If a ear of corn is filched in an empty field, will anybody miss it?

1 medium-size red pepper
4 tablespoons (55 g) butter
1 pound (450 g) frozen corn kernels, thawed,
    or the kernels cut from 6 ears of blanched corn
2 tablespoons (5 g) minced fresh basil

Core the pepper and remove the seeds. Cut out the ribs and cut the pepper into small (¼-inch, or ½-cm) dice. Heat the butter in a wide sauté pan or skillet over medium-high. When the butter melts, add the red pepper and sauté for 1 to 2 minutes. Add the corn, basil, and salt and pepper to taste. Sauté, tossing often, for 3 to 4 minutes.

YIELD: 6 to 8 servings

NOTE: *This is great with Flank Steak with Peppers and Onions (page 191).*

LIME-GARLIC ROASTED CORN

What a terrific burst of flavor lime and garlic impart to what is already an incredibly tooth-some vegetable! Wait until the corn is at its seasonal height and have a grilling fiesta with the corn, marinated flank steak, and grilled crusty bread. Don't forget the fresh sliced tomatoes to go with it.

4 ears of corn
1 lime
1 tablespoon (10 g) minced garlic
2 tablespoons (28 g) butter

Soak the corn, with the husk on, for 30 to 40 minutes in cold water. Prepare a grill.

Remove some of the outer layer of husk from each ear, then peel the husk down halfway and remove the silk. Peel and finely mince the zest from the lime, then squeeze the juice.

In a small pot, melt the butter with the lime zest, lime juice, and garlic, along with salt and pepper to taste. Brush each ear liberally with the butter mixture and close up the husk. Grill the ears for about 10 minutes, turning so all sides are cooked. Don't worry if the husks char some, or if the kernels get a bit scorched.

YIELD: 4 servings

STEWED CORN WITH ANCHO CHILES

Our supermarket has a big display of various chiles, both dried and fresh, including anchos. Ancho chiles are dried poblano chiles and have a smoky, low-heat flavor.

> 1 pound (450 g) frozen corn kernels, thawed
> 2 ancho chiles
> 2 tablespoons (2 g) chopped fresh cilantro
> 2 tablespoons (28 g) butter

Put the corn in a 1-quart (1-L) pot and add water to cover. Remove the stem and seeds from the chiles and break them up into the pot. Salt and pepper to taste, then cover and cook over medium heat for 20 to 25 minutes, until the peppers have kind of melted into the corn and most of the water is gone. Stir in the cilantro and butter.

YIELD: 6 to 8 servings

ADD IT!
Add a can of chopped tomatoes with pepper to the stewing corn.

LEMON-TAHINI EGGPLANT

Try this with the Broiled Lamb Chops and Tomatoes (page 264).

- 1 large eggplant
- 3 cloves minced garlic
- ½ cup (120 ml) lemon-tahini dressing (see note)

Preheat oven to 400°F (200°C, gas mark 6).

Peel the eggplant and cut it into ½-inch (1-cm) cubes. Toss the eggplant with ½ cup (120 ml) olive oil and the garlic, while seasoning with salt and pepper. Spread the eggplant out on a baking sheet and roast for 15 to 20 minutes, until it is soft but still holds its shape. Toss with the lemon-tahini dressing in a large bowl.

YIELD: 4 servings

NOTE: *To make a cup of your own dressing, blend the juice of 2 lemons, ¼ cup (60 g) tahini, ½ cup (120 ml) olive oil, 1 teaspoon minced garlic, and salt and pepper to taste in a blender until smooth.*

EGGPLANT BRAISED WITH TOMATO AND GARLIC

This is also great tossed with the pasta of your choice, sprinkled with a little shaved Parmesan cheese.

    1 large eggplant
    1 can (14 ounces, 400 g) diced tomatoes
    2 tablespoons (20 g) minced garlic

Peel and cut the eggplant into ½-inch (1-cm) cubes. Put them into a 2-quart (2-L) pot with a tight-fitting cover. Mix in the tomato and garlic and season with salt and pepper. Cook over medium-low heat for 30 minutes, until the eggplant is soft but not falling apart.

YIELD: 6 servings

ADD IT!
Add a handful of chopped fresh basil to the pot for extra zip.

Braised Endive with Stilton

Endive takes wonderfully to braising, losing some of its bitterness and acquiring a nutty taste. This is an elegant dish that would pair well with a festive roast beef dinner.

4 heads Belgian endive
2 cups (475 ml) chicken stock or broth
1 cup (120 g) Stilton cheese, crumbled

Preheat the oven to 350°F (180°C, gas mark 4).

Split the endives lengthwise and put them in a shallow baking dish that accommodates them in one layer. Pour the broth over them, season with salt and pepper, and bake for 30 minutes. Sprinkle the Stilton over the endive and continue baking for another 30 minutes.

YIELD: 4 servings

Sautéed Escarole

Escarole, another member of the endive family, is one of those slightly bitter greens that can punch up a salad when used in moderation. It's also delicious in soups or as a side dish on its own.

1 small head escarole
1 tablespoon (10 g) minced garlic
2 tablespoons (17 g) capers, drained

Remove the core from the escarole and tear into pieces 1 to 2 inches (2½ to 5 cm) large. Wash well and spin-dry. Heat 2 tablespoons (30 ml) olive oil in a wide sauté pan or skillet over high heat. When the oil is hot but not quite smoking, add the escarole. Season with salt and pepper, add the garlic and capers, and sauté, tossing often, until the escarole wilts, about 4 to 5 minutes.

YIELD: 4 to 6 servings

Fiddleheads

Fiddlehead ferns are one of the first gifts of spring in the northern woods—we first ran across them as kids. They are increasingly available in supermarkets on a strictly seasonal basis. If you find them, dig in. There are canned fiddleheads, but don't bother with those.

1 pound (450 g) fiddleheads
4 tablespoons (55 g) butter
2 tablespoons (20 g) minced shallot
¼ cup (60 ml) red wine vinegar

Trim the ends of the fiddleheads. Heat 1 quart (1 L) salted water to a boil in a 2-quart (2-L) pot and add the fiddleheads. Cook at a rolling boil for 6 to 8 minutes, then drain.

While the fiddleheads are cooking, melt the butter in a medium-size sauté pan or skillet and add the shallot. Cook over medium heat until the shallot is softened, 4 to 5 minutes. Add the vinegar and salt and pepper to taste. Add the drained fiddleheads and cook for 2 to 3 minutes, tossing to coat them with the butter sauce.

YIELD: 4 to 6 servings

GREEN BEANS WITH CREAM AND MINT

Another good springtime dish—try serving this with lamb!

- 1 pound (450 g) green beans
- 1 cup (235 ml) heavy cream
- 2 tablespoons (12 g) chopped fresh mint

Prepare a bowl of ice water.

Trim the beans. Heat 2 quarts (2 L) salted water in a 4-quart (4-L) pot. When it is at a full boil, cook the beans, in batches of about ⅓ pound (150 g) until just cooked. This will give the beans room and allow the water to return to a boil quickly. Test a bean after 8 minutes. It is done when it does not crunch but squeaks against the tooth. Immediately plunge the cooked beans into cold water.

Put the cream in a wide sauté pan or skillet and season with salt and pepper. Heat to a boil and reduce by a third. Add the beans and mint. Cook until the beans are heated through and are coated with the cream.

YIELD: 4 servings

GREEN BEANS WITH DILL

1 pound (450 g) green beans
4 tablespoons (55 g) butter
2 tablespoons (4 g) chopped fresh dill
2 tablespoons (30 ml) sherry vinegar

Prepare a bowl of ice water.

Trim the beans. Heat 2 quarts (2 L) salted water in a 4-quart (4-L) pot. When it is at a full boil, cook the beans, in batches of about ⅓ pound (150 g) until just cooked. This will give the beans room and allow the water to return to a boil quickly. Test a bean after 8 minutes. It is done when it does not crunch but squeaks against the tooth. Immediately plunge the cooked beans into cold water.

In a wide sauté pan or skillet heat 1 cup (235 ml) water to a boil. Season with salt and pepper. Whisk in the butter and vinegar, not allowing the water to boil again. Add the dill and beans and allow them to heat through. Drain and serve.

YIELD: 4 servings

Green Beans with Lemon and Almonds

In this recipe we use a technique called beurre monté, which allows the beans to be finished with butter without becoming greasy.

1 pound (450 g) green beans
1 lemon
4 tablespoons (55 g) butter
½ cup (60 g) toasted sliced almonds

Prepare a bowl of ice water.

Trim the beans. Heat 2 quarts (2 L) salted water in a 4-quart (4-L) pot. When it is at a full boil, cook the beans, in batches of about ⅓ pound (150 g) until just cooked. This will give the beans room and allow the water to return to a boil quickly. Test a bean after 8 minutes. It is done when it does not crunch but squeaks against the tooth. Immediately plunge the cooked beans into cold water. In a wide sauté pan or skillet heat 2 cups (475 ml) water over high heat until it boils. Cut the butter into bits and whisk into the water, not allowing it to boil again. Squeeze the lemon juice into to the pan, then season the sauce with salt and pepper. Add the beans and reheat them in the sauce. Drain the beans and sprinkle almonds over them to serve.

YIELD: 4 servings

LONG-SIMMERED KALE

Kale is another of those leafy green vegetables that the FDA recommends we eat in bales, but we somehow never do. Perhaps this dish—great with a pot roast—will rectify the situation.

> 1 bunch kale
> ¼ pound (115 g) salt pork, diced
> ¼ cup (60 ml) red wine vinegar

Remove the stems and ribs from the kale and chop it roughly. Cut the pork into small cubes. Put all the ingredients, plus some pepper, into a large pot, cover with water, and simmer for 1½ to 2 hours. The kale should be quite soft. Serve in bowls with some of the cooking liquid.

YIELD: 4 to 6 servings

🥫 ADD IT!
Substitute chicken stock for the water.

CREAMED KOHLRABI

Kohlrabi looks somewhat like a turnip but has a milder, nutty flavor and a texture almost like an artichoke heart. Try kohlrabi if you never have. It's one of our favorites.

> 2 pounds (900 g) kohlrabi, about 3 medium
> 1 cup (235 ml) heavy cream
> 1 teaspoon nutmeg

Trim the outer stems and the bottom of the kohlrabi and peel the globes. Cut into wedges and put them in a 1-quart (1-L) pot with salted water to cover. Bring to a boil over high heat and reduce heat to a low boil. Cook for 12 to 15 minutes, until tender.

As the kohlrabi is cooking, preheat oven to 350°F (180°C, gas mark 4).

Drain and put the kohlrabi in a mixing bowl with the cream, nutmeg, and salt and pepper to taste. Put into a shallow casserole dish and bake for 30 to 35 minutes.

YIELD: 6 servings

BRAISED LEEKS WITH TOMATO AND BLUE CHEESE

Be sure to wash your leeks in many changes of water; they are very tricky and subversive when it comes to disgorging all the dirt in their many layers.

4 leeks
2 cups (500 g) bottled marinara sauce
½ cup (60 g) blue cheese crumbles

Trim the root ends of the leeks, cut off the green part, and split the leeks lengthwise. Carefully wash the leeks, being sure to get any dirt hiding at the base of the stalks. Put the leeks in a medium-size sauté pan or skillet, season them with salt and pepper, and just cover them with water. Cook them at a simmer for 25 to 30 minutes, until soft.

Meanwhile, preheat the oven to 400°F (200°C, gas mark 6).

Carefully remove the leeks and put them in a baking dish in one layer. Pour the tomato sauce over the leeks and sprinkle the blue cheese over all. Bake for 15 to 20 minutes, until the cheese is melted and browned on top.

YIELD: 4 servings

NOTE: *Leeks pair well with a variety of fish and meats. Try this with Beef Rib Roast with Horseradish and Garlic Crust (page 180).*

CREAMED MUSHROOMS

Mushrooms are one of the many vegetables reviled by small fry and beloved of adults. Our theory is that the mouthfeel of a cooked mushroom is off-putting to little people. That's okay—all the more for us!

> 1 pound (450 g) button mushrooms
> 1 tablespoon (10 g) minced garlic
> 1 cup (235 ml) light cream

Combine all the ingredients in a 1-quart (1-L) saucepan and season with salt and pepper. Cook over medium heat for 30 to 40 minutes, until the sauce is thickened.

YIELD: 4 servings

GRILLED PORTOBELLO CAPS

These meaty mushrooms can take center stage, fill a sandwich to admiration, or serve as a sidekick to grilled steak or lamb.

> 4 portobello mushroom caps
> 2 tablespoons (30 ml) balsamic vinegar
> ¼ cup (60 ml) olive oil
> 1 tablespoon (10 g) minced garlic

Prepare a grill.

Using a spoon, scrape off and discard the gills from the mushrooms. Whisk together the vinegar, oil, garlic, and salt and pepper to taste in a small mixing bowl. Add the mushrooms and toss to coat them with the marinade. Allow to marinate for 10 minutes. Grill the mushrooms for 4 to 5 minutes per side.

YIELD: 4 servings

Mustard Greens Simmered with Ancho Chile and Garlic

Ancho chiles are dried poblano chiles. They have a rich, earthy flavor and low heat.

- 1 bunch mustard greens
- 1 medium-size ancho chile
- 4 cloves garlic, peeled

Remove the stems and ribs from the greens and roughly chop the greens. Put them in a 2-quart (2-L) pot and add water to just cover them. Remove the stem from the ancho, break the chile in half, and remove the seeds. Add the chile to the pot along with the garlic and salt and pepper to taste. Simmer the mustard greens over low heat for 45 minutes to an hour. They should get quite tender. In fact, many Southern cooks would simmer their greens for much longer and you can, too. Add water if needed, but since you are not boiling the greens, this should not be much of a problem. Serve with some of the cooking water.

YIELD: 4 to 6 servings

Stewed Okra

Okra is a vegetable indelibly associated with the South, but it's time for this delicious veggie to take up worldwide residence.

- 1 pound (450 g) fresh okra, or 1 package frozen
- 1 can (14 ounces, or 400 g) diced tomato with garlic
- 2 tablespoons (5 g) chopped fresh basil

If using fresh okra, remove the stem tops and cut the okra into ½-inch (1-cm) rounds. Put the okra and tomatoes into a 1-quart (1-L) pan and simmer over medium heat for 30 to 40 minutes.

Season with salt and pepper, add the basil, and simmer for another 5 minutes.

YIELD: 6 servings

Roasted Parsnips with Tarragon and Lemon

We weren't properly introduced to parsnips until relatively late in life, but are now firm friends with this sweet, sharp root vegetable. If you grow your own parsnips, leave them in the ground until after several frosts to get very sweet roots.

- **1 pound (450 g) parsnips**
- ¼ cup (60 ml) olive oil
- **2 lemons**
- **2 tablespoons (2 g) chopped fresh tarragon**

Peel the parsnips and cut into sticks ½ x 2 inches (1 x 5 cm). Put them into a 1-quart (1-L) pot and cover with salted water. Cover the pot and bring the parsnips to a boil. Cook them for 5 to 8 minutes, until somewhat softened but not fully cooked. Drain the parsnips and set aside.

Preheat the oven to 350°F (180°C, gas mark 4).

Squeeze the lemons into a bowl. Toss the parsnips with the lemon juice, oil, and tarragon, along with salt and pepper to taste. Spread the parsnips onto a baking sheet and bake for 15 minutes, until a bit browned and quite soft.

YIELD: 4 to 6 servings

Peas with Mint and Mushrooms

Shelling peas may be time consuming, but it's also strangely fun. By concentrating on this one small chore, we're forced to sit still. It's also useful for entertaining small children, although admittedly they tend to consume any peas that get shelled by their small fingers.

2 cups (200 g) sliced button mushrooms
2 cups (300 g) shelled fresh peas, or ½ pound (225 g) frozen peas
2 tablespoons (28 g) butter
2 tablespoons (12 g) chopped fresh mint

Fill a 2-quart (2-L) pot halfway with water; salt and set to boil. Meanwhile, heat 2 tablespoons olive oil in a wide sauté pan or skillet. Add the mushrooms and sauté for 5 to 6 minutes, until they have absorbed any liquid they release. Set aside.

When the water boils, drop in the peas and cook, uncovered, for 2 to 3 minutes. Drain the peas and combine with the mushrooms in the pan. Add the butter, mint, and salt and pepper to taste. Cook over medium heat until the butter melts and the vegetables are heated through.

YIELD: 4 to 6 servings

> **NOTE:** *Okay, this isn't really for eating, but you can make a small flotilla of peapod boats by shelling carefully and propping them open with a small twig. Toothpick masts and paper sails complete the armada.*

SAUTÉED SNAP PEAS

This is a simple but very satisfying presentation that pairs very well with Szechuan Stir-Fried Tenderloin with Tangerine Peel (page 195).

- ½ pound (225 g) sugar snap peas, about 2 cups
- 1 tablespoon (10 g) minced garlic
- 1 tablespoon (15 ml) toasted sesame oil (see note)

Trim the stem ends from the peas and remove the strings if there are any (some varieties of sugar snaps are stringless, while others aren't). Heat 2 tablespoons (30 ml) vegetable oil in a wide sauté pan or skillet over high heat. When the oil begins to smoke, add the peas, garlic, and sesame oil, along with salt and pepper to taste. Sauté, tossing often, for 5 to 6 minutes, until the peas are just done but still crisp.

YIELD: 4 servings

NOTE: *Be sure to use the dark, highly flavored oil used in Asian cooking, not the lighter variety.*

🫙 ADD IT!
Toss the snap peas with soy sauce for an added kick.

Spring Pea Puree

Wait until the crop comes in for this one; frozen peas don't do it justice.

2 cups (300 g) shelled fresh peas
½ cup (120 ml) cream
2 tablespoons (8 g) chopped fresh parsley

Fill a 2-quart (2-L) pot halfway with salted water and bring to a boil. Add the peas and cook for 3 to 4 minutes, until just done. Drain the peas, reserving ½ cup (120 ml) of the water.

Put the peas into a food processor fitted with a cutting blade and add the cream and parsley, as well as salt and pepper to taste. Process until smooth, adding water as needed to make the puree a smooth consistency.

YIELD: 4 servings

SAUTÉED RAPINI WITH GARLIC AND RED PEPPER FLAKES

This is a vegetable of a thousand names: broccoli raab, broccoli rabe, and broccoli de rape, to name just a few. Rapini's pungent, slightly bitter flavor is a great favorite in Italy, but it's just catching on in the U.S. It's best to use the leaves and florets and discard the tough last couple of inches of the stems, which are very bitter indeed.

1 bunch rapini
2 tablespoons (20 g) minced garlic
1 teaspoon red pepper flakes

Prepare a bowl of ice water. Wash and trim the rapini. Fill a 4-quart (4-L) pot halfway with water and bring to a rapid boil. Drop in the rapini and cook, uncovered, for 3 to 4 minutes, then drain and plunge immediately into the ice water.

Drain and cut the rapini into bite-size pieces, discarding the last couple of inches of the stems. Heat 2 tablespoons (30 ml) olive oil in a wide sauté pan or skillet over high heat. When it begins to smoke, add the rapini, garlic, and red pepper, along with salt and pepper to taste. Sauté, tossing for 4 to 5 minutes.

YIELD: 4 servings

Sautéed Radishes

Most people think of radishes as a visual exclamation point in a salad, but their peppery punch works especially well with white fish such as cod, haddock, and halibut.

- 2 bunches radishes, about 1 pound (450 g)
- 1 tablespoon (10 g) minced garlic
- 2 tablespoons (30 ml) rice vinegar, or other light vinegar

Trim the radishes and split them in half lengthwise. Heat ¼ cup (60 ml) olive oil in a medium-size sauté pan or skillet over medium-high heat. Add the radishes and season with salt and pepper to taste. Add the garlic. Sauté for 5 to 6 minutes, tossing every so often. Add the vinegar, stir one last time, and serve.

YIELD: 4 servings

Red Pepper stuffed with Eggplant and Goat Cheese

Here, we are trying to exorcise the memory of the vile stuffed peppers that regularly appeared on our family table. We figure that baba ghanoush—a smoky, creamy eggplant dip generally found in the produce aisle—ought to do the trick.

> 2 red bell peppers
> ½ cup (110 g) baba ghanoush
> ½ cup (75 g) goat cheese—a creamy, fresh type

Preheat the oven to 450°F (230°C, gas mark 8).

Core the peppers and cut them into quarters. Combine the baba ghanoush and goat cheese and spoon some of the mixture into each piece of pepper. Put the peppers on a baking sheet and bake for 12 to 14 minutes.

YIELD: 4 servings

🫙 ADD IT!
Sprinkle chopped mint and toasted chopped almonds over the peppers before serving.

Sage-Scented Rutabaga

Rutabagas are first cousins to turnips. They're larger and slightly sweeter and have yellow flesh. They are generally available year-round, with a peak season of July through April.

> 1 rutabaga, about 2 pounds (900 g)
> ½ cup (120 ml) maple syrup
> 2 teaspoons rubbed (ground) sage
> 4 tablespoons (55 g) butter

Peel and cut the rutabaga into 1-inch (2½-cm) cubes. Put the rutabaga into a 2-quart (2-L) pot, cover with water, and bring to a boil over high heat. Reduce the heat and cook at a gentle boil, covered, until they are soft, 25 to 30 minutes. Drain the rutabaga and mash them in a large mixing bowl. Stir in the rest of the ingredients, along with salt and pepper to taste.

YIELD: 6 to 8 servings

CREAMED SALSIFY

Salsify, also known as goatsbeard or oyster plant, is a long, stalklike vegetable with the taste and texture of an artichoke heart. (Given our preoccupation with all things artichoke, no wonder we like it.) Like artichokes, peeled salsify must be immediately put into acidulated water to prevent it from turning brown. If you can't find salsify, you can substitute parsnips or artichoke hearts.

> 1 pound (450 g) salsify
> 1 cup (235 ml) heavy cream
> ½ cup (25 g) fresh bread crumbs
> 2 tablespoons (28 g) butter

Peel the salsify and cut it into lengths of 2 to 3 inches (5 to 7½ cm). Put the salsify into a 2-quart (2-L) pot, cover with water, and cook at a low boil for 20 minutes, until just tender.

Preheat the oven to 350°F (180°C, gas mark 4).

Drain and put the salsify into a shallow baking dish. Pour the cream over the salsify and season with salt and pepper. Cover with the crumbs and dot with butter. Bake for 20 to 25 minutes, until golden brown.

YIELD: 6 to 8 servings

🧂 ADD IT!
After you cut the salsify, you can soak it in acidulated water to prevent browning. Squeeze the juice of one lemon in 2 quarts (2 L) water.

ROASTED SPAGHETTI SQUASH

Spaghetti squash is known as a fun food because when cooked, the squash innards come out in strands that look a lot like pasta. One big difference, however: a 4-ounce (115 g) serving of spaghetti squash has only 37 calories.

> 1 spaghetti squash, about 2 pounds (900 g)
> ½ cup (110 g) light brown sugar, packed
> 1 teaspoon nutmeg
> 4 tablespoons (55 g) butter

Preheat the oven to 350°F (180°C, gas mark 4).

Split the squash lengthwise and remove the seeds. Place the squash, cut side down, on a shallow baking sheet pan and pour 1 cup (235 ml) of water on the sheet. Roast the squash for 45 minutes to 1 hour, until it is quite soft. Remove from the oven and allow to cool.

When cool enough to handle, scoop out the squash, discarding the shell. Put the squash in a 2-quart (2-L) pot, add the remaining ingredients along with salt and pepper to taste, and reheat over medium heat. Stir to distribute the sugar and spices. Serve when the butter is melted and the squash is heated.

YIELD: 6 to 8 servings

CREAMED SPINACH

A classic steakhouse side dish. Serve it with Filet Mignon with Maytag Blue Cheese and Port Wine Sauce (page 187).

- 1 pound (450 g) spinach
- 1 cup (235 ml) heavy cream
- 1 tablespoon (10 g) minced garlic

Pick through the spinach and remove any large stems and spoiled leaves. Wash the spinach well and put it into a 4-quart (4-L) pot with 2 to 3 cups (475 to 700 ml) water. Cook over high heat until the spinach wilts, which will take just a couple of minutes after it comes to a boil.

Drain the spinach; when cool enough to handle, further squish out excess water by hand and chop it. Put the cooked spinach, cream, garlic, and salt and pepper to taste into a 1-quart (1-L) pot and cook it over medium-low heat for 20 minutes. The spinach will have broken down and the cream will be absorbed.

YIELD: 4 servings

GARLICKY SPINACH

- 1 pound (450 g) spinach
- 2 cloves minced garlic
- 2 tablespoons (30 ml) fresh lemon juice

Pick through the spinach and remove any large stems and spoiled leaves. Wash and spin-dry the spinach. Heat ¼ cup (60 ml) olive oil in a large sauté pan or skillet over high heat. When it begins to smoke, add the spinach, then the garlic, as well as salt and pepper to taste. Sauté the spinach, stirring, until it begins to wilt (2 to 3 minutes), then add the lemon juice and sauté for a few seconds more.

YIELD: 4 servings

SQUASH BLOSSOM FRITTERS

Use the male blossoms (so you don't waste potential squash), or the blossoms sometimes marketed on the end of baby squash from any kind of squash, or even pumpkins, to make these delicious treats. You can find blossoms at farmers' markets, upscale produce vendors, or in your own garden.

8 squash blossoms
½ pound (225 g) soft, fresh goat cheese
1 cup (110 g) tempura batter mix

Rinse the blossoms and make sure no insects lurk within. Stir the goat cheese until it is soft, season it with salt and pepper, and stuff a teaspoon or so into each squash flower.

Heat 1 inch (2½ cm) oil in a sauté pan, skillet, or deep-fat fryer to 350°F (180°C).

Prepare the tempura mix according to package instructions. Dip each blossom into the tempura batter and fry until golden brown, 4 to 5 minutes. Drain on paper towels and season with salt and pepper.

YIELD: 4 servings

Summer Squash with Thyme

A very quick, very tasty, very satisfying take on summer squash.

- 2 medium-size summer squash
- 1 medium-size onion, diced
- 1 tablespoon (2 to 3 g) minced fresh thyme

Cut the ends off the squash and split the squash lengthwise. Cut each side into strips and then cut the strips into cubes. Heat ¼ cup (60 ml) olive oil in a wide sauté pan or skillet over high heat. When the oil is hot but not quite smoking, add the onion and sauté for 1 to 2 minutes, then add the squash and thyme. Season with salt and pepper. Sauté, tossing every minute or so, for 4 to 5 minutes, until the squash has softened but still holds its shape.

YIELD: 4 servings

Dill Roasted Sunchokes

Sunchokes are also known as Jerusalem artichokes, although they are neither artichokes nor from Jerusalem. This brown, bumpy root is actually from a variety of sunflower, and it boasts crunchy, sweet flesh that is good raw, roasted, or steamed. It also makes a fine soup.

- 1 pound (450 g) sunchokes
- 2 tablespoons (4 g) chopped fresh dill
- 1 tablespoon (10 g) minced garlic

Preheat the oven to 350°F (180°C, gas mark 4).

Peel the sunchokes and cut into 1-inch (2½-cm) pieces. Put the sunchokes into a shallow 1- or 2-quart (1- or 2-L) baking dish. Mix in the dill and the garlic, then drizzle with ¼ cup (60 ml) olive oil and season with salt and pepper to taste. Bake for 45 to 50 minutes, until the sunchokes are soft and golden brown.

YIELD: 4 servings

Orange-Scented Sweet Potato Puree

Here's a way to zest up the Thanksgiving sweet potatoes.

4 medium-size sweet potatoes, about 2 pounds (900 g)
1 cup (235 ml) orange juice
1 teaspoon cinnamon
4 tablespoons (55 g) butter

Peel the sweet potatoes and cut into chunks 1 to 2 inches (2½ to 5 cm) long. Put the potatoes in a 2-quart (2-L) pot, cover with salted water, and bring to a boil over high heat. Reduce the heat and cook at a gentle boil for 25 to 30 minutes, until the potatoes are soft.

Drain the potatoes and put them and the remaining ingredients, along with salt and pepper to taste, in a mixing bowl. Mash well to make a smooth puree.

YIELD: 4 to 6 servings

Sweet Potato with Ginger and Maple

Try serving this with Orange-Coriander Pork Chops (page 243) and a salad of bitter greens.

4 medium sweet potatoes, about 2 pounds (900 g)
½ cup maple syrup
1 teaspoon minced fresh ginger
4 tablespoons (55 g) butter

Peel the sweet potatoes and cut into 1-inch (2½-cm) pieces. Put the potatoes in a 2-quart (2-L) pot, cover with salted water, and bring to a boil over high heat. Reduce the heat and cook at a gentle boil for 25 to 30 minutes, until the potatoes are soft.

Drain the potatoes and put them and the remaining ingredients, along with salt and pepper to taste, in a mixing bowl. Mash well to make a smooth puree.

YIELD: 4 to 6 servings

TOMATO CASSEROLE

This casserole depends on beautifully ripe tomatoes for the highest level of taste sensation, but it won't let you down even in the dead of winter, what with the profusion of tomato choices we have these days.

2 pounds (900 g) ripe tomatoes
2 cups (230 g) seasoned dried bread crumbs
½ cup (130 g) pesto
4 tablespoons (55 g) butter

Preheat the oven to 350°F (180°C, gas mark 4). Prepare a bowl of ice water.

Bring a large pot of water to a boil. Core the tomatoes and mark an X at the base with a paring knife. Drop the tomatoes in the boiling water for 10 to 12 seconds, then remove and plunge immediately into the ice water. (If the tomatoes aren't summer ripe, you may have to leave them in the boiling water longer. Watch for the skin to start splitting, and then yank them.) Drain the tomatoes and peel them—the skin should slip right off. Slice the tomatoes crosswise into ½-inch (1-cm) slices.

Layer a shallow 1-quart (1-L) baking dish with tomatoes. Spread the pesto over the tomatoes and season with salt and pepper. Sprinkle with some of the bread crumbs. Repeat the layers, finishing with bread crumbs. Dot with butter. Bake for 35 to 40 minutes, until the crumbs are golden brown and the tomatoes are bubbling. Allow to sit for a few minutes to cool and set.

YIELD: 6 servings

ADD IT!
Sprinkle shredded extra-sharp cheddar on the top of the casserole.

FRIED GREEN TOMATOES

This dish may be a Southern favorite, but up here in New England we like it too—perhaps because not all of our tomatoes ever get ripe before the first frost.

2 medium-size green tomatoes
½ cup (70 g) cornmeal
½ cup (110 g) all-purpose flour

Core the tomatoes and slice them crosswise ¼-inch (½-cm) thick. Mix the cornmeal and flour in a small mixing bowl and season with salt and pepper. Dredge the tomato slices in the flour mixture, pressing it into the slices well.

Heat ½ inch (1 cm) vegetable oil in a large sauté pan or skillet until hot. Test it by dropping a small piece of bread into the pan. (It should sizzle readily.) Fry the tomato slices for 3 to 4 minutes per side. You may have to do this in batches, as it is important not to crowd the pan. Add oil as needed. Drain on paper towels and serve.

YIELD: 4 servings

STEWED TOMATOES

This is a gentle and old-fashioned recipe that makes us think of faded china and well-worn aprons.

  2 pounds (900 g) ripe tomatoes
  1 medium-size onion
  1 tablespoon (2 to 3 g) chopped fresh thyme

Prepare a bowl of ice water. Bring a large pot of water to a boil. Core the tomatoes and mark an X at the base with a paring knife. Drop the tomatoes in the boiling water for 10 to 12 seconds, then remove and plunge them immediately into the ice water. (If the tomatoes aren't summer ripe, you may have to leave them in the water longer. Watch for the skin to start splitting, and then yank them.) Drain the tomatoes and peel them—the skin should slip right off. Cut into quarters and set aside.

Peel and cut the onion into small pieces. Put the onion in a 2-quart (2-L) pot and add 2 to 3 tablespoons olive oil. Cover and cook over medium heat until the onions are softened and translucent, about 5 to 7 minutes. Add the tomato, thyme, and salt and pepper to taste. Cook at a simmer for 15 to 20 minutes.

YIELD: 4 servings

DIJON MASHED TURNIPS

Turnips can be cooked any number of ways: roasted, boiled, or mashed, as here. Rutabagas make a good substitute for turnips if none are to be found.

  1 pound (450 g) purple-top turnips
  2 tablespoons (30 g) tarragon-Dijon mustard
  ½ cup (120 ml) heavy cream
  2 tablespoons (28 g) butter

Cut off the stems and roots of the turnips, then peel the turnips and cut them into quarters. Put the turnips into a 1-quart (1-L) pot, cover with salted water, and cook over medium-high heat until they are easily pierced by a knife, about 30 minutes. Drain the turnips and place them in a mixing bowl. Add the mustard, cream, and butter, along with salt and pepper to taste. Mash until smooth.

YIELD: 4 servings

ZUCCHINI FRITTERS

These are great as a light dinner. Cook up a platter full and serve with salsa and a salad.

> 1 medium-size zucchini
> 1 egg
> ½ cup (110 g) self-rising flour

Shred the zucchini on a box grater and put it into a mixing bowl. Add the egg and stir well with a fork. Add the flour and salt and pepper to taste. Stir together, adding enough water to form a fairly loose batter, like pancake batter.

Heat ½ inch (1 cm) oil in a large sauté pan or skillet over medium-high heat. When the oil is hot, drop in the batter by spoonfuls. Fry for 3 to 4 minutes per side, turning carefully. Do not crowd the pan. Cook in batches if need be. Drain the cooked fritters on paper towels.

YIELD: 4 servings

 ADD IT!
You could add a multitude of things here: a shot of hot sauce, some chopped oregano, or chicken stock instead of the water are just three options.

FRIED ZUCCHINI

These are good hot or at room temperature and make a great appetizer as well as a side dish for a main meal.

2 medium-size zucchini
2 eggs
2 cups (230 g) seasoned dried bread crumbs

Cut the ends off the zucchini, then cut the zucchini into ¼-inch (½-cm) rounds. Whisk the eggs with 2 tablespoons (30 ml) water in a pie plate. Put the crumbs in another pie plate. Season the squash with salt and pepper. Dip each piece into the egg, then into the crumbs, turning to coat well. Set the coated squash on waxed paper.

Heat ¼ inch (½ cm) oil in a sauté pan or skillet over medium-high heat. When the oil starts to smoke, fry the zucchini, in batches, for 2 to 3 minutes per side. Drain on paper towels.

YIELD: 4 servings

18

Potatoes

The ultimate comfort food in many cuisines, potatoes remain a basic starch at dinner tables across the country. It's hard to serve a bad potato dish—you can mash them, roast them, fry them, boil them—you can turn them into soup, for goodness' sake, and still get a tasty result.

Potatoes have an honest, earthy taste that serves as a terrific base for many different flavors—classic combinations involve dairy and onions, or garlic and rosemary.

Potatoes are moving out their position as the third leg of the dinnertime meat-vegetable-potato triumvirate and are beginning to take center stage on occasion. As meatless dinners become more commonplace, the idea of a salad or vegetable with a potato-based accompaniment has become increasingly popular.

MASHED POTATO BASICS

This is an all-purpose master recipe for mashed potatoes, to which any number of third ingredients may be added. In the following recipes we suggest quite a few.

First off, when cooking mashed potatoes, the goal is a fluffy product—not one that can be used as wallpaper paste. Here's how to accomplish this feat:

◆ Use a boiling potato (not a russet)—Yukon gold is a good choice.

◆ Peel the potatoes, but then leave them whole if they are roughly the same size. If they are all different sizes leave the pieces as large as you can and still have them finish cooking at the same time.

◆ Start the potatoes in cold water.

◆ When you drain the potatoes, allow them to dry out in a colander for 2 to 3 minutes before mashing—but not for much longer.

◆ Never rinse potatoes after cooking.

◆ Add cream, butter, and other ingredients after mashing and add these ingredients in three stages, incorporating them fully before adding more.

MASHED POTATOES FOR 4

2 pounds (900 g) boiling potatoes, such as Yukon gold
½ cup (120 ml) heavy cream
4 tablespoons (55 g) Butter

Peel the potatoes and put them in a 4-quart (4-L) pot. Add cold water to cover the potatoes and cover the pot. Heat on high until the potatoes boil, then reduce the heat to medium and simmer until they are easily pierced with a knife, 25 to 30 minutes.

While the potatoes are cooking, combine the cream and butter in a small saucepan and heat over medium heat until the butter is melted and the cream is hot.

Drain the potatoes and allow them to sit in a colander for 2 to 3 minutes. Mash the potatoes or put them through a potato ricer. Stir in the cream mixture by thirds. Season to taste with salt and pepper.

YIELD: 4 servings

MASHED POTATOES WITH BACON

2 pounds (900 g) boiling potatoes, such as Yukon gold
6 slices bacon, cooked
½ cup (120 ml) heavy cream
4 tablespoons (55 g) butter

Peel the potatoes and put them in a 4-quart (4-L) pot. Add cold water to cover the potatoes and cover the pot. Heat on high until the potatoes boil, then reduce the heat to medium and simmer until they are easily pierced with a knife, 25 to 30 minutes. Dice the bacon. While the potatoes are cooking, combine the cream, butter, and bacon in a small saucepan and heat over medium heat until the butter is melted and the cream is hot.

Drain the potatoes and allow them to sit in a colander for 2 to 3 minutes. Mash the potatoes or put them through a potato ricer. Stir in the cream mixture by thirds. Season to taste with salt and pepper.

YIELD: 4 servings

MASHED POTATOES WITH SAUTÉED CABBAGE

In Ireland they have a similar dish named Colcannon.

2 pounds (900 g) boiling potatoes, such as Yukon gold
4 cups (280 g) green cabbage, shredded
½ cup (120 ml) heavy cream
4 tablespoons (55 g) butter

Peel the potatoes and put them in a 4-quart (4-L) pot. Add cold water to cover the potatoes and cover the pot. Heat on high until the potatoes boil, then reduce the heat to medium and simmer until they are easily pierced with a knife, 25 to 30 minutes.

While the potatoes are cooking, heat 2 tablespoons (30 ml) oil in a sauté pan or skillet over medium-high heat. Sauté the cabbage for 8 to 10 minutes, until soft and a bit browned.

Combine the cream and butter in a small saucepan and heat over medium heat until the butter is melted and the cream is hot.

Drain the potatoes and allow them to sit in a colander for 2 to 3 minutes. Mash the potatoes or put them through a potato ricer. Stir in cream mixture by thirds. Stir in the cabbage. Season to taste with salt and pepper.

YIELD: 4 servings

Mashed Potatoes with Cheddar Cheese

2 pounds (900 g) boiling potatoes, such as Yukon gold
1 cup (120 g) shredded cheddar cheese
½ cup (120 ml) heavy cream
4 tablespoons (55 g) butter

Peel the potatoes and put them in a 4-quart (4-L) pot. Add cold water to cover the potatoes and cover the pot. Heat on high until the potatoes boil, then reduce the heat to medium and simmer until they are easily pierced with a knife, 25 to 30 minutes.

While the potatoes are cooking, combine the cream and butter in a small saucepan and heat over medium heat until the butter is melted and the cream is hot.

Drain the potatoes and allow them to sit in a colander for 2 to 3 minutes. Mash the potatoes or put them through a potato ricer. Stir in the cream mixture by thirds. Stir in the cheese. Season to taste with salt and pepper.

YIELD: 4 servings

MASHED POTATOES WITH HORSERADISH

2 pounds (900 g) boiling potatoes, such as Yukon gold
¼ cup (60 g) prepared horseradish
½ cup (120 ml) heavy cream
4 tablespoons (55 g) butter

Peel the potatoes and put them in a 4-quart (4-L) pot. Add cold water to cover the potatoes and cover the pot. Heat on high until the potatoes boil, then reduce the heat to medium and simmer until they are easily pierced with a knife, 25 to 30 minutes.

While the potatoes are cooking, combine the cream, butter, and horseradish in a small saucepan and heat over medium heat until the butter is melted and the cream is hot.

Drain the potatoes and allow them to sit in a colander for 2 to 3 minutes. Mash the potatoes or put them through a potato ricer. Stir in the cream mixture by thirds. Season to taste with salt and pepper.

YIELD: 4 servings

MASHED POTATOES WITH PESTO

2 pounds (900 g) boiling potatoes, such as Yukon gold
¼ cup (65 g) basil pesto
½ cup (120 ml) heavy cream
4 tablespoons (55 g) butter

Peel the potatoes and put them in a 4-quart (4-L) pot. Add cold water to cover the potatoes and cover the pot. Heat on high until the potatoes boil, then reduce the heat to medium and simmer until they are easily pierced with a knife, 25 to 30 minutes. While the potatoes are cooking, combine the cream, butter, and pesto in a small saucepan and heat over medium heat until the butter is melted and the cream is hot.

Drain the potatoes and allow them to sit in a colander for 2 to 3 minutes. Mash the potatoes or put them through a potato ricer. Stir in the cream mixture by thirds. Season to taste with salt and pepper.

YIELD: 4 servings

MASHED POTATOES WITH ROASTED GARLIC

2 pounds (900 g) boiling potatoes, such as Yukon gold
8 to 10 cloves garlic, roasted until soft (see note)
½ cup (120 ml) heavy cream
4 tablespoons (55 g) butter

Peel the potatoes and put them in a 4 quart pot. Add cold water to cover the potatoes and cover the pot. Heat on high until the potatoes boil, then reduce the heat to medium and simmer until they are easily pierced with a knife, 25 to 30 minutes.

While the potatoes are cooking, combine the cream, butter, and garlic in a small saucepan and heat over medium heat until the butter is melted and the cream is hot.

Drain the potatoes and allow them to sit in the colander for 2 to 3 minutes. Mash the potatoes or put them through a potato ricer. Stir in the cream mixture by thirds. You can leave the garlic cloves whole or mash them in. Season to taste with salt and pepper.

YIELD: 4 servings

NOTE: *To roast garlic, preheat the oven to 325°F (170°C, gas mark 3). Put 2 whole garlic bulbs, unpeeled, on a small baking pan and brush with 2 teaspoons olive oil. Bake for 45 minutes to 1 hour, until the garlic cloves are quite soft. Remove from the oven and allow to cool. Cut off the top ½ inch (1 cm) of the bulb and squeeze out the roasted garlic flesh.*

MASHED POTATOES WITH SCALLION

Scallions and potatoes and cream—the most potent triple-play combo in Spudland. Think of vichysoisse, think of what you put on baked potatoes. We prefer Yukon gold to russets because they don't get as watery when boiled.

2 pounds (900 g) boiling potatoes, such as Yukon gold
1 bunch scallions
½ cup (120 ml) heavy cream
4 tablespoons (55 g) butter

Peel the potatoes and put them in a 4-quart (4-L) pot. Add cold water to cover the potatoes and cover the pot. Heat on high until the water boils, then reduce the heat to medium and simmer until they are easily pierced with a knife, 25 to 30 minutes.

While the potatoes are boiling, prepare the scallions by removing and discarding the top inch of the scallion and then slicing the rest of the green part into ½-inch (1-cm) pieces.

Melt the butter in a small saucepan over low heat and gently sauté the scallions. Add the cream and heat over medium heat until the mixture is hot.

Drain the potatoes and allow them to sit in a colander for 2 to 3 minutes. Mash the potatoes or put them through a potato ricer. Stir in the cream mixture by thirds. Season to taste with salt and pepper.

YIELD: 4

SINFUL ROASTED POTATOES

You may scoff at this recipe, saying, "How can they expect me to have duck fat?!" Simple! Whenever you prepare a duck recipe, save the trimmed scrap fat, render the fat, and store in a jar in the refrigerator. It lasts forever, and you can use it for making confit, these potatoes, the crust for cassoulet, and more.

> **2 pounds (900 g) baby red potatoes, or other baby or fingerling potatoes**
> **2 tablespoons (3 g) chopped fresh rosemary**
> **1 cup (200 g) duck fat**

Preheat the oven to 325°F (170°C, gas mark 3).

Cut the potatoes into halves or quarters, depending on their size. Put the potatoes in a roasting pan and season with salt and pepper. Sprinkle the rosemary over them.

Melt the duck fat and toss it with the potatoes. Spread the potatoes out in the pan and roast them for 45 minutes, until golden brown and crisp outside, but quite soft when pierced with a paring knife.

YIELD: 4 servings

GERMAN-FRIED POTATOES

We call this "German fried" because a dear friend from Germany first made them for us.

> **¼ pound (115 g) bacon**
> **2 medium-size onions**
> **2 pounds (900 g) Yukon gold potatoes, unpeeled**

Cut the bacon into ½-inch (1-cm) squares. Peel and dice the onion. Wash the potatoes and slice thin, skin on. Heat a sauté pan or skillet over medium heat. Add the bacon and onion. Cook for 6 to 8 minutes, then add the potatoes, season with salt and pepper, and stir well. Cook for 30 minutes or so, turning the whole thing with a spatula every 4 to 5 minutes, until the potatoes are quite soft inside but have a nice brown crust outside, the bacon is crisp, and the onions are caramelized. The potatoes may break up some—no problem.

YIELD: 4 to 6 servings

SIMPLE POTATO GRATIN

The trick to a great gratin is slow cooking at a low temperature. This technique allows the cream and cheese to melt into the potatoes and the finished product to remain smooth and creamy. Cooking at a higher temperature will cause the cream and cheese to break, leaving you with a greasy gratin.

2 pounds (900 g) potatoes—yellow Finns, Yukon golds, and russets are all good choices
4 tablespoons (55 g) butter
1½ cups (165 g) shredded Gruyère cheese
1 cup (235 ml) heavy cream

Preheat the oven to 250°F (120°C, gas mark ½).

Peel the potatoes and slice thin, putting them into a container of cold water as you work. Grease the bottom and sides of an ovenproof medium-size sauté pan or skillet with the butter. Cover the bottom of the pan with the potato slices, overlapping them slightly and making a concentric ring design. Sprinkle one-third of the cheese over the potatoes and season with salt and pepper. Repeat the layering twice more, then finish with a last covering of potatoes. Pour the cream over the potatoes and cover the pan with foil, sealing the edges.

Put the pan on a baking sheet to catch any drips and bake for 1½ to 2 hours, until the potatoes are easily pierced by a knife. Allow to cool for 15 minutes, remove the foil, and carefully invert the gratin onto a serving platter. Slice into wedges.

YIELD: 8 to 10

LIGHT SCALLOPED POTATOES

All right, we know it's an oxymoron, but by "light" we mean lighter than traditional scal-loped potatoes made with flour and milk.

> 2 pounds (900 g) potatoes—yellow Finn, Yukon gold,
>   and russet are all good choices
> 4 tablespoons (55 g) butter
> 1 pound (about 2 cups, or 450 g) sliced onion
> 2 cups (475 ml) chicken stock or canned broth

Peel and slice the potatoes thin, dropping them into a container of cold water as you work. Peel and slice the onions thin. Melt 3 tablespoons (43 g) of the butter in a medium-size sauté pan or skillet over medium heat, and add the onions. Sauté them for 8 to 10 minutes, until they are softened and slightly caramelized.

Preheat the oven to 325°F (170°C, gas mark 3).

Grease a 2-quart (2-L) casserole with the remaining butter and layer the potatoes on the bottom. Season with salt and pepper, spread some of the onions over the potatoes and repeat the process, finishing with a layer of potatoes. Pour the stock over the potatoes and cover with foil or parchment paper. Bake for 1 hour, until the potatoes are quite easily pierced with a knife.

YIELD: 4 to 6 servings

TWICE-BAKED POTATOES

These are a treat served with chops, a steak, or a rib roast. Heck, they are great all by themselves. Next time you are baking potatoes, throw in a few extra and try this the next day.

4 russet potatoes
4 tablespoons (55 g) butter
½ cup (115 g) sour cream
½ cup (55 g) shredded cheddar cheese

Preheat the oven to 400°F (200°C, gas mark 6).

Wash the potatoes well and pierce each one once with a paring knife. Bake for 45 minutes to 1 hour, until soft. Cool the potatoes until you can handle them.

Again, preheat the oven, this time to 350°F (180°C, gas mark 4).

Cut the top third off each potato, lengthwise. Scoop out the insides, leaving the skin intact and set aside the larger, bottom part of each potato. Put the potato flesh in a mixing bowl and mash with a potato masher or pass through a potato ricer. Mix in the butter (melted if the potato is cold), the sour cream, the cheese, and salt and pepper to taste.

Spoon the mixture into your reserved potato skins—they should be heaping full. Put your stuffed potatoes on a baking sheet and bake them for 20 to 30 minutes.

YIELD: 4 servings

ADD IT!
Many items mix in with alacrity: sautéed mushrooms or onions, chopped scallions, chopped fresh herbs. Let the sky be the limit!

OVEN FRIES

4 russet potatoes
½ cup (120 ml) olive oil
1 tablespoon (7 g) paprika
1 tablespoon (2 to 3 g) chopped fresh thyme

Preheat the oven to 375°F (190°C, gas mark 5).

Wash the potatoes well. You can peel them or not, as you choose. Cut the potatoes into wedges, about 8 per potato. Toss the potatoes in a mixing bowl with the oil, paprika, thyme, and salt and pepper to taste. Spread the potatoes out on a baking sheet and bake for 40 to 45 minutes, until tender through and nicely browned.

YIELD: 4 servings

STEAMED NEW POTATOES WITH HERBS

This recipe should be reserved for the tiny new potatoes fresh dug from your garden or obtained from a local farmer. It's great with salmon and fresh peas to celebrate spring.

2 pounds (900 g) baby new potatoes
   (if you can't find those, small red-skinned potatoes will do)
2 tablespoons (2 g) chopped fresh chervil
2 tablespoons (8 g) chopped fresh flat-leaf parsley
4 tablespoons (55 g) butter, melted

Wash the potatoes, lightly scrubbing off any dirt, then put in the top of a steamer. Pour 2 cups (475 ml) water in the bottom of the steamer and steam the potatoes over high heat for 15 to 20 minutes, depending on the size of the potatoes. They should be cooked through but still slightly firm, not mushy. Toss in a bowl with the herbs, butter, and salt and pepper to taste.

YIELD: 4 servings

🧂 ADD IT!
Try a spritz of fresh lemon juice when you toss the potatoes together.

Potato Pancakes

3 russet potatoes
1 egg
½ cup (60 g) all-purpose flour

Peel the potatoes and shred them on a box grater. Add the egg and flour, along with salt and pepper to taste, and mix. Heat a wide sauté pan or skillet over medium heat and add ½ cup oil. Drop in spoonfuls (about 2 to 3 tablespoons, or 30 to 45 ml) of the potato batter and fry for 5 to 6 minutes per side. Do not crowd the pan.

Drain on paper towels and keep the pancakes warm while the rest are cooking.

YIELD: 4 servings

🥫 ADD IT!
Try some chopped fresh oregano in the potato batter.

Indian-Style Potatoes

4 medium-size boiling potatoes, such as Yukon gold
1 medium-size onion
2 teaspoons tumeric

Peel the potatoes and cut them into 1-inch (2½-cm) cubes. Put the potatoes into a 1-quart (1-L) pot, cover with water, and cook them at a low boil for 15 to 20 minutes, until just tender. While the potatoes are cooking, peel and finely dice the onion. Heat ¼ cup (60 ml) olive oil in a medium-size sauté pan or skillet over medium heat. Sauté the onions until they are soft, translucent, and slightly browned. Stir in the tumeric. Drain the potatoes and put them into the pan. Season with salt and pepper and toss the potatoes to coat them well with the onions and spices.

YIELD: 4 servings

Sweet Stuff

19

Desserts

The more we played, the more we realized that we didn't have to force dessert, that inherently lush and extravagant concept, into a three-ingredient mold. It fit just fine, all by itself.

INDIVIDUAL APPLE CHARLOTTES

Here's a three-ingredient take on the traditional apple charlotte. Unlike other charlottes, this one is served hot.

    4 Granny Smith apples
    ½ cup (100 g) cinnamon sugar (see recipe, page 37)
    7 to 8 slices home-style white bread
    8 tablespoons (115 g) unsalted butter

Peel, core, and dice the apples. Put the apples, sugar, and ½ cup (120 ml) water into a heavy-bottomed 1-quart (1-L) saucepan. Cook over medium heat until the apples are soft, about 20 minutes. Using a fork or potato masher, mash them to form a thick apple sauce.

Clarify the butter: Put the butter in a sauté pan or skillet and slowly melt over low heat. Skim any foam off the top, and carefully pour the clear yellow liquid at the top of the pan into a container. Discard the whitish milk solids on the bottom.

Preheat the oven to 350°F (180°C, gas mark 4).

With a round cutter or a paring knife, cut out circles of bread to fit the bottoms of four 8-ounce (235 ml) ramekins. Dip the bread into the clarified butter and sauté over medium heat in a nonstick pan until golden brown on both sides, 1 to 2 minutes per side. Put a piece of bread in the bottom of each ramekin. Remove the crusts from the rest of the bread and cut into strips ½ inch (1 cm) wide and as tall as the ramekins. Dip in the butter and line the walls of the ramekins, slightly overlapping. Spoon the applesauce into the ramekins and bake for 40 to 45 minutes, until the bread against the walls of the ramekins is browned. Allow to cool, then invert the charlottes out of the ramekins onto plates.

YIELD: 4 servings

🧂 ADD IT!
Nice with some crème anglaise or whipped cream as a garnish.

APPLE TARTE TATIN

This rich French classic is surprisingly quick and easy to make. Serve with a scoop of vanilla ice cream if you wish.

6 Granny Smith apples
8 tablespoons (115 g) butter, softened
¾ cup (150 g) sugar
1 sheet puff pastry dough, 13 x 9 inches (33 x 23 cm), thawed

Peel the apples, split them in half, and remove the cores. (We find a melon baller works best for this.) With the butter, grease the bottom and sides of a medium-size ovenproof sauté pan or skillet. Sprinkle the sugar over the butter. Arrange the apples, cut side up, in the pan. Roll out the puff pastry so that it will fit over the pan. Drape the pastry over the pan and cut off any excess, leaving ½ inch or so of overhang. Tuck in the overhanging pastry.

Preheat the oven to 400°F (200°C, gas mark 6).

On the stovetop, heat the pan on medium-high heat for 15 to 20 minutes, until the sugar starts to caramelize on the apples and the apples are softened. You can check by using a pair of tongs to lift the pastry dough and peek underneath. Put the pan in the oven and bake for 12 to 15 minutes, until the pastry is golden brown. Remove from the oven, wait 3 to 4 minutes, and flip the pan over onto a large plate. Don't worry if the apples stick in the pan or fall out of place; you can easily put them back in their proper spot. Spoon any caramel left in the pan over the top of the apples.

YIELD: 6 servings

APPLE-WALNUT BREAD PUDDING

Bread puddings used to be a way to use up stale bread—now we go buy fancy breads specifically to make these fiendishly addictive desserts.

> 1 loaf (1½ pounds, or 675 g) apple-walnut bread
> 3 eggs
> 2 cups (475 ml) light cream

Slice the apple-walnut bread and lay the pieces in a bread loaf pan, cutting them to make them fit as needed. Whisk together the eggs and cream in a mixing bowl. Pour over the bread and let it sit for 30 minutes.

Preheat the oven to 325°F (170°C, gas mark 3).

Cover the loaf pan with foil, set it into a larger baking pan and pour in boiling water halfway up the side of the loaf pan. Bake for 1 hour. Remove from the oven and leave in the water bath to cool until the pudding is warm. Invert the pudding out of the pan and slice.

YIELD: 6 to 8 servings

ADD IT!
Feel free to sprinkle dried cherries, raisins, or cranberries into the pudding before baking. Serve with whipped cream or vanilla ice cream if desired.

BAKED ALASKA

This is always a crowd-pleaser. The notion of cooking ice cream is particularly appealing to kids.

1 pint (285 g) of your favorite ice cream (we like coffee)
4 egg whites
½ cup (100 g) sugar

Preheat the oven to 500°F (250°C, gas mark 10).

Scoop the ice cream into 4 mounds and put them on a baking sheet. Put the sheet in the freezer. The ice cream needs to freeze pretty solid to withstand the oven's assault, so give it time to cool.

Make the meringue by putting the egg whites in the bowl of an electric mixer. Start to beat them with the whisk attachment. When they are fluffy, add one-third of the sugar. Continue beating, adding the rest of the sugar in 2 parts. Beat until the whites are stiff, smooth, and glossy. Using a spatula or spoon, top each mound of ice cream with meringue and smooth it out so the ice cream is completely covered. Use the back of the spoon to make decorative curls in the meringue. Bake for 6 to 8 minutes, until the meringue is browned. Remove, put on plates using a spatula and serve immediately.

YIELD: 4 servings

🥫 ADD IT!
You can garnish with your favorite sliced fruit, or even better, chocolate sauce.

BAKED PEACHES

August is when peaches ripen in New England, and we always try to get to a pick-your-own farm to fill a basket of succulent native peaches, one of summer's true delights.

> 4 freestone peaches
> 1 cup (225 g) brown sugar, packed
> 1 teaspoon nutmeg
> 4 tablespoons (55 g) butter

Prepare a bowl of ice water. Blanch the peaches: Bring a large pot of water to a boil. Drop the peaches in the boiling water for 15 to 20 seconds, then remove and plunge immediately into the cold water. Drain the peaches and peel them—the skin should slip right off.

Preheat the oven to 400°F (200°C, gas mark 6).

Cut the peaches in half along the "line" that bisects the fruit and remove the stone. Put the peaches cut side up in a shallow baking pan so that they all fit in one layer. In a small bowl, mix together the brown sugar and the nutmeg, then cut in the butter using your fingertips. Sprinkle over the peaches. Bake for 20 to 25 minutes.

YIELD: 4 servings

🥫 ADD IT!
Serve with a scoop of vanilla ice cream.

BASIC POACHED PEARS

Poached pears have a reputation as an elegant dessert as well as the virtue of being easy to make. And on top of everything else, they're delicious. This is a basic recipe; feel free to use it as a springboard, experimenting with poaching liquids and drizzling with sauces of your own choosing.

4 firm ripe pears, Bartlett or Anjou
2 cups (400 g) sugar
1 lemon

Peel the pears, split them in half (leave the stem on and try to split that too), then scoop out the cores with a melon baller. Put the sugar in a 2-quart (2-L) pot and add 1 quart (1 L) water. Heat over medium heat, stirring occasionally, until the sugar dissolves. Peel the zest from the lemon and add it to the pot. Add the pears, making sure they are fully covered; if they're not, add more water. Poach over low heat for 40 to 45 minutes, until the pears are easily pierced with a knife but are still firm. Remove the pears from the poaching liquid.

YIELD: 4 servings

ADD IT!
Replace the water with red wine or orange juice, as you prefer. After removing the pears, reduce the cooking liquid to a syrup as a sauce for the pears.

CARAMEL CRÈME BRÛLÉE

The flavor of caramel is infused into this crème brûlée and then melted on top.

½ cup (100 g) sugar, plus 5 to 6 tablespoons (up to 75 g) for the crust
2 cups (475 ml) heavy cream
6 egg yolks

Preheat the oven to 300°F (150°C, gas mark 2).

Put the sugar in a heavy 2-quart (2-L) saucepan and add enough water to make the sugar the consistency of wet sand. Put the pot on high heat and bring to a boil. Boil until the steam stops rising from the pot, then stick close by. As soon as the water (the steam) is all gone, the temperature of the sugar will start to rise quickly. When the sugar has turned a nice golden brown, remove from the heat and add half the cream. It will bubble furiously—when it dies down, add the rest of the cream. Reduce the heat to medium, return the pot to the heat, and stir until the caramel is all melted into the cream—1 to 2 minutes. Set aside.

Whisk the egg yolks briefly in a mixing bowl. Temper in the hot cream—meaning, pour it into the bowl, while whisking, in a thin stream—you don't want to scramble the egg yolks. Ladle the mixture into five 6-ounce (175 ml) ramekins or other baking dishes. Put the ramekins into a shallow baking dish and add hot water until it comes halfway up the sides of the ramekins. Cover the whole pan with foil, press the foil onto the rim of each ramekin for a loose seal, and carefully put the whole dish into the oven. Bake for about 20 minutes, until the custard is just set. Be careful not to overcook, or you will end up with sweet scrambled eggs!

Remove from the oven and allow to cool in the water. Remove from the water and refrigerate until cold. To serve, sprinkle 1 tablespoon or so (15 g) sugar on top of each crème brûlée, and either under the broiler, or using a torch, melt the sugar into a thin crust. Allow to cool for a minute, then serve.

YIELD: 5 servings

CHERRY GRANITA

This amazingly refreshing summer ice is a far cry from the neon-colored confections we used to get from the ice cream truck.

1 pound (450 g) cherries
2 cups (400 g) sugar
1 lemon

Squeeze the lemon and set the juice aside. Pit the cherries (they make cherry pitters, but you can just cut them in half with a paring knife—they don't have to be pretty.) Put the cherries, sugar, and lemon juice into a food processor fitted with the metal blade. Puree, then add 1 to 2 cups (235 to 475 ml) water, as needed, to make a smooth and fairly thick puree.

Heat in a 2-quart (2-L) pot over medium heat to simmer until the sugar is dissolved. Pour into a loaf pan and freeze. Serve by scraping off the top with a spoon to make crystals. The granita ice should be rather grainy, not smooth like a sorbet.

YIELD: 4 to 6 servings

CHOCOLATE BREAD PUDDING

This recipe is quite adaptive to personal muffin tastes. Our supermarket has chocolate chip muffins, cappuccino muffins, lemon poppy seed muffins, carrot muffins—all would make a fine base for this bread pudding.

2 tablespoons (28 g) butter
4 large chocolate muffins, broken into bite-size pieces (about 4 cups, or 560 g)
4 large eggs
2 cups (475 ml) light cream

Preheat the oven to 350°F (180°C, gas mark 4).

Butter a 9 x 5 x 3-inch (23 x 13 x 6-cm) loaf pan with half the butter. (You can use a similar-size casserole dish if you want a prettier vessel.)

In a large bowl, beat together the eggs and cream until well mixed. Add the muffin pieces and stir together. Let sit about 30 minutes, stirring occasionally, until the muffins absorb lots of moisture.

Pour the mixture into the prepared pan. Dot with the rest of the butter and bake until the pudding is set in the center, approximately 50 minutes. Remove and cool on stovetop.

YIELD: 6 to 8 servings

🥫 ADD IT!
Serve with melted chocolate drizzled on top, or whipped cream, or sliced strawberries, or all of the above.

STRAWBERRIES WITH CHOCOLATE FONDUE

Use a good-quality chocolate here—it will make a difference. This is a fun way to end a casual dinner party among close friends. The sauce is also great with other fruits, pieces of angel food cake, pretzels, or whatever you want to dip.

12 ounces (340 g) semisweet chocolate
12 ounces (355 ml) half-and-half
1 quart (700 g) strawberries, washed and hulled

Melt the chocolate. We use the microwave and a glass bowl, heating and mixing alternately to prevent scorching. You can also easily use a metal bowl over a pot of simmering water to melt the chocolate. When the chocolate is melted, stir in the half-and-half until smooth. Put in a fondue pot with the heat source set low. Serve with the strawberries.

YIELD: 8 to 10 servings

ADD IT!
Stir in 2 to 3 tablespoons (30 to 45 ml) dark rum with the half-and-half, if desired.

HAZELNUT CHOCOLATE TORTE

This makes a surprisingly light cake. Top it with whipped cream and fresh raspberries, and you'll have a dessert for any occasion.

7 ounces (200 g) finest-quality semisweet or bittersweet chocolate, chopped fine
8 tablespoons (115 g) butter
1 cup (150 g) hazelnuts, toasted and ground fine
5 large eggs, separated

Preheat oven to 350°F (180°C, gas mark 4) and butter an 8-inch (20-cm) cake pan.

In a double boiler (or a metal pan set over a saucepan of simmering water), melt the chocolate and butter, stirring occasionally, until everything is completely melted. Remove from the heat and set aside to cool for about 10 minutes.

In a large bowl, whip the egg yolks until pale yellow and somewhat frothy. Add the hazelnuts and mix to form a stiff batter. When the chocolate has cooled, slowly mix the chocolate into the batter.

Whip the egg whites with a mixer until stiff peaks form and hold their shape, 5 to 10 minutes. Slowly fold the egg whites into the chocolate batter.

Pour the mixture into the pan and bake in the middle of the oven 25 to 40 minutes. Cool on a rack for 10 minutes and invert the pan to remove the cake.

YIELD: 6 to 8 servings

Chocolate "Lasagna" Filled with Apricot and Almonds

Dessert lasagnas are a fun twist on the usual interpretation of that word. Here, we satisfy our taste for chocolate and fruit simultaneously.

1 pound (450 g) semisweet chocolate
1½ cups (480 g) apricot preserves
1 cup (125 g) sliced almonds, toasted

Line the bottoms of two 9-inch (23-cm) square baking pans with waxed paper.

In a double boiler (or a metal pan set over a saucepan of simmering water), heat the chocolate, stirring occasionally, until completely melted. Spread the chocolate out in a thin layer in both baking pans.

When cooled and hardened, invert a layer of chocolate onto a cutting board and peel off the waxed paper. Spread the apricot preserves evenly over the chocolate and sprinkle the almonds on top. Invert the other chocolate layer onto the assembly and remove the waxed paper. Cut into 3-inch (7½-cm) squares and, using a spatula, put each on a plate.

YIELD: 4 servings

ADD IT!
You can garnish with whipped cream and more toasted almonds if you wish.

CHOCOLATE-PEANUT BUTTER PHYLLO PURSES

16 frozen phyllo sheets, thawed, each 14 x 18 inches (about 35 x 46 cm)
12 tablespoons (170 g) butter
1 cup (175 g) peanut butter morsels
1 cup (175 g) semisweet chocolate morsels

Preheat oven to 400°F (200°C, gas mark 6).

Unwrap and unroll the package of phyllo; place on a clean, dry surface and cover—first with a sheet of plastic wrap, and then a damp towel.

Melt the butter over low heat. Lay out a phyllo sheet and brush with the butter. Lay another sheet on top of the first, and repeat the buttering. Repeat again with third and fourth sheets. Make two equidistant cuts crosswise on the phyllo, dividing it into thirds, and make one lengthwise cut to divide the pastry into 6 pieces.

Put about 5 peanut butter and 5 chocolate morsels on each square. Pull up the sides of each phyllo square and twist it into a small sack, like a paper bag with a twist at the top.

Repeat with the process three more times with the remaining ingredients.

Place the sacks on a cookie sheet covered with parchment paper. Brush with melted butter and bake for 10 to 15 minutes, or until phyllo is golden brown and somewhat crackly looking.

YIELD: Makes 24 purses

CHOCOLATE-STRAWBERRY PINWHEELS

1 sheet frozen puff pastry, 9 x 10 inches (23 x 25½ cm)
1 tablespoon (20 g) strawberry preserves
½ cup (65 g) finely grated semisweet chocolate, finest quality

Preheat oven to 400°F (200°C, gas mark 6). Put a sheet of parchment paper on a cookie sheet.

Defrost the puff pastry at room temperature, about 30 minutes. Remove from the package and unfold. Gently roll with a rolling pin until it increases in size by one-quarter.

Spread the pastry evenly with the preserves (you may want to chop up any large chunks of strawberries), leaving an inch (2½ cm) of pastry uncovered at the far long side. Sprinkle the grated chocolate evenly over the pastry, again leaving an inch (2½ cm) uncovered at the far long side. Starting with the long side nearest you, roll the pastry jelly-roll fashion.

Cut the roll into disks ½-inch (1-cm) wide and lay them on a cookie sheet. Bake until golden brown, about 15 minutes.

Remove from the sheet with a spatula and let cool on baking rack. Store in an airtight container, separated in layers by waxed paper.

YIELD: 4 servings

DOUBLE CHOCOLATE TRUFFLES

These are easy, rich, and elegant confections. And best of all, they don't require that imple-ment of evil, the candy thermometer. As always, go for the deluxe chocolate, like Scharffen Berger or something equally sinful.

We find crème fraîche in the specialty cheese section of our supermarket. If you can't find it, substitute heavy cream.

> 9 ounces (255 g) best-quality bittersweet or semisweet chocolate
> 9 ounces (255 g) best-quality milk chocolate
> 1 cup (225 g) crème fraîche

Spray a 9 x 5-inch (23 x 13-cm) loaf pan with vegetable cooking spray and then line with plastic wrap, doing your best to smooth out the wrinkles in the wrap.

In a food processor, pulse the bittersweet chocolate until roughly chopped. Put the chocolate and half of the crème fraîche in a double boiler and melt, stirring gently, until smooth. (If you lack a double boiler, a small metal bowl set over a pan of simmering water also works just fine.) Spoon the mixture into the loaf pan and level the surface with a spreading knife. Put the pan in the freezer to cool.

Take a minute to clean the equipment and repeat the process with the milk chocolate. After making sure that the dark chocolate layer has cooled and formed a crust, carefully pour the milk chocolate over a spoon or spatula onto the dark chocolate layer. Cover the loaf pan with plastic wrap and chill in the refrigerator; overnight is a good bet.

Remove the candy from its pan and cut into small squares. We like truffles that are just under 1 inch (2½ cm) square, but you can choose whatever size fits your inclination. Place on waxed paper in a container with an airtight lid. Use waxed paper to separate each layer of candy. Chill until ready to serve.

🫙 ADD IT!
Roll your truffle pieces in chopped nuts, cocoa powder, or confectioner's sugar.

CRÈME CARAMEL

It is best to make this dessert a day or two ahead, so that the caramel softens and makes the sauce.

    2 cups (400 g) vanilla sugar (see recipe on page 37)
    4 eggs
    3 cups (700 ml) whole milk

Preheat the oven to 300°F (150°C, gas mark 2).

Put 1 cup (200 g) of the sugar in a heavy 2-quart (2-L) saucepan and add enough water to make the sugar the consistency of wet sand. Put the saucepan on high heat and bring to a boil. Boil until the steam stops rising from the pot, then stick close by. As soon as the water (the steam) is all gone, the temperature of the sugar will start to rise quickly. Pour the caramel into six 6-ounce (175 ml) ramekins or other small containers.

Put the other cup of sugar and the eggs into a mixing bowl and whisk together. Heat the milk almost to a boil and temper into the eggs—meaning, pour it into the bowl, while whisking, in a thin stream—you don't want to scramble the eggs. Pour the egg mixture into the ramekins and put the ramekins into a baking dish that can accommodate all of them. Pour in very hot water until it reaches halfway up the sides of the ramekins. Bake for 30 to 40 minutes, uncovered, until the custards are set. Refrigerate overnight, or better, for 2 days.

To serve, carefully slip a thin knife around the edge of the custard. Invert the ramekin onto a plate and shake to release the custard. Allow the caramel sauce to flow around the custard.

YIELD: 6 servings

🧂 ADD IT!
Serve with a spoonful of fresh raspberries, mulberries, or sliced peaches.

CRÊPES SUZETTE

This classic dish is a lot of fun to make and usually evokes intense admiration from the crowd. Just don't singe your eyebrows. Vanilla ice cream is good with this.

1 cup (200 g) sugar
4 tablespoons (55 g) butter
½ cup (120 ml) Grand Marnier or other orange liqueur
8 dessert crêpes

Put the sugar and butter in a medium-size sauté pan or skillet and heat over high heat until the sugar is dissolved and a syrup forms. Add the liqueur; light a match and carefully apply to the side of the liquid, setting it alight. When the flames subside, use tongs to dip a crêpe into the syrup and fold it into quarters. Repeat until you have 2 crêpes on each of 4 plates. Spoon the remaining sauce over the crêpes. Garnish with a sprinkle of powdered sugar.

YIELD: 4 servings

NOTE: *We find dessert crêpes near the berries in the produce section of our supermarket.*

DESSERT WONTONS

We are indebted to personal chef Kim Savage for this fun recipe.

16 wonton wrappers, any size
2 cups (340 g) sliced strawberries
2 cups (350 g) semisweet chocolate morsels

Place a wonton wrapper on a flat surface and put a spoonful of strawberries and a spoonful of chocolate morsels on it. Fold the wrapper around the mixture, tucking in the ends like a burrito. Repeat until all the dessert wontons are built.

In a large saucepan, heat ¼ cup (60 ml) oil on medium heat and gently sauté the wontons, turning occasionally, until the confections are golden brown on all sides. Be sure to do this a few at a time—you don't want to crowd the pan or they won't brown properly. Place the wontons on a plate with a couple layers of paper towels to help drain the oil.

Serve warm.

YIELD: 16 wontons

ADD IT!
Sprinkle shredded coconut in with the fruit and chocolate, or add another type of fruit, such as raspberries or peaches. These wontons are always good with a scoop of vanilla ice cream, too.

EGGNOG RICE PUDDING

A comforting dessert, reminiscent of Christopher Robin and English nurseries.

1 cup (200 g) arborio rice
3 cups (700 ml) eggnog
½ cup (80 g) raisins

Combine all the ingredients in a heavy-bottomed 2-quart (2-L) saucepan and cook over low heat, stirring occasionally, until the rice has absorbed the eggnog, about ½ hour. Spoon into serving bowls and serve hot, warm, or cold.

YIELD: 4 to 6 servings

FLOATING ISLAND

A classic dessert that has stood the test of time and is actually quite easy to make. The crème anglaise can be made up to a day in advance and kept in the refrigerator.

> 2 cups (475 ml) whole milk
> 1 cup (200 g) vanilla sugar (see recipe, page 37)
> 3 eggs

Make the crème anglaise:

Separate the eggs, putting the yolks in a bowl with half the sugar. Set the whites aside. Heat the milk in a heavy-bottomed pan until hot but not boiling. While the milk is heating, whisk the yolks with the sugar. Pour the milk into the eggs in a thin stream while whisking. Return to the saucepan and heat, stirring constantly with a wooden spoon, until the custard thickens to the point of coating the back of a spoon. Do not allow to boil. As soon as the sauce has thickened, transfer it to a bowl and cool it in the refrigerator, with a sheet of plastic wrap right on the surface of the custard.

Make the meringue islands:

Beat the egg whites in a mixing bowl, adding the remaining ½ cup (100 g) sugar in 3 parts, until you have a smooth, thick, and shiny meringue. Over medium heat, heat a sauté pan or skillet filled with 2 inches (5 cm) water to a simmer. Spoon in the meringue in 4 piles. Poach the islands for 1 to 2 minutes, then turn them over and poach for another 1 to 2 minutes. Set aside on a towel to drain. Serve by dividing the crème anglaise among 4 bowls and floating a meringue on each.

YIELD: 4 servings

FONDUE S'MORES

Who says campfire fare can't go upscale? This dessert is a little whimsical, very interactive, and quite delicious. If you really want to go all gourmet, you could buy fancy organic marshmallows, but the supermarket variety work just fine.

> 3 cups (300 g) shaved finest-quality semisweet chocolate
>   (if you prefer milk chocolate, feel free to substitute)
> 8 tablespoons (115 g) butter
> 10 ounces (280 g) marshmallows
> 14 ounces (400 g) graham crackers

Put the chocolate and butter in a double boiler and melt, stirring gently, until smooth. (If you lack a double boiler, a small metal bowl set over a pan of simmering water also works.)

Transfer the chocolate to a fondue pot set over a can of Sterno to keep the chocolate melted. Set out bowls of marshmallows and plates of graham crackers.

Using fondue forks, dip the marshmallows into the chocolate and twirl until liberally covered. Remove each marshmallow from the pot and transfer to a graham cracker. Pop another cracker on top and enjoy!

YIELD: 6 to 8 servings

ADD IT!
Purists might be aghast, but rolling the chocolate-covered marshmallow in toasted coconut shreds before consuming is also quite good.

FRESH FIGS WITH SWEETENED MASCARPONE

This light summertime dessert features mascarpone cheese, which is kind of a cross between cream cheese and sour cream.

> 1 pint (300 g) fresh figs
> 1 cup (240 g) mascarpone cheese
> ½ cup (50 g) confectioner's sugar

Split figs lengthwise into quarters. In a small mixing bowl whisk together the mascarpone and powdered sugar until smooth. Divide the mascarpone mixture among 4 plates and surround the mascarpone with the fig quarters. To eat, dip a piece of fig into the mascarpone.

YIELD: 4 servings

GRAPEFRUIT BRÛLÉE

You thought that a propane blow torch was only for plumbing work, didn't you? In fact, the mini kind sold for the kitchen are all kinds of fun to use. (The broiler works, too.)

> 2 grapefruit
> ½ cup (110 g) brown sugar, packed
> 4 scoops orange sorbet

Cut the grapefruit in half. Sprinkle the cut surfaces with the brown sugar. Using the blowtorch, or under the broiler, caramelize the sugar until bubbling and brown. Put 1 grapefruit half on each of 4 plates and top with a scoop of sorbet.

YIELD: 4 servings

Ice Cream "Tiramisu"

A delicious return on a minimal work investment.

> 1 package (12 ounces, or 340 g) ladyfinger cookies
> 1 quart (570 g) vanilla ice cream, softened
> ½ cup (120 ml) coffee syrup (see note)

Cover the bottom of a 9-inch (23-cm) square baking pan with ladyfingers laid side by side. Pour half of the coffee syrup over the cookies. Put the ice cream into a mixing bowl and beat it with a wooden spoon until it is easily spreadable. Working quickly to minimize further melting, spread half of the ice cream on the ladyfingers. Add another layer of ladyfingers and repeat the process with the coffee syrup and ice cream. Freeze for at least 1 hour. Cut lengthwise and crosswise into thirds.

YIELD: 9 squares, each 3 inches (7½ cm) square

 ADD IT!
Serve with whipped cream, powdered cocoa, or cinnamon as a garnish.

> NOTE: *If you can't find coffee syrup, you can make a cup by combining ¼ cup (12 g) instant coffee powder, 1 cup (235 ml) water, and 1 cup (200 g) sugar in a small saucepan and cook until the sugar is dissolved.*

APPLES BAKED IN MAPLE SYRUP

4 sweet-tart cooking apples, such as Cortland, McIntosh, or Granny Smith
½ cup (120 ml) pure maple syrup
2 teaspoons cinnamon

Preheat the oven to 325°F (170°C, gas mark 3).

Peel the apples and remove the cores using an apple corer. Put the apples in a shallow baking dish that fits them snugly, but does not crowd them. Mix the syrup and cinnamon in a small bowl and pour over and into the center of the apples. Bake for 30 to 40 minutes, until the apples are browned and soft, but not totally losing shape. Use any sauce in the pan as a sauce for the apples.

YIELD: 4 servings

⬭ ADD IT!
Like pretty much any other dessert in the free world, these are delicious served with vanilla ice cream. You can also add a pinch of nutmeg to the maple syrup.

Individual Apple Dumplings

2 frozen pie shells, thawed
4 sweet-tart cooking apples, such as Cortland or McIntosh
¼ cup (50 g) cinnamon sugar (see recipe, page 37)
4 tablespoons (55 g) butter

Preheat the oven to 350°F (180°C, gas mark 4).

Cut each dough circle in half and roll out to a kind of circular shape, so you have four pieces. Peel the apples and remove the cores using an apple corer. Put 1 apple on the center of each piece of dough. Put one-fourth of the cinnamon sugar in the hollowed center of each apple. Top with one-fourth of the butter. Fold up the sides of the dough so that it meets at the top of the apple and twist the dough together so that it stays in place. Put the dumplings on a baking sheet and bake for 40 to 45 minutes, until the crust is golden brown and some caramel is oozing out the bottoms.

YIELD: 4 servings

LEMON CARDAMOM ICE

This is refreshing on a hot summer evening like nothing else we know.

> 6 lemons
> 1 teaspoon ground cardamom
> 2 cups (400 g) sugar

Squeeze the lemons to get 1 cup (235 ml) lemon juice. Put the lemon juice, cardamom, sugar, and 1 cup (235 ml) water in a 1-quart (1-L) pot and heat over medium heat to a simmer, stirring occasionally until the sugar has dissolved. Pour into a loaf pan and freeze at least 8 hours. Scrape off with a spoon and serve in chilled glass bowls. The ice with be grainy, not smooth.

YIELD: 4 servings

MANGO MOUSSE

Since our kids are unswervingly devoted to mangos, we developed this recipe for them.

> 1 jar (16 ounces, or 450 g) mangos in juice
> 2 eggs
> 2 cups (475 ml) heavy cream

Puree the mangos and juice in a food processor fitted with the metal blade. Put the eggs in a small metal mixing bowl or the top half of a double boiler and whisk them smooth. Add the mango and mix well. Heat 2 to 3 inches (5 to 7½ cm) water to a simmer in a 2-quart (2-L) pot; put the bowl containing the egg mixture on the pot and whisk until the mixture lightens and thickens, 10 to 12 minutes. Set aside to cool a bit.

Whip the cream to stiff peaks. Fold the cream into the mango mixture and spoon into wine glasses. Refrigerate 2 hours.

YIELD: 8 to 10 servings

ADD IT!
You can add a couple teaspoons of sugar and a dash of vanilla to the cream before whipping.

MELON GRANITA

1 small honeydew melon
1 cup (200 g) sugar
2 limes

Cut off the peel of the melon, split in half, and remove the seeds. Cut the melon into 1 inch (2½ cm) cubes and put them in a food processor with the metal blade attached. Squeeze the limes and add the juice to the melon with the sugar. Puree until smooth. Spoon into a loaf pan and freeze (4 to 6 hours at least) until hard. Serve by scraping off the top with a spoon and serving in bowls. A granita should be crystal ice, not smooth like a sorbet.

YIELD: 6 to 8 servings

PEACH COBBLER

When fresh peaches are in season, this is a dinner-table favorite.

1 pound (450 g) peaches
1 cup (200 g) cinnamon sugar (see recipe, page 37)
1 box (8 ounces, or 225 g) buttermilk biscuit mix

Preheat the oven to 350°F (180°C, gas mark 4). Prepare a bowl of ice water.

Blanch the peaches: Bring a large pot of water to a boil. Drop the peaches in the boiling water for 15 seconds, then remove and plunge immediately into cold water. Drain the peaches and peel them—the skin should slip right off. Remove the pits and cut into wedges.

Combine the peaches and sugar in a mixing bowl and put the mixture into a 9-inch (23-cm) square baking dish. Make the biscuit batter and spoon over the peaches.

Bake for 20 to 25 minutes, until the biscuits are golden brown and the peaches are bubbling.

YIELD: 6 servings

Orange-Ginger Ice Cream Roll

20 or so gingersnap cookies
1 quart (570 g) vanilla ice cream
1 cup (320 g) orange marmalade

Put the cookies in a food processor fitted with the metal blade and pulse until you have crumbs. Alternatively, put the cookies in a plastic bag and roll a rolling pin over them.

Line a cookie sheet with waxed paper.

Allow the ice cream to soften, then beat it with a wooden spoon in a mixing bowl until it reaches a spreadable consistency. Lay a piece of plastic wrap on a cutting board. Spread the ice cream to make a rectangle about 9 x 12 inches (23 x 30 cm). Spread the marmalade over the ice cream. Sprinkle half of the cookie crumbs evenly over the marmalade. Using the plastic wrap to start the process, roll up the ice cream jelly-roll fashion. Transfer to the cookie sheet. Coat the outside of the roll with the remaining cookie crumbs. Freeze for 2 to 3 hours. Slice to serve.

YIELD: 8 to 10 servings

ORANGE TERRINE

This is a updated and elegant take on the gelatin desserts of our youth. Serve with whipped cream, sour cream, or crème fraîche.

10 oranges
2 envelopes (2 tablespoons, or 15 g) unflavored gelatin
1 cup (200 g) sugar

Squeeze 6 of the oranges and put the juice in a small saucepan. Add the gelatin to the juice; stir to distribute the gelatin and let it sit for 8 to 10 minutes to soften. Add the sugar and cook over low heat to a simmer, until the gelatin and sugar are dissolved. Put the mixture into a steel mixing bowl and chill in an ice bath, stirring every so often. With a sharp knife, remove the peel and inner membrane from the remaining oranges. With a paring knife, working over a bowl, cut out the segments from the inner membranes. Mix these segments and any accumulated juice into the gelatin mixture. Put the whole thing into a small loaf pan, lightly press plastic wrap onto the surface of the terrine and chill for at least 4 hours. To serve, unmold the terrine and slice.

YIELD: 6 servings

PEANUT BUTTER COOKIES

Simple to make, easy to eat. These are great for those who need to avoid wheat products.

> 2 eggs
> 1 cup (225 g) peanut butter
> 1 cup (200 g) sugar

Preheat the oven to 350°F (180°C, gas mark 4).

Lightly beat the eggs in a mixing bowl and stir in the remaining ingredients. Drop by spoonfuls onto a lightly greased cookie sheet. Bake until puffy, golden, and still soft, about 6 to 8 minutes. Cool on the sheet for 5 minutes, then remove to a cooling rack.

YIELD: About 24 cookies

QUICK STRAWBERRY WHIP

Strawberry season usually calls for strawberry shortcake, but if you don't have time to bake the shortcake, this dessert is a tasty alternative.

> 1 quart (700 g) strawberries
> 1 cup (235 ml) heavy cream
> 3 tablespoons (45 ml) orange juice concentrate, thawed

Wash, hull, and slice the strawberries; puree half and leave the rest sliced. Whip the cream and fold in the orange juice concentrate. Reserve a few strawberry slices for garnish and fold in the rest. Spoon into serving bowls or wine glasses and refrigerate for an hour to let it set. Garnish with reserved berries.

YIELD: 4 servings

RASPBERRY NAPOLEONS

This is a pretty spectacular-looking dessert for pretty minimal effort.

1 sheet puff pastry dough, thawed, 9 x 10 inches (23 x 25½ cm)
1 cup (235 ml) heavy cream
1 pint (300 g) raspberries

Preheat the oven to 400°F (200°C, gas mark 6).

Roll out the puff pastry dough very thin and put it onto a baking sheet lined with parchment paper. Prick the dough all over with a fork. Select a flat roasting rack with a surface area large enough to cover the dough. This will keep the pastry from puffing up. If your rack is not large enough, you may cut the dough and bake it in batches. Spray the rack with pan spray and invert it onto the puff pastry. Put another baking sheet on top and weight it with pie weights or dried beans. Bake for 15 to17 minutes, until the puff pastry is golden brown.

Remove the top baking sheet and the rack and allow the pastry to cool. Using a bread knife and a sawing motion, cut the pastry sheet into 8 rectangles, 2 x 4 inches (5 x 10 cm). There will be some pastry left over. (You may increase the dimensions of the rectangles if you like.)

Whip the cream. Layer a piece of the pastry with whipped cream, arrange raspberries on the whipped cream, and top with a bit more cream, then another piece of the pastry. Garnish with a spoonful of cream and a few more berries. Repeat with remaining ingredients.

YIELD: 4 servings

RHUBARB CRISP

While rhubarb is traditionally paired with strawberries in crisps and pies, it's pretty mouth-watering all on its own. Crisps are always delightful with a dairy accompaniment of either the whipped or the frozen variety. Your choice.

> 1 pound (450 g) rhubarb stalks, cut into ½-inch pieces (about 4 cups)
> 2 cups (400 g) cinnamon sugar (see recipe, page 37)
> 1½ cups (185 g) all-purpose flour
> 8 tablespoons (115 g) butter

Preheat the oven to 350°F (180°C, gas mark 4).

Mix the rhubarb with 1 cup (200 g) of the sugar and put the mixture in a shallow baking dish. Put the other cup of sugar and the flour in a mixing bowl and stir together. Add a pinch of salt. Cut in the butter, using your fingertips or a pastry cutter, until the mixture has pea-size lumps. Spread over the rhubarb. Bake for 40 to 45 minutes, until the top is golden brown and the rhubarb is soft and bubbling.

YIELD: 6 to 8 servings

STRAWBERRY CRÊPES

You can use whipped cream instead of the crème fraîche, but we like the tangy sweetness of the latter. We find dessert crêpes near the berries in the produce section of our supermarket.

> 1 quart (700 g) strawberries
> 8 dessert crêpes
> 2 cups (450 g) crème fraîche

Wash, hull, and slice the strawberries. Turn the crème fraîche into a bowl and stir to soften. Lay out the crêpes and spread a spoonful of the crème fraîche into the center of each, reserving some for garnish. Spoon the strawberries over the crème fraîche, again reserving a bit for garnish. Roll up the crêpes and put 2 on each of 4 plates. Garnish with a spoonful of crème fraîche and a few strawberry slices.

YIELD: 4 servings

TEMPURA BANANAS

In a word, these are fantastic. When Bob tested them, his family followed him around with their tongues hanging out, hoping for seconds.

> 4 bananas
> 2 cups (250 g) tempura batter mix
> 1 cup (350 g) honey

Heat a deep fryer, or a pot with 2 inches of clean oil, to 350°F (180°C).

Peel the bananas and slice on the bias into 4 to 5 pieces each. Prepare the tempura batter. Dip the banana slices into the tempura batter and fry in batches until golden brown. Drain on paper towels and keep warm while the rest is frying. Heat the honey in a small saucepan only until warmed. Drizzle over bananas and serve.

YIELD: 4 to 6 servings

ADD IT!
You can also drizzle melted chocolate over these delicacies should you so desire.

TRIPLE CHOCOLATE PIE

12 ounces (340 g) semisweet chocolate
3 eggs
1 Oreo pie crust (see note)

Melt the chocolate in a steel bowl over a simmering water bath. Separate the eggs. Put the yolks in another steel mixing bowl and whisk over the simmering water until they are light and streaks of the bowl show as you whisk. Fold in two-thirds of the chocolate and remove from heat. Whip the egg whites into stiff peaks and fold into the chocolate-egg mixture.

Pour the rest of the melted chocolate into the pie crust and spread out to cover the bottom. Spoon the chocolate-egg mousse into the pie crust and smooth with a spatula. Chill for 2 to 3 hours.

YIELD: 6 servings

NOTE: *If your market does not carry these crusts, you can make your own by grinding 12 to 15 Oreo cookies in a food processor, mixing them with 8 tablespoons (115 g) melted butter, and pressing the crumbs into an 8-inch (20-cm) pie pan. Bake for 8 to 10 minutes and cool.*

TROPICAL MOUSSE PIE

1 cup (150 g) mixed tropical fruit, mango, or pineapple sorbet
1 cup (235 ml) heavy cream
1 graham cracker pie shell

Melt the sorbet. Whip the cream, then fold the melted sorbet into the whipped cream. Fill the pie shell with this mixture and refrigerate for at least 2 hours.

YIELD: 6 servings

ADD IT!
You can garnish this pie with slices of the fresh fruit that matches your sorbet choice.

ZABAGLIONE

This classic dessert sauce is great warm or cold with fresh fruit. Try it with strawberries, raspberries, peaches, apricots, plums, or a mixture of all of the above!

4 egg yolks
⅓ cup (80 ml) marsala wine
⅓ cup (65 g) sugar

Combine all the ingredients in a large steel mixing bowl. Heat a pan of water; when it simmers, put the bowl on the pan. Whisk constantly, until the sauce is foamy, light colored, and thick and you can see streaks of the bowl bottom as you whisk. Serve soon after making, or the sauce will deflate.

YIELD: 4 to 6 servings

ZEBRA CAKE

This is a classic recipe from the '70s that originally called for whipped dessert topping. Switch to real whipped cream, and you have a heavenly cake that's simultaneously light and rich. We must confess: This is one of our all-time favorite desserts. We have been known to eat it for breakfast.

  1 pint (475 ml) whipping cream
  ¼ cup (50 g) sugar
  1 package (14 ounces, or 400 g) dark-chocolate wafer cookies
    (we use Nabisco's Famous Chocolate Wafers)

Combine the cream and sugar in a mixing bowl and whip with a mixer until stiff peaks form. With a wide spreading knife, spread a dollop of whipped cream on a wafer, and top it with another cookie. Keep alternating whipped cream and cookies until you've created a stack of about 5 or 6 cookies. Then turn the stack on its side on a long plate.

Repeat the process with another stack and add to the first. Keep doing this until you run out of cookies; you should have a log about 14 to 18 inches (35 to 45 cm) long. You can also place the cookie stacks next to each other to make a shorter, wider cake.

Frost the cake with the remainder of the whipped cream and cover with plastic wrap. We generally porcupine the cake with a few toothpicks to keep the wrap from sticking to the whipped cream. Refrigerate overnight.

To serve: Slice at a 45-degree angle so that the cake comes out striped like a zebra. Be sure to save some for breakfast the next day.

YIELD: 6 to 8 servings

🥫 ADD IT!
Add ¼ teaspoon vanilla to the cream before whipping, and top the cake with fresh raspberries or serve with fresh sliced strawberries. Further heaven.

20

Drinks

There's no doubt that we've gotten lazy about drinks, opting to pop the top on a can of soda instead of creating our own elixirs. And that's too bad, because we're missing out on a lot of fun.

Many of these drink recipes, such as the Black and White Milkshake and Lime Rickey, harken back to old-fashioned recipes. Perhaps it's time to rediscover them. A mug of hot cocoa doesn't have to involve water and an envelope of powdered mix (although there's certainly a time and place for that, too). Ironically, a three-ingredient mug of cocoa is little more complicated than that.

Big coffee chains, with their arcane and complicated mixological methodologies, could represent a return to more complicated drinks. How soon can it be until we're experimenting with them ourselves?

BANANA-STRAWBERRY SMOOTHIE

Our kids love these. They think they're getting a big ol' treat, and we think they're getting a healthy snack.

> 1 banana
> 1 cup (300 g) frozen strawberries (you can use fresh if they're in season)
> 1 cup (245 g) vanilla yogurt

Place all the ingredients in a blender and add 3 to 4 ice cubes. Blend on high speed until smooth—you may need to add a little water.

YIELD: 2 servings

BLACK AND WHITE

Our dad spent his formative years working the soda fountain at his local drugstore, building old-fashioned ice-cream-shop favorites such as these. We can't get him to come out of retirement for us, so we whip them up at home.

> ½ cup (120 ml) chocolate syrup
> 4 scoops (½ cup, or 70 g) vanilla ice cream
> 2 cups (475 ml) milk

Blend all the ingredients in a blender until smooth. Pour into glasses and serve with 1 straw or 2.

YIELD: 2 servings

Black Currant Spritzer

Long popular in Europe, black currant juice syrup is finding its way into American super-markets. A terrific summer refresher—add white wine if you'd like.

> ½ cup (120 ml) black currant syrup
> 2 cups (475 ml) sparkling water
> 2 lime wedges

Fill 2 glasses with ice. Divide the syrup between the glasses, then pour the sparkling water over it. Squeeze a lime wedge in each glass.

YIELD: 2 servings

Blood Orange Iced Tea

Blood orange juice is a trendy, ruby-red liquid that has been showing up in our local mar-kets. If you can't find any, substitute a good-quality regular orange juice, or try squeezing your own blood oranges!

> 2 cups (475 ml) blood orange juice
> 2 cups (475 ml) strong brewed tea, cooled
> ¼ cup (50 g) sugar

Mix together all the ingredients and serve in tall glasses over ice.

YIELD: 4 servings

BLOODY MARY MIX

1 cup (235 ml) lemon vegetable juice cocktail
1 tablespoon (15 g) prepared horseradish
½ teaspoon Worcestershire sauce

Mix all the ingredients with a liberal dose of fresh ground black pepper. Pour over ice and garnish: Popular items include lime and lemon wedges and the traditional celery stick, although we prefer cucumber spears. Oh yes, you can add vodka too.

YIELD: 1 serving

GENUINE LIME RICKEY

This was a great favorite in the old days of Boston ice cream parlors. Nowadays, lime rickeys are a pale shadow of their formerly sprightly selves. We have had some horrid renditions over the years, reminiscent of melted lime Popsicles. Here is the real—and refreshing—deal.

1 lime
2 tablespoons (25 g) sugar
10 ounces (285 ml) soda water

Squeeze the lime and put the juice in a tall glass with the sugar. Stir with a spoon to mix and add the soda water. Stir gently to dissolve the sugar. Add a piece of the squeezed lime and several ice cubes.

YIELD: 1 serving

ADD IT
For a raspberry lime rickey, add 2 tablespoons (30 g) raspberry puree.

GINGER LEMONADE

Different and very refreshing on a hot summer day.

2 tablespoons (12 g) minced fresh ginger root
1 cup (200 g) sugar
6 lemons

Combine the ginger, sugar, and 3 cups (700 ml) water in a small saucepan. Bring to a boil, remove from the heat, and let stand for 30 minutes to 1 hour. Strain the liquid to remove the ginger. Squeeze the lemons, and remove any seeds that might have sneaked into the juice. Add the lemon juice to the sugar water and stir. Pour over ice and serve.

YIELD: 2 to 3 servings

ADD IT!
A sprig of mint in each class provides a festive touch.

HORCHATA

A traditional Mexican drink. Although it's milky white and smooth, this contains no dairy. Just the thing for the lactose-intolerant crowd.

1 cup (200 g) uncooked white rice
¼ cup (50 g) sugar
1 teaspoon vanilla extract

Grind the rice to a fine powder in a blender, and mix in a bowl with the sugar. Bring 3 cups (700 ml) water to a boil and pour over the rice. Let the mixture sit for 2 hours. Add the vanilla and 3 cups (700 ml) cold water. Strain through a fine-mesh strainer. Serve over ice.

YIELD: 3 to 4 servings

ADD IT!
Good additions are ½ cup blanched almonds, ground fine with the rice, and ½ teaspoon cinnamon.

Iced Coffee

The Mason-Dixon line used to have a beverage equivalent—the line between sweet tea and iced coffee. Long a favorite in New England, iced coffee is finally getting its just deserts—and desserts—everywhere, thanks to the proliferation of coffee chains. But you don't need some barista to build you a supersweet, fancy-pants coffee drink: you can make your own. It's easy.

- 1 cup (235 ml) strong black coffee, cold
- 1 cup (235 ml) milk
- 2 tablespoons (30 ml) simple syrup, or to taste (see note)

Mix all the ingredients together and pour into glasses over ice.

YIELD: 2 servings

NOTE: *Simple syrup is simply equal parts sugar and water briefly boiled together.*

Lemon Raspberry Smoothie

Serve this in tall glasses for an unorthodox dessert.

- 2 scoops (½ cup, or 75 g) lemon sorbet
- 1 cup (250 g) frozen raspberries
- 1 cup (245 g) vanilla or plain yogurt

Combine all the ingredients in a blender. Add 4 to 5 ice cubes and ½ cup (120 ml) water. Blend until smooth.

YIELD: 2 servings

Mango Lhassi

It's hot in India, and they have devised great ways over the millennia to cool off. Lhassi is one of the best.

    1 cup (175 g) diced fresh mango, or bottled fresh-pack mango, drained
    1 cup (245 g) plain yogurt
    ¼ cup (75 g) honey

Combine all the ingredients in a blender. Add 4 to 5 ice cubes and ½ cup (120 ml) water. Blend until smooth.

YIELD: 2 servings

Mocha Hot Chocolate

This is the grown-up version of the post-skating hot chocolate our mom used to make for us. If you really want to gild the lily, top with a dollop of whipped cream.

    2 cups (475 ml) milk
    2 tablespoons (30 ml) coffee syrup
    ¼ cup (60 ml) chocolate syrup

Combine all the ingredients in a small saucepan and heat over medium heat until it just starts to bubble. Remove from the heat immediately and stir to make sure everything is combined. Pour into mugs and serve.

YIELD: 2 servings

OLD-FASHIONED ROOT BEER FLOAT

10 ounces (285 ml) root beer
1 scoop (½ cup, or 70 g) vanilla ice cream
Whipped cream

Pour the root beer into a tall glass over ice. Hang the ice cream on the edge of the glass. Top with whipped cream. Serve with a straw and a tall spoon.

YIELD: 1 serving

POMEGRANATE JUICE SPARKLER

This is a new product making its way into supermarkets. There are several flavor combos based on pomegranate juice. Just choose one that sounds good to you for this recipe.

1 cup (235 ml) pomegranate juice cocktail
1 cup (235 ml) sparkling water
2 lime or lemon wedges

Mix together the pomegranate juice and sparkling water. Pour over ice cubes in tall glasses. Squeeze in lime or lemon.

YIELD: 2 servings

Rosewater Lhassi

Rosewater is available at our local supermarket, but you may need to find a Middle Eastern or Latino grocery store to obtain it.

½ cup (120 ml) rosewater
1 cup (245 g) plain yogurt
½ cup (50 g) sugar

Combine all the ingredients in a blender. Add 4 to 5 ice cubes and ½ cup (120 ml) water. Blend until smooth, adding a bit of water if needed.

YIELD: 2 servings

White Cranberry Juice Spritzer

We were intrigued with white cranberry juice and found it has a livelier and more sophisticated taste than its red cousin.

1 cup (235 ml) white cranberry juice cocktail
1 cup (235 ml) soda water
2 lime or lemon wedges

Fill 2 tall glasses with ice. Pour half of the cranberry juice and soda water into each, then stir. Squeeze in the citrus of your choice.

YIELD: 2 servings

INDEX

ACKNOWLEDGMENTS

Cookbooks are never a solo effort—even those with one author—and this one is no exception. We drew deeply from a well of support from our families, friends, and colleagues and are hugely grateful to them all; without them, this book would not have been written.

First, we'd like to thank our families:

Don Eburne—for heroic childcare far, far above and beyond the call of duty, for many thoughtful and much-appreciated cups of chamomile tea, and for being an all-around mensch.

Sarah Hildebrand—for letting Bob chuck his suit and tie for cooking school.

Our parents, George and Margery, and our brother and sister, Charles and Amy, for aiding and abetting us, and for having the dubious distinction of sharing the strange Hildebrand sense of humor.

Our kids—Erica, Sam, Olivia, and Nicholas, for being delightful human beings.

Also, our colleagues: Thanks to Sam, Jinny, Martina, Erik, and Levi for fostering a fun, creative team environment at the Three Stallion Inn.

In particular, we'd like to thank our team of recipe testers for adding yet another task to their already busy lives and providing us with helpful, thoughtful, and useful feedback. As well, we truly appreciate those folks who came up with some pretty ingenious recipes. And finally, we also want to thank our patient friends who put up with our endless yammering about what ingredient would or would not fit in what recipe. So, many and heartfelt thanks to:

Leslie and Geol Barnes, Barbara Bilodeau, David Bromley, Laurie Brustlin, Lois Conroy, Susan Crockett, Todd and Sheila Datz, Margery Hildebrand, Charles and Jerrie Hildebrand, Amy and Darrell Jones, Alice Kelly, Kim Nash, Chris Lindquist, and Barbara Rogers—not to mention their families, who actually ate the recipes. Thank you, thank you, thank you!

Lastly: Thank you to our editor and publisher, Holly Schmidt, for giving us a chance to have great fun writing this book and for guiding us along the way.

And an extra hug to Alice Kelly for telling us about this opportunity in the first place. Alice, you rock!

ABOUT THE AUTHORS

Robert Hildebrand is the executive chef at The Three Stallions Inn in Randolph, Vermont. His work has been featured in *Bon Appetit*, as well as several newspapers.

Carol Hildebrand is an award-winning writer and editor with work appearing in *Boston Magazine*, *The Old Farmer's Almanac*, *CIO*, *Darwin*, and many others.